# Politicizing the Poor

# Biliana C. S. Ambrecht

The Praeger Special Studies program—utilizing the most modern and efficient book production techniques and a selective worldwide distribution network—makes available to the academic, government, and business communities significant, timely research in U.S. and international economic, social, and political development.

# Politicizing the Poor

## The Legacy of the War on Poverty in a Mexican-American Community

PRAEGER SPECIAL STUDIES IN U.S. ECONOMIC, SOCIAL, AND POLITICAL ISSUES

**Praeger Publishers**  New York  Washington  London

Library of Congress Cataloging in Publication Data

Ambrecht, Biliana C   S
   Politicizing the poor.

  (Praeger special studies in U.S. economic, social, and political issues)
   Bibliography: p.
   Includes index.
   1. Mexican Americans—California—Los Angeles. 2. Mexican Americans—Economic conditions.   3. Political participation—Los Angeles.   4. Los Angeles—Politics and government.
I. Title.
F869.L89M422        362.8'4        74-31501
ISBN 0-275-05900-6

PRAEGER PUBLISHERS
111 Fourth Avenue, New York, N.Y. 10003, U.S.A.

Published in the United States of America in 1976
by Praeger Publishers, Inc.

*All rights reserved*

© 1976 by Praeger Publishers, Inc.

Printed in the United States of America

To My Mother and Father

# ACKNOWLEDGMENTS

The assistance of a number of individuals and institutions that have made this study possible is gratefully acknowledged. Most of all, many thanks are due to the many advisory council members and officials in the East Los Angeles community who were kind enough to submit to several hours of intensive interviewing. I only hope that this study ultimately may prove to be of some value to them. Special thanks are owed to my research assistants at Loyola Marymount University (especially Deborah Barthel and Gilbert Garcia) who worked tirelessly and with enthusiasm in collecting and coding the advisory council data. The assistance of the Los Angeles City Board of Education Committee on Research and Evaluation in providing access to the school advisory councils in the East Los Angeles area is also gratefully acknowledged.

The Ford Foundation and Loyola Marymount University provided the financial assistance necessary to complete this study. Leo Grebler, Joan W. Moore, Ralph C. Guzman, Frank G. Mittelbach, and Douglas Scott made available the 1965 Mexican American Study Project data. A special debt of thanks is owed to Harry R. Pachon with whom I collaborated in conducting a follow-up study of the Mexican American Study Project and whose ideas and data evaluation assistance are reflected in the discussion of the panel study in Chapter 6. Part of that chapter is reprinted from our coauthored article, "Ethnic Political Mobilization in a Mexican American Community: An Exploratory Study of East Los Angeles 1965-1972," The Western Political Quarterly 27, no. 3 (September 1974): 500-19. (Reprinted by Permission of the University of Utah, Copyright Holder).

A special intellectual debt is owed to Professors John C. Ries and Francine F. Rabinovitz, who gave generously of their time and knowledge to supervise this study as a doctoral dissertation. Their guidance and support are much appreciated. For skilled advice in the data processing stages of this study, I am indebted to John Light and Ricardo Klorman. Carl P. Hensler provided suggestive comments on an earlier draft of this manuscript. Nancy Davidson brought skill and experience to the task of preparing the index. Finally, a special personal debt of gratitude is owed my husband for his unfailing moral support and encouragement.

# CONTENTS

|  | Page |
|---|---|
| ACKNOWLEDGMENTS | vi |
| LIST OF TABLES AND FIGURE | x |

Chapter

1. THE POLITICAL SOCIALIZATION EFFECTS OF "MAXIMUM FEASIBLE PARTICIPATION" . . . . . . 1

    "Maximum Feasible Participation" as a Catalyst for the Creation of Community Advisory Councils . . . . . . 2
    Studies of the War on Poverty: Substantive Problems . . . . . . 3
    Studies of the War on Poverty: Methodological Problems . . . . . . 7
    Major Purpose of This Study . . . . . . 10
    If the Poor are Politicized, So What? . . . . . . 13
    Notes . . . . . . 15

2. INVOLVEMENT IN ADVISORY COUNCILS AS AN ALTERNATIVE ROUTE TO POLITICAL PARTICIPATION . . . . . . 21

    Studies on Political Participation: the Status Quo Bias . . . . . . 22
    Studies on Political Socialization: the Deterministic Bias . . . . . . 25
    Political Participation: the Standard SES Model and "Enabling Antecedents" . . . . . . 27
    Alternative Routes to Political Participation: Organizational Involvement and Group Consciousness . . . . . . 29
    Major Hypotheses to be Explored and Operationalization of Key Variables . . . . . . 34
    Research Strategy . . . . . . 46
    Notes . . . . . . 50

| Chapter | Page |
|---|---|
| 3. DATA COLLECTION PROCEDURES | 61 |

    Definition of Key Concepts    61
    The Universe of Advisory Councils    65
    Membership of the Advisory Councils    67
    Composition of the Advisory Councils    68
    Drawing the Sample    72
    Questionnaire Design    72
    Conducting the Field Work    74
    Analysis of the Data    76
    Notes    76

4. THE ADVISORY COUNCILS AND THEIR MEMBERSHIP    84

    Descriptive Analysis of the Advisory Councils    84
    "Representativeness" of Advisory Council Members: A Comparison with the General Population and with the 1972 Panel Study    92
    The Operation of "Self-Selection": Extent and Correlates    95
    Notes    98

5. THE POLITICIZATION OF ADVISORY COUNCIL MEMBERS    99

    The Development of Politicization    100
    The Correlates of Politicization    128
    Politicization: A Product of "Self-Selection"?    139
    Notes    142

6. GROUP CONSCIOUSNESS AS AN ALTERNATIVE EXPLANATION    149

    Ethnic Consciousness in East Los Angeles: An Exploration of the Panel Data    149
    Group Consciousness and Politicization    162
    Group Consciousness and Organizational Involvement: Interactive Effects    164
    Notes    168

| Chapter | Page |
|---|---|
| 7. THE LIKELIHOOD OF SUSTAINED POLITICIZATION AND TYPE OF LEADERSHIP LIKELY TO EMERGE | 172 |
|     Likelihood of Sustained Politicization: An Assessment | 173 |
|     Type of Leadership Likely to Emerge | 175 |
|     Conclusions | 181 |
|     Notes | 182 |
| 8. CONCLUSIONS: THE POLITICIZING LEGACY OF THE WAR ON POVERTY | 183 |
| BIBLIOGRAPHY | 187 |
| APPENDIX: EAST LOS ANGELES ADVISORY COUNCIL QUESTIONNAIRE | 202 |
| INDEX | 221 |
| ABOUT THE AUTHOR | 224 |

## LIST OF TABLES AND FIGURE

| Table | | Page |
|---|---|---|
| 3.1 | Total Population and Proportion of Spanish-Surnamed Persons for Los Angeles-Long Beach SMSA and East Los Angeles Community (1960, 1970) | 62 |
| 3.2 | Median Family Income for Los Angeles-Long Beach SMSA and East Los Angeles Community (1960, 1970) | 63 |
| 3.3 | Advisory Councils: Breakdown by Government Level and Service Area | 66 |
| 3.4 | Composition of Advisory Council Membership by Type of Representation | 69 |
| 3.5 | Sex of Advisory Council Members by Type of Member | 70 |
| 3.6 | Replacement and Refusal Rates | 75 |
| 3.7 | Replacements by Type of Lack of Availability | 75 |
| 4.1 | Distribution of Family Income for Council and Panel Respondents and East Los Angeles Population | 92 |
| 4.2 | Education: Years of School Completed for Council and Panel Respondents and East Los Angeles Population | 93 |
| 4.3 | Members' Previous Involvement by Type of Council | 96 |
| 4.4 | Members' Previous Involvement by Language of Interview | 97 |
| 4.5 | Members' Previous Involvement by Education | 97 |
| 5.1 | Awareness of the Impact of the Local Government Among Council and Panel Respondents | 100 |
| 5.2 | Awareness of the Impact of the National Government Among Council and Panel Respondents | 101 |

| Table | | Page |
|---|---|---|
| 5.3 | Evaluation of Local and National Government Among Council and Panel Respondents | 103 |
| 5.4 | Evaluation of War on Poverty Programs Among Council Respondents | 104 |
| 5.5 | Political Efficacy Among Council and Panel Respondents as Measured by the SRC Political Efficacy Scale | 106 |
| 5.6 | Political Efficacy Toward the Local and National Government Among Council and Panel Respondents | 107 |
| 5.7 | "Passivity-Activity" Orientations Among Council and Panel Respondents | 110 |
| 5.8 | Perceptions of Past, Present, and Future Life Situations Among Council and Panel Respondents | 111 |
| 5.9 | "Trust in People" Among Council and Panel Respondents | 112 |
| 5.10 | Type of Skills Learned | 118 |
| 5.11 | Learned New Things as Member by Extent of Previous Involvement | 119 |
| 5.12 | Cognition of Community Organizations Among Panel and Council Respondents | 120 |
| 5.13 | Membership in Organizations Among Council and Panel Respondents | 122 |
| 5.14 | Membership in Religious Organizations Among Council and Panel Respondents | 123 |
| 5.15 | Attendance at Protests, Marches, and Demonstrations | 123 |
| 5.16 | Evaluation of Protest Activity | 124 |
| 5.17 | Electoral Behavior Among Council and Panel Respondents | 125 |

| Table | | Page |
|---|---|---|
| 5.18 | Perception of Impact of Council Experience on Own Involvement in Community Affairs | 125 |
| 5.19 | Perception of Impact of Council Experience on Own Involvement in Community Affairs by Previous Involvement | 126 |
| 5.20 | Joining Community Organizations Subsequent to Council Membership by Previous Involvement | 126 |
| 5.21 | Factor Loadings of Politicization Items | 130 |
| 5.22 | Organizational Correlates of Dimensions of Politicization | 136 |
| 5.23 | Personal Efficacy Among Council and Panel Respondents Controlling for Council Members' "Self-Selection" | 140 |
| 5.24 | Political Efficacy Among Panel and Council Respondents Controlling for Council Members' "Self-Selection" | 141 |
| 5.25 | Awareness of Government Among Council and Panel Respondents Controlling for Council Members' "Self-Selection" | 141 |
| 5.26 | Involvement in Community Organizations Among Council and Panel Respondents Controlling for Council Members' "Self-Selection" | 142 |
| 6.1 | Likelihood of Assimilation into American Society | 151 |
| 6.2 | Value of Assimilation into American Society | 151 |
| 6.3 | What Children Should Keep of the Mexican Heritage | 152 |
| 6.4 | Self-Stereotypes Among East Los Angeles Respondents | 153 |

| Table | | Page |
|---|---|---|
| 6.5 | Perceptions of Discrimination | 155 |
| 6.6 | Cognition Rates of Ethnic Organizations | 156 |
| 6.7 | Self-Identification (English, Spanish) | 156 |
| 6.8 | Orientations Toward Work Performance | 157 |
| 6.9 | Sense of Neighborliness | 159 |
| 6.10 | Opinions on Resolution of Problems in the East Los Angeles Community (1972) | 161 |
| 6.11 | Dimensions of Politicization by Group Consciousness Among 1972 Panel Respondents | 163 |
| 6.12 | Dimensions of Politicization by Group Among Council Respondents | 165 |
| 6.13 | Learned Skills on the Council by Group Consciousness | 166 |
| 6.14 | Perception of Increased Involvement in Community Affairs as a Result of the Council Experience by Group Consciousness | 166 |
| 6.15 | "Not Group Conscious" Council Members and "Group Conscious" Panel Respondents Rating High on Politicization Measures | 167 |
| 7.1 | Strategies that Should be Employed to Solve Problems in the East Los Angeles Community | 177 |
| 7.2 | Awareness of, Attendance at, and Opinions of Protest Activity | 178 |
| 7.3 | Evaluation of Presumably Radically Oriented Organizations | 178 |
| 7.4 | Perceptions of Discrimination | 179 |
| 7.5 | Orientations Toward Ethnic Group Organization | 180 |

| Figure | | |
|---|---|---|
| 2.1 | Major Hypotheses | 35 |

CHAPTER

# 1

## THE POLITICAL SOCIALIZATION EFFECTS OF "MAXIMUM FEASIBLE PARTICIPATION"

With the passage of the Economic Opportunity Act on August 20, 1964, President Lyndon Baines Johnson ushered in the War on Poverty, which was to prove that "for the first time in the history of the human race, a great nation is able to make and is willing to make a commitment to eradicate poverty among its people."[1] A little over a decade later, many of the programs associated with the War on Poverty are being dismantled and a new philosophy denying that the federal government is either responsible for resolving the problems of the poor or is capable of doing so is replacing the old liberalism.[2]

The current reversal of social policy—this "counterrevolution" as some have called it[3]—brings into focus more sharply than ever the need for evaluation of a seemingly passing stage in American politics, initially marked by high idealism and zealousness and later marred by disappointment and intensive criticism by conservatives and liberals alike. As various poverty programs of the 1960s are eliminated in the 1970s, practitioners and academics alike must ask what effects (if any) the variety of programs associated with the War on Poverty have had on the lives of the individuals they were supposed to affect and on the communities they were supposed to lift from the misery of poverty. Will some of the processes initiated by these programs be more lasting than the programs themselves?

This book assesses the long-range impact of one major procedural change implemented by the War on Poverty programs: the notion that change targets or clients must be involved actively if change endeavors are to be effective—the alternatively lauded, misunderstood, and much criticized notion of "maximum feasible participation."

## "MAXIMUM FEASIBLE PARTICIPATION" AS A CATALYST FOR THE CREATION OF COMMUNITY ADVISORY COUNCILS

"Maximum feasible participation" was undoubtedly the most controversial component of the War on Poverty, eliciting heated debate from all sides of the political spectrum. That it was a poorly understood concept at the time of its enactment as part of the Economic Opportunity Act is a problem that has been well documented elsewhere and need not be discussed directly in this book.[4] This book is concerned with what consequences (if any) that concept has elicited, and what impact it has had on the lives of the individuals taking part in the process and on the communities where it has been established. To explore these consequences, first the operationalization of the "maximum feasible participation" concept will be discussed, then the numerous scholarly efforts to evaluate it.

The notion that community action programs were to be "developed, conducted, and administered with the 'maximum feasible participation' of residents of the areas and of the groups served,"[5] was interpreted and operationalized diversely in different communities across the country.[6] Although most of the original Community Action Programs (CAPs) complied with the federal requirement by creating private, nonprofit, nongovernmental agencies governed by boards in which at least one-third of the membership was selected from the ranks of "poor" communities,[7] most of the Office of Economic Opportunity (OEO) delegate agencies, as well as the subsequent Model Cities program and other programs, operationalized the concept of resident participation primarily by creating advisory bodies. Generally, these groups were known as advisory councils or advisory boards.

Although citizen participation in the form of advisory councils to public agencies long has been an established practice in the American political system, it has been limited to different groups at different times in our history. As John Strange put it, "Only propertied, well-educated, white males have always been eligible to participate in our government processes."[8] Traditionally, advisory councils to public agencies have been composed of leading citizens, primarily professional and business "nonamateur" types.

By and large, the specific efforts to induce more "grass roots" participation prior to the 1960s were unsuccessful. Two major examples can be found in the Tennessee Valley Authority (TVA), and in the urban renewal programs established by the Housing Act of 1954.[9] In his widely acclaimed study, <u>TVA and the Grass Roots</u>, Philip Selznick concludes that the TVA's policy of grass roots administration, which channeled the administration of the program through established local institutions, in fact served to reinforce the legitimacy of the existing leadership to the detriment of potential opposition groups. Reliance on the existing leadership structure inhibited a direct approach to the local citizenry and precluded the articulation of interests outside the preestablished local elite.[10] In terms of the second example, urban renewal, most cities responded to the citizen participation requirements of the Housing Act of 1954 by "creating citywide advisory committees composed of leading citizens with little or no representation from the neighborhoods affected by urban renewal."[11]

In essence, the "maximum feasible participation" requirement cannot be considered as a "revolutionary" innovation. Citizen participation, in rhetoric at least, always has been part of American political tradition. However, the element that was undeniably novel and perhaps revolutionary in the War on Poverty programs was that, for the first time and on a large scale, a different class of people was being asked to participate in the operation of public programs. Not the professionals, nor the businessmen, nor the established local elites, but rather the amateurs, the poor, "the common community people" were asked to be involved.

This novel practice of including representatives of the poor (or laymen) in advisory councils to public agencies has "caught on" and has been adopted by a wide variety of agencies, some connected with the War on Poverty, some clearly outside its boundaries. While in the early 1960s participation of the poor largely was confined to a few programs such as the CAPs and later the Model Cities program, today many agencies encompassing all levels of government (that is, federal, state, county, and city) and most policy areas (such as, education, health, welfare, or senior citizens services) have adopted the practice of creating advisory councils largely composed of community representatives.[12] Thus it is likely that the procedural innovation represented by the "maximum feasible participation" requirement will last beyond and independently of the longevity of the War on Poverty programs.[13]

Although the growing practice of including community representatives in advisory councils to public agencies attracted unparalleled attention on the part of social scientists,[14] its effects are still not clearly understood. Scholarly efforts to evaluate this type of participation made throughout the 1960s and early 1970s are characterized by a number of shortcomings—both substantive and methodological.

## STUDIES OF THE WAR ON POVERTY: SUBSTANTIVE PROBLEMS

Although it is difficult to make generalizations about various studies of War on Poverty programs given their variety, divergent approaches, and extensive number, an overview of this literature suggests that most have been concerned primarily with assessing the short-range effects of participation of the poor. Two types of short-range effects have been the object of intensive study: (1) the question of power distribution (that is, has participation resulted in the redistribution of political power to formerly powerless classes of people, or has participation been primarily of a cooptative nature, a facade?), and (2) the question of optimal delivery of services (that is, how does participation of poverty clientele groups add to or detract from the quality of services delivered?).

### Focus on Power

Of these two concerns, the question of power distribution seems to have received the most attention. Three related lines of inquiry are manifested in research on power distribution effects: (1) determination of the extent of power redistribution (if any) on the basis of empirical findings from one or more programs, (2) research on the correlates of different types of power configurations, and (3) research on the outcomes of different types of power configurations.

In terms of the first line of inquiry—research on the extent of power redistribution—the evidence gathered is inconclusive. As Hans Spiegel and Stephen Mittenthal point out, ". . . the evidence that we do have is contradictory, inconclusive, particularistic, and overly qualified by the dictates of time, place, and circumstances."[15] Examples range from cases where residents actually gained control of programs[16] to cases where participation was totally cooptative and tokenistic,[17] to cases where participation, in Elliot Krause's terms, was purely "bureaucratic ideology."[18] Indeed, variation of effects according to diverse local conditions is the primary finding of several major studies of War on Poverty programs.[19]

Notwithstanding the diversity of results reported however, if a tentative generalization about the question of power distribution were to be made, it would appear that the weight of the evidence falls on the side of those cases where participation proved to be largely cooptative and tokenistic and where no effective redistribution of power occurred.[20]

Research efforts also have been made to determine the correlates of different modes of power distribution, that is, what conditions tend to produce "adversary" versus "cooptative"[21] modes of power distribution. Research on this question, however, is more sparse. It is known, for example, that power relationships predominant in the councils tend to be related to the type of city in which the councils operate; that is, "boss" cities tend to be associated with "cooptative" councils, but "reform" cities tend to be associated with more "adversary" type councils.[22] Also, controversy and conflict seem to have prevailed only in those local settings where conditions were already ripe for conflict, where groups of the poor were mobilized already and organized for action.[23]

Controversy and divergent findings also have dominated the final category of research associated with the question of power distribution—what are the outcomes of different modes of power distribution? The major controversy in this area hinges on whether the "adversary" form of decision making is conducive to program efforts that are racially separatist.[24] The problem of bias, so endemic to most of the literature on citizen participation in the War on Poverty, is particularly evident in research on this question. As Spiegel and Mittenthal put it in a general statement of the problem,

> A scientific approach to citizen participation is extraordinarily difficult, suffused as it is with normative judgements, value laden preconceptions, lack of objective criteria, and standards of measurement, and a host of differentiated perspectives from which anyone can draw whatever meaning his predilections desire. If one concludes, for example, that citizen participation is, by nature, good and desirable, then nearly every instance of it demonstrates a modicum of value, regardless of how much rationalization is accommodated in the process. Conversely, if one has reservations about the efficacy of this process, it is not at all difficult to uncover situations which substantiate such doubts. Few absolutes adhere to citizen participation. Much of it is relative and contingent upon a wide variety of variables, not the least of which is the non-objective perception of the beholder.[25]

### Focus on Quality of Services

The second major area of concern in research on "maximum feasible participation" has been focused on the optimal delivery of services and on the challenges that citizen participation poses for the planning process. As Ronald A. Warren suggested, "Resident participation . . . has changed the entire conception of what the planning process would be like and what goals might be accomplished."[26] Indeed, the concept of citizen participation in the planning and delivery of social services brings into sharp focus the issue of "who knows their needs best, the poor or the technicians?" Or, as Robert Aleshire put it, "Is the better decision for the neighborhood that which arises from a factual examination or that which is the product of intergroup participation and pressure?"[27]

Extensive controversy[28] has been engendered on this question basically because it touches on two crucial yet often conflicting requisites of democracy—effectiveness and responsiveness—and because it is a question that assumes increasing preeminence as the society becomes more technocratic and as deference to expertise as the *modus operandi* comes increasingly under attack.[29] The real controversy in this area seems to revolve around a conflict of values, rather than around divergent empirical findings. Do the costs associated with increased participation outweigh its benefits? Some studies have shown that where there has been participation ineffective delivery of services has been common. How much loss in delivery, then, is acceptable for a gain in participation?

The major criticism that can be leveled at this body of literature is that, by focusing largely on the short-range effects of "maximum feasible participation," it was shortsighted to neglect considering possible long-range effects. This criticism is not meant to suggest that the major questions that were posed—i.e., power distribution and quality of services—were not important. On the contrary, these represent crucial areas of concern. Certainly, finding out whether previously aggrieved classes have been able to gain their rightful share of political power is a question that should concern most political scientists.[30] Similarly, the concern over the quality of services delivered and research on the conflict between the expert and common citizen are questions that have gained prominence as society has grown more technocratic and the individual more powerless.

Nevertheless, an important gap in this literature remains neglecting to consider the possible long-range effects of "maximum feasible participation:" the political socialization effects of increased citizen participation. It is clear that most evaluations of the effects of increased participation took a limited time perspective. As Nathan Glazer suggests, "Thus it turned out we had much better studies of the beginnings of programs than of how they operated once started and once the initial phases of conflict were overcome. . . . After it [the CAP program] was more or less running at the end of the sixties, our data—at least in the form of good studies by social scientists—becomes sparser."[31]

It is possible that the limited time referent evidenced in the majority of studies has helped to overemphasize the shortcomings of War on Poverty programs and has accentuated the general dissatisfaction and dissappointment pervading discussions of increased community participation.[32] This is easy to understand given the rhetoric of the early 1960s, and the high expectations raised by the vision of a "massive war on poverty" and by "maximum feasible participation"—both in the scholarly community and in the poor communities themselves.

This generalized disappointment, while understandable, is not readily justifiable from a social science perspective. It can be argued that it was almost naive to hold very high expectations regarding the immediate consequences of the new process. Social change, after all, does not generally occur overnight. Political power, in particular, is not a commodity that can easily be given to those who do not possess it or taken away from those who do. Rarely, if ever, in the history of mankind has one seen politically powerful groups relinquish their power voluntarily. How could one then expect that established local elites would not attempt to gain control over the new resources handed out by the federal government and try to coopt or manipulate possibly emerging opposition groups?

Whatever the immediate results of "maximum feasible participation" have been, the fact remains that this federal requirement has resulted in the institutionalization and diffusion of the notion that the layman ought to have an input into the operation of government agencies. Procedural changes, whether "real" or solely "formal," have been made. Whether they hold effective political power, the fact remains that poor people and unskilled citizens by the hundreds of thousands are taking part in advisory councils all over the country. And, as previously noted, this participatory process is likely to continue independently of the War on Poverty programs that fostered it.

The major question posed in this study, then, is what long-range effects are likely to ensue as a result of increased citizen participation in community advisory councils? More specifically, what are the political socialization effects of this new process? Are the individuals engaged in this process becoming more politicized? Are they making gains in terms of political skills, information, and sophistication? Are new community leaders emerging? And, ultimately, what effects is this process likely to have on the poor communities themselves?

In essence, the ultimate purpose of this research is in many ways similar to the concern that has dominated previous studies. That is, will political power eventually be redistributed to previously powerless groups? Yet the perspective taken and the assumptions made are different here. Basically, the author assumes that redistribution of power will not occur through some kind of _deus ex machina_ process. Rather, she assumes that transferral of power _may_ occur only when and if the poor gain the political competition skills to intervene effectively in the political arena. The focus of the study thus rests on an empirical investigation of citizen participation in advisory councils as a process that may (or may not) be conducive to the acquisition of certain skills, attitudes, and behavior, which in turn may (or may not) lead ultimately to the redistribution of power.

## STUDIES ON THE WAR ON POVERTY: METHODOLOGICAL PROBLEMS

Three major methodological shortcomings characterize studies of the War on Poverty: (1) the lack of scientific rigor, (2) limited coverage, and (3) overly "micro" or overly "macro" approaches to the subject.

### Lack of Scientific Rigor

The bulk of research on the effects of "maximum feasible participation" consists of impressionistic, mainly descriptive and unsystematic, case studies of one or more programs. For example, after reviewing 200 reports coming from research on antipoverty programs, Peter Rossi concluded that 85 percent of them were " . . . primarily descriptive accounts of how many people were being reached by the program. They tended to be written in a loosely narrative form, with virtually no systematic observation on the effectiveness of the programs included."[33] Part of this problem, of course, is due to inherent difficulties of conducting evaluative research.[34] Notwithstanding the seriousness of the evaluation problem, there is a clear need for more empirically oriented and rigorous research on the basis of which more theoretically relevant conclusions may be made.[35]

### Limited Coverage

Most of the studies of the War on Poverty focused on the experience of citizen participation in the most important programs, CAPs and Model Cities, neglecting the experience of other agencies, which have adopted the practice of creating community advisory councils. As previously noted, the "maximum feasible participation" requirement of the Economic Opportunity Act served as a catalyst for the diffusion and institutionalization of citizen participation in many public agencies outside those two programs. The effects of participation in these agencies, however, is, by and large, unstudied.

Moreover, it is possible, given such focus on the major programs (CAP and Model Cities), that the problems of "cooptation" of the poor may have been overemphasized. S. M. Miller and his associates call this process the "creaming of the poor," or the "process by which mainly the least poor are included in the poverty programs . . . and which seems to maintain the status quo needs of the larger society. It coopts the potential or actual leaders of the poor and leaves untouched those poor who may be too miserable to pressure for change."[36] Many studies did find that this process was operative in the CAP and Model Cities programs. Yet it should be kept in mind that both of these programs involved high stakes: the disbursement of millions of dollars and of new resources so readily handed out by the federal government. Other programs adopting the practice of citizen participation involved much lower stakes, at least in financial terms. In this respect it is possible that the issues that arise in the councils and the conflicts that divide agencies and councils may be different. As essentially disbursing programs, CAP and Model Cities generally involved conflict over two main issues: (1) program priorities (that is, what kind of programs should be funded or not) and (2) administration priorities (who should administer them—established agencies, newly created agencies, or community groups). Personal observation of agency-council conflicts in other agencies (schools, health clinics, and service centers[37]) suggests that the issues that arise tend to be of a different nature. They seem to involve conflict over details of program implementation and, most prominently, conflicts over personnel matters. In this sense, if the nature of the issues differs, possibly the nature of the power configurations differs also.

This possibility highlights even more prominently the need for extensive empirical investigation of citizen participation in agencies other than CAP and Model Cities.

### Too "Micro" or Too "Macro" Approaches

Studies of the War on Poverty primarily have pursued either of two approaches: (1) idiosyncratic case studies of single agencies mainly done in an unsystematic and impressionistic way[38] or (2) more empirically oriented macro aggregate studies of CAPs all over the country.[39] Each of these approaches appears to suffer from opposite shortcomings. The first sacrifices theoretical relevance at the expense of depth. The second, because of its broad and aggregate nature, emphasizes theoretical relevance at the expense of depth. Moreover, the macro approach necessarily involves focusing on measurable and easily comparable short-range, tangible outputs, to the neglect of more intangible (and not readily measurable on a national basis), long-range effects.

This study seeks to avoid some of the methodological problems evident in previous studies of War on Poverty programs by following an empirical, middle-range approach. As the study's primary substantive interest lies in exploring the long-range socialization effects of increased lay participation in the context of the full variety of agencies that have adopted this practice, the study focuses on <u>all</u> the advisory councils operative in one community: the predominantly Mexican-American community of East Los Angeles, California. If participation in advisory councils serves as a politicizing and skills-acquiring experience, it is at the community level that its effects ultimately will be felt. Moreover, by focusing on all the advisory councils in one community, the approach avoids the problem of particularism so endemic to the micro or single program study approach. Finally, the focus on a single community allows us to retain some of the depth and focus on "intangibles," which is exceedingly difficult to obtain through the use of a national macro or aggregate approach.

Any conclusions empirically derived from this study, of course, are only applicable to that community. Hence, any conclusions made

## MAJOR PURPOSE OF THIS STUDY

The major purpose of this study is suggested by Peter Bachrach and Morton Baratz in Power and Poverty: Theory and Practice. They suggest that

> Cooptative participation within the antipoverty effort can help the poor develop a set of political interests, increase their political resources, and acquire the know how to intervene effectively in the political process. In other words, cooptative participation by the poor can lead to interest oriented participation and the development of indigenous leadership.[40]

First, the discussion will focus on the general evidence available on this proposition; subsequently it will turn to a more detailed analysis of its component parts.

There is little empirical evidence available on the notion that, regardless of the quality of participation (that is, cooptative or adversary), the participative process itself works to foster certain values and to teach political skills, which ultimately can lead to the emergence of indigenous leadership in poverty communities. In fact, the few references to this question in the literature consist of highly impressionistic statements based on personal observation rather than on rigorous empirical research. Consider, for example, the following two commentaries, neither of which cites any empirical evidence for the "conventional wisdom" posited:

> New leaders numbering in the tens of thousands have emerged from among the poor, near poor, and minority groups, including many militants who now call the poverty program "mickey mouse," but who got considerable experience on the CAP payroll.[41]

And, in a similar vein,

> All the same, Community Action has probably led to such lasting consequences as the development of new black leaders and the opening of opportunities for paraprofessionals who in New York City have secured effective union advocates. What works in the long run is political power. Even though the Nixon administration is neither

> beholden to the black community nor particularly
> sympathetic to its aspirations, the impetus for
> black political organization given by the Great
> Society is likely in a more promising post-Nixon
> national administration to produce both legislative
> and administrative benefits.[42] (emphasis added)

This conventional wisdom about the emergence of leaders is further marred by critics who suggest, also primarily in an impressionistic fashion, that even though leaders may be emerging, they are the "wrong type of leaders." Consider, for example, Tom Kahn's statement on this matter.

> By playing on the theme of the poor as lonely non-participants, The Other America helped set the stage for the notion that we had to give the poor something to belong to, somebody to belong to. The somebody turned out to be John Lindsay . . . and the something turned out to be boards—poverty boards, planning boards, school boards, boards of directors, boards of trustees—all in the unshakable conviction of the middle class activist that everyone shares his fondness, or need for, going to meetings, articulating like blazes, and "relating" all over the place. The result? Instead of the invisible poor and the silent poor, we got the vivid poor and the noisy poor—and the terribly participatory poor.[43]

Or, as Edward Banfield suggests,

> Where motivation developed, it may have done so in spite of these programs rather than because of them. The people who gained most, however, were "middle class," not culturally deprived.[44]

The concern over the "representative" nature of indigenous poverty leadership evidenced in these statements represents a theme evoked in many other studies. It is the author's expectation that the information gained in compiling this book may shed additional light on that question. As the research strategy followed focuses on all the advisory councils operative in one community, aggregate data on the characteristics of members of councils should reveal how "representative" they are of the general population, thus avoiding possibly idiosyncratic findings based on case studies of single programs.

This study focuses on the possible politicization effects of involvement in advisory councils—a research question that either has been overlooked in previous studies or has been mentioned in passing on the basis of highly impressionistic analysis. The major questions posed, to be fully explicated in Chapter 2, are listed below.

(1) Does involvement in advisory councils lead to the acquisition of attitudes that are conducive to political participation?

(2) Does involvement in advisory councils lead to the acquisition of political skills and to an increase in political information and sophistication?

(3) Does involvement in advisory councils lead to behavioral changes in the direction of increased involvement in community activities?

(4) If the first three conditions are empirically operative, is involvement in advisory councils conducive to the formation of indigenous leaders?

In regard to the first question, there is some evidence to support it. A few case studies focusing directly on the War on Poverty have found that the participation of the poor has resulted in sociopsychological changes, that is, in the reduction of feelings of powerlessness, normlessness, and anomie, and in an increase in achievement orientations and feelings of self-competence.[45] The hypothesized link between participation in the councils and attitudinal changes, however, needs to be tested more extensively and, in particular, in varied ethnic settings. The findings of Louis Zurcher's study suggest that patterns of attitudinal change may vary according to culture or ethnicity; Mexican-Americans in the sample did not manifest attitudinal changes in the hypothesized direction but showed increases in anomie, isolation, powerlessness, and alienation.[46] The Mexican-American community of East Los Angeles thus represents an excellent setting where the relationship between attitudinal changes and ethnicity can be explored further.

In terms of the second question, to this author's knowledge no study has attempted to ascertain empirically whether experience in advisory councils can lead to the acquisition of new skills by the participants. This question becomes of key concern when one is attempting to ascertain the potential development of an indigenous leadership group capable of effective intervention in the political arena. Potentially effective political action requires, among other things, the ability to organize and the knowledge to deal with government bureaucracies at all levels. Hence a major focus of this study is to ascertain whether participants in advisory councils become more politically skilled and knowledgeable as a result of the advisory council experience.

To this author's knowledge, there are no empirical data in the War on Poverty literature[47] bearing on the third question—does involvement in advisory councils lead to behavioral changes in the direction of increased participation in community affairs? This is a crucial area for analysis because, while changes in attitudes and skill levels may demonstrate a "latent" propensity for political action, behavioral changes may demonstrate a "manifest" propensity for political action, thus greatly enriching the analysis.

On the basis of the results obtained on the first three questions, one can further speculate about the potential effects of increased individual politicization at the group or community level. Two main questions are explored: is individual politicization likely to endure, and what type of leadership is likely to emerge? This study thus seeks to obtain empirically grounded answers to the overall question of how the advisory council experience affects attitudes and behavior at the individual level and to speculate about what consequences individual changes may elicit at the group level.

Before turning in Chapters 2 and 3 to a more detailed discussion of the central hypotheses and of the research methodology, an assumption implicit throughout this chapter must be discussed: increasing the level of participation of a largely politically inactive and politically deprived class of people—the poor—may potentially bring about a variety of necessary socioeconomic changes.

## IF THE POOR ARE POLITICIZED, SO WHAT?

Increasing the level of political participation of the poor is a notion that, paradoxically, has been viewed with skepticism by political scientists embracing opposite conceptions about how the American political system is run, and widely divergent views about democracy and the proper role of the social scientist. On the one hand, those in the mainstream of the discipline (those who tend to believe that the American system is pluralistic and who tend to define democracy in accordance with the Anglo-American empirical reality[48] have viewed any rise in the level of participation of the lower classes as a potential threat to the stability of the system. The conceptions of these theorists are not discussed here because their views are elaborated upon in Chapter 2. Suffice it to say that, guided by an overriding concern with stability and by a particular interpretation of democracy, these theorists, until recently, either have not been concerned with redressing class inequalities in levels of political participation or have tended to view any such efforts with suspicion.

On the other hand, another set of theorists holding opposite views about pluralism, democracy, and the role of social science[49] also have viewed increased participation of the poor with skepticism, but for different reasons. They contend that the politicization of the poor may be fruitless because the political structures are inherently unresponsive. Michael Parenti, for example, espouses this position in "Power and Pluralism: A View from the Bottom." After reviewing three case studies in Newark, New Jersey, in which the poverty community, although highly mobilized and organized, was unable to prevail on some minor issues, Parenti concludes that the poor lack the "exchange power" necessary to bargain in the political arena: That is, they lack "marketable" resources that can create the kinds of inducements that would make it in the political leaders' interest to take positive measures. Lacking as they do in money, status, and expertise, the only bargaining resource that the poor might have—numbers in the form of votes—is still ineffective. Parenti argues, "Unlike the indigent in many other countries, the poor in America are a minority and therefore even when mobilized for electoral participation, may only have a limited impact. The power of numbers can be employed when countervailing efficacy by the majority that identifies with the 'haves' and against the 'have nots'."[50]

This type of analysis obviously raises some question as to the possible futility of conducting research on increased citizen participation. If increased participation may be fruitless, why study how it can be brought about? In this author's view, a priori assumptions about the responsiveness (or lack thereof) of the American political system ought not be allowed to circumscribe research. Political scientists do not agree on the extent to which the American system of government is (or can be) responsive. The "elitist-pluralist" debate[51] and the "participatory democracy-democratic elitism" debate,[52] to mention only two examples, clearly attest to this uncertainty. In this regard, the discipline is undoubtedly in a state of flux, in a transition stage searching for a new paradigm.[53] While the dominant model (pluralism), the dominant approach (behavioralism), and the dominant emphasis (stability) are the object of extensive questioning and criticism, no consensus exists regarding an alternative model, approach, or emphasis. More "creative speculation"[54] and research departing from alternative perspectives and employing alternative methodologies will have to be conducted before any definitive answers can be given to the question of how the American system is run, how it should be run, and how it can be run.

Adherence to a particular model of American politics, given the state of flux in the discipline's orientation and style, is thus unwise, and, moreover, unnecessary for the purposes of this book. The only assumption made here about the American political system is that increased citizen participation potentially _may_ alter the nature and quality of political outputs and affect the distribution of socioeconomic benefits. In this sense, citizen participation is viewed as a potentially _necessary_ but not _sufficient_ condition for socioeconomic changes to occur. Though in many respects this is a normative assumption, it is also supported by empirical research.

In their recent study, <u>Participation in America: Political Democracy and Social Equality,</u>[55] Sidney Verba and Norman Nie address themselves to this question, that is, does citizen participation make a difference in regard to policy outcomes and the policy preferences of the elites? Their findings clearly demonstrate that the policy preferences of those who participate (largely those in the middle and upper classes) are congruent with the policy preferences of the elites and with actual policy outcomes.[56] Moreover, the relationship between the policy preferences of the elites and those who participate is "not the result of the social characteristics of participants, but appears to be an independent effect of participation."[57] The authors conclude,

> Participation, looked at generally, does not necessarily help one social group rather than another. The general model of the sources and consequences of participation that we have presented could work in a number of ways. It could work so that lower status citizens were more effective politically and used that political effectiveness to improve their social and economic circumstances. Or it could work, as it appears to do in the United States, to benefit upper class citizens more. It depends on what organizations, parties, and belief systems exist, and how these affect participation rates. Participation remains a powerful social force for increasing or decreasing inequality. It depends on who takes advantage of it.[58]

Increased participation by the lower classes <u>may</u> offer a potential means for inducing socioeconomic policy changes. This potential validates conducting research on redressing the class bias of political participation.

A discussion of research on political socialization and political participation, which provides the broader framework against which this study is cast, follows. In Chapter 2, the major hypotheses to be explored are defined and operationalized, and the adopted research strategy is discussed.

NOTES

1. Johnson's statement as quoted in Daniel Patrick Moynihan, <u>Maximum Feasible Misunderstanding</u> (New York: The Free Press, 1969), pp. 3-4.

2. Manifestations of this trend are the dismantling of much of the OEO bureaucracy and the displacement of many of the categorical grants-in-aid programs of the 1960s with federal revenue sharing in 1972. On the OEO, see "Nixon's Call to Counter-Revolution," <u>Time</u> (February 5, 1973): 24-29, and Robert A. Diamond, ed., <u>Future of Social Programs</u>, (Washington, D.C.: Congressional Quarterly Inc., 1973). For some documentation of the anti-social-welfare bias of revenue sharing, see Ellen Boneparth and Terry Christensen, "Revenue Sharing in Santa Clara County: Take the Money and Run," paper presented at the Annual Meeting of the Western Political Science Association, 1974, Denver.

3. See comments to this effect in Edward C. Banfield et al., "A Symposium: Nixon, the Great Society, and the Future of Social Policy," <u>Commentary</u> 55, no. 5 (May 1973): 31-62.

4. See, for example, Lillian Rubin, "Maximum Feasible Participation: The Origins, Implications, and Present Status," <u>Poverty and</u>

Human Resources Abstracts 2, no. 6 (November-December 1967): 5-18; and Harry Scoble, "The Political Scientist's Perspective on Poverty," in Poverty: New Interdisciplinary Perspectives, edited by Thomas Weaver and Alvin Magid (San Francisco: Chandler, 1969), pp. 134-152.

5. From the Economic Opportunity Act of 1964, Title II: Urban and Rural Community Action Programs; Part A: General Community Action Programs, sec. 202 (a).

6. See John H. Strange, "Citizen Participation in Community Action and Model Cities Programs," Public Administration Review 32, Special Issue (October 1972): 656.

7. Richard W. Boone, "Reflections on Citizen Participation and the Economic Opportunity Act," Public Administration Review 32, Special Issue (September 1972): 448.

8. John H. Strange, "The Impact of Citizen Participation on Public Administration," Public Administration Review 32, Special Issue (September 1972): 458.

9. Robert A. Aleshire, "Power to the People: An Assessment of the Community Action and Model Cities Experience," Public Administration Review 32, Special Issue (September 1972): 429.

10. Philip Selznick, TVA and the Grass Roots: A Study in the Sociology of Formal Organization (Berkeley, Calif.: University of California Press, 1949).

11. Howard Hallman, "Federally Financed Citizen Participation," Public Administration Review 32, Special Issue (September 1972): 421.

12. See, for example, a survey of agencies making participation a requirement in Melvin Moguloff, "Citizen Participation: A Review and Commentary on Federal Policies and Practices," and "Citizen Participation: The Local Perspective," Working Papers (Washington, D.C.: The Urban Institute, 1970). See also comments in Strange, op. cit., p. 467. In addition, in the area surveyed in this study (East Los Angeles) 70 advisory councils were found to be operative.

13. Further evidence suggesting that the notion of citizen participation indeed has become institutionalized is found in recent developments in the health area. One of the major provisions of the National Health Planning and Resources Development Act of 1974 (which calls for the reorganization of health planning across the country) is the creation of governing boards composed of a plurality of citizen consumers. Citizen participation is also a requirement in some Law Enforcement Assistance Administration programs; see Marjorie P. Stern, "Citizen Participation in the War on Crime: Accountability Insurance?," paper presented at the Annual Meeting of the American Society for Public Administration, April 4, 1975, Chicago.

14. See, for example, an extensive bibliography of studies on the War on Poverty compiled by U.S. Department of Housing and Urban Development, "Citizen and Business Participation in Urban Affairs" (Washington, D.C.: U.S. Government Printing Office, 1970); and

extensive bibliographies cited in two special issues of the <u>Public Administration Review</u>: "Curriculum Essays on Citizens, Politics, and Administration in Urban Neighborhoods" <u>Public Administration Review</u> 32, Special Issue (October 1972): 566-738; and "Citizens Action in Model Cities and CAP Programs: Case Studies and Evaluation" <u>Public Administration Review</u> 32, Special Issue (September 1972): 377-470.

15. Hans B. C. Spiegel and Stephen D. Mittenthal, "The Many Faces of Citizen Participation: A Bibliographic Overview," in <u>Citizen Participation in Urban Development</u>, vol. 1, edited by Hans B. C. Spiegel (Center for Community Affairs: NTL Institute for Applied Behavioral Research, 1968), p. 3.

16. See, for example, Ralph M. Kramer, <u>Participation of the Poor: Comparative Community Case Studies in the War on Poverty</u> (Englewood Cliffs, N.J.: Prentice Hall, 1969); and Judy V. May, "Two Model Cities: Political Development on the Local Level," paper presented at the Sixty-Fifth Annual Meeting of the American Political Science Association, September 1969, New York City.

17. This is particularly true of studies that examined a large number of councils. In the large-scale study conducted by the Florence Heller Graduate School, Brandeis University, for example, 17 of 20 councils in 20 different cities were found to be largely cooptative. See David M. Austin, "Resident Participation: Political Mobilization or Cooptation," <u>Public Administration Review</u> 32, Special Issue (September 1972): 409-420. See also Stephen M. Rose, <u>The Betrayal of the Poor: The Transformation of Community Action</u> (Cambridge, Mass.: Schenkman, 1972); Roberta S. Sigel, "Citizen Advisory Groups: Do They Really Represent the People or Are They Rubberstamp Decisions of the 'Experts'?," <u>Nation's Cities</u> 6 (May 1968): 15-21; and Kenneth J. Pollinger and Annette C. Pollinger, <u>Community Action and the Poor: Influence versus Social Control in a New York City Community</u> (New York: Praeger Publishers, 1972).

18. Elliott A. Krause, "Functions of a Bureaucratic Ideology: Citizen Participation," <u>Social Problems</u> 16, no. 2 (Fall 1968): 129-143.

19. See, for example, Howard Hallman, "The Community Action Program: An Interpretative Analysis," in <u>Urban Poverty: Its Social and Political Dimensions</u>, edited by Warner Bloomberg, Jr., and Henry J. Schmandt (Beverly Hills, Calif.: Sage, 1970); and Florence Heller School of Advanced Studies in Social Welfare, Brandeis University, Report no. 5, "Community Representation in Community Action Programs" (Waltham, Mass.: Brandeis University, 1969).

20. See studies cited in Note 17.

21. Austin's dichotomy in op. cit.

22. David Greenstone and Paul Peterson, "Reformers, Machines, and the War on Poverty," in <u>Cities and Suburbs</u>, edited by Bryan T. Downes (Belmont, Calif.: Wadsworth, 1971): 377-399.

23. See Hallman, op. cit.

24. For opposing views on this question, see Alan A. Altshuller, Community Control: The Black Demand for Participation in Large American Cities (New York: Pegasus, 1970); and Melvin Moguloff, "Black Community Development in Five Western Cities," Social Work 15, no. 1 (January 1970): 12-18. For empirical data on this question, see also Richard L. Cole, Citizen Participation and the Urban Policy Process (Lexington, Mass.: D. C. Heath and Co., 1974), ch. 5.

25. Spiegel and Mittenthal, op. cit., p. 4.

26. Ronald A. Warren, "Model Cities First Round: Politics, Planning, and Participation," Journal of the American Institute of Planners 35, no. 4 (July 1969): 245.

27. Robert A. Aleshire, op. cit., p. 434.

28. See, for example, Howard Hallman, Community Control: A Study of Community Corporations and Neighborhood Boards (Washington, D.C.: Center for Metropolitan Studies, 1969); Robert C. Wood, "A Call for Return to Community," Public Management 51, no. 7 (July 1969): 2-9; Edmund M. Burke "Citizen Participation Strategies," Journal of the American Institute of Planners 34, no. 5 (September 1968): 287-294; and Robert A. Aleshire, "Planning and Citizen Participation: Costs, Benefits, and Approaches," Urban Affairs Quarterly 5, no. 4 (June 1970): 369-393.

29. For a statement about this problem, see Theodore Roszack, The Making of a Counterculture (Garden City, N.Y.: Anchor Books, 1969).

30. This is so even though many in the mainstream of the discipline have not been concerned with this problem. This point is discussed in Chapter 2.

31. Nathan Glazer's statement in Banfield et al., op. cit., pp. 34-35.

32. Ibid.; this pessimistic tone is very much in evidence in the separate commentaries in that symposium.

33. Peter H. Rossi, "Practice, Methods, and Theory in Evaluating Social Action Programs," in On Fighting Poverty: Perspectives from Experience, edited by James L. Sundquist (New York: Basic Books, 1969), p. 222.

34. Vague and unclear program goals, goals that are not readily measurable, and political obstacles are among the most serious problems. This question is discussed more extensively in Chapter 2.

35. The current trend seems to be in this direction. See Pollinger and Pollinger, op. cit., and Cole, op. cit.

36. S. M. Miller, Pamela Roby, and Alwine A. de Vos Van Steenwijk, "Creaming the Poor," Transaction 7, no. 8 (June 1970): 44.

37. The author was a participant observer in a number of advisory councils in the East Los Angeles area in 1971-72.

38. See Rossi, op. cit.

39. See, for example, Rose, op. cit.

40. Peter Bachrach and Morton S. Baratz, Power and Poverty: Theory and Practice (London: Oxford University Press, 1970), p. 210.
41. Hallman, "Federally Financed Citizen Participation," op. cit., p. 424.
42. Robert Leachman's statement in Banfield et al., op. cit., p. 48.
43. Ibid., p. 43 (Tom Kahn's statement).
44. Ibid., p. 32 (Banfield's statement).
45. Louis A. Zurcher, "The Poverty Board: Some Consequences of 'Maximum Feasible Participation'," The Journal of Social Issues 26, no. 3 (Summer 1970): 85-107; Dale Rogers Marshall, The Politics of Participation in Poverty: A Case Study of the Economic and Youth Opportunities Agency of Greater Los Angeles (Berkeley: University of California Press, 1971); Harry Gottesfeld and Gerterlyn Dozier, "Changes in Feelings of Powerlessness in a Community Action Program," Psychological Reports 19, no. 3 (1966): 978; and Helene Levens, "Organizational Affiliation and Powerlessness: A Case Study of the Welfare Poor," Social Problems 16, no. 1 (Summer 1968): 18-32.
46. Zurcher, op. cit.
47. In other bodies of literature, however, considerable evidence suggests that this is so. This is discussed at length in Chapter 2.
48. The author is referring here to Dahl, McClosky, Lipset, Sartori, and Eckstein, among others. See, for example, views expressed in Robert Dahl, Who Governs? (New Haven, Conn.: Yale University Press, 1961); Herbert McClosky, "Political Participation," in International Encyclopedia of the Social Sciences, vol. 12, edited by David L. Sills (New York: Macmillan, 1968), pp. 252-264,; Seymour Martin Lipset, Political Man (New York: Doubleday and Co., 1960); Giovanni Sartori, Democratic Theory (Detroit: Wayne State University Press, 1962); and Harry Eckstein, Division and Cohesion in Democracy (Princeton: Princeton University Press, 1966).
49. See, for example, Frances Fox Piven and Richard A. Cloward, Regulating the Poor: The Functions of Social Welfare (New York: Pantheon Books, 1971); and Michael Parenti, "Power and Pluralism: A View from the Bottom," Journal of Politics 32, no. 3 (August 1970): 501-530. For views reflecting a similar orientation in the literature on minority groups, see Joan W. Moore, "Colonialism: The Case of the Mexican American," Social Problems 17, no. 4 (Spring 1970): 463-472; Robert Blauner, "Colonialism and Ghetto Revolts," Social Problems 16, no. 4 (Spring 1969): 393-407; and Marrio Barrera, Carlos Munoz, and Charles Ornelas, "The Barrio as an Internal Colony," in People and Politics in Urban Society, edited by Harlan H. Hahn (Beverly Hills, Calif.: Sage, 1972), pp. 465-499.
50. Parenti, op. cit., p. 528.
51. See Dahl, op. cit.; Floyd Hunter, Community Power Structure (Chapel Hill, N.C.: University of North Carolina Press, 1953); Terry N. Clark, ed., Community Structure and Decision Making:

Comparative Analyses (San Francisco: Chandler, 1968); Robert Presthus, Men at the Top (New York: Oxford University Press, 1964); and Nelson Polsby, Community Power and Political Theory (New Haven, Conn.: Yale University Press, 1963); among others.

52. See Peter Bachrach, The Theory of Democratic Elitism: A Critique (Boston: Little, Brown and Co., 1967); Joseph Schumpeter, Capitalism, Socialism, and Democracy (New York: Harper and Brothers, 1942); Robert A. Dahl, "Hierarchy, Democracy, and Bargaining in Politics and Economics," in Political Behavior: A Reader in Theory and Research, edited by Heinz Eulau (Glencoe, Ill.: The Free Press, 1969), pp. 83-90; T. B. Bottomore, Elites and Society (Baltimore: Penguin Books, 1967); and Charles A. McCoy and John Playford, eds., Apolitical Politics: A Critique of Behavioralism (New York: Crowell, 1967).

53. For an elaboration of the functions of paradigms, see Thomas Kuhn, The Structure of Scientific Revolutions (Chicago: University of Chicago Press, 1962).

54. David Easton's terminology in his statement on the "postbehavioral revolution": in "The New Revolution in Political Science," American Political Science Review 63, no. 4 (December 1969): 1058.

55. Sidney Verba and Norman H. Nie, Participation in America: Political Democracy and Social Equality (New York: Harper and Row, 1972).

56. Ibid., ch. 15.
57. Ibid., p. 332.
58. Ibid., p. 342.

CHAPTER

# 2

**INVOLVEMENT IN
ADVISORY COUNCILS AS
AN ALTERNATIVE
ROUTE TO
POLITICAL PARTICIPATION**

Increasing the level of political participation of lower status groups is a subject that has received little attention from social scientists studying the intertwined processes of political participation and political socialization. In fact, research aimed at exploring those processes whereby citizen participation may be fruitfully increased has endured sustained neglect. First this chapter will explore some of the reasons why this area of research has been neglected, and subsequently it will examine findings that indicate a change in research orientation in a direction more congruent with this book.

Major reasons why questions about changing the structure of political participation in the United States generally have not been raised are evident in the assumptions that underlie most studies of political participation and political socialization—assumptions that, in turn, are deeply rooted in the undeniably status quo-oriented ideology that has long dominated the discipline. On the one hand, the majority of studies on political participation have operated under the assumption (implicit or explicit) that the existing level of political participation in the Anglo-American democracies must be taken as given and as adequate to sustain the democratic process. Any appeal to increase the level of existing citizen participation thus has generally been viewed as a potential threat to the stability of the system—the overriding concern of these theorists.

In a similar vein, research on political socialization can be characterized as intrinsically deterministic. The underlying assumption of most political socialization studies has been that most politically relevant attitudes are learned during the preadult period; "early acquired attitudes are usually viewed as likely to remain virtually unchanged during the entire life cycle."[1] Such an assumption obviates conducting research on how attitudes and behavior can be altered through adult socialization inputs and, instead, focuses attention on the child's acquisition of politically relevant norms and attitudes.

Both of these assumptions are rooted in a similar research orientation, which is embodied in a tendency to focus on existing reality and to neglect the possible. There is also a tendency to accept the functioning of the Anglo-American democracies as "the good society" in operation, thus neglecting the question of "who benefits?" and the inevitable concomitant changes that evokes. The following sections explore these reasons in detail.

## STUDIES ON POLITICAL PARTICIPATION: THE STATUS QUO BIAS

Undoubtedly one of the major and most consistent findings of empirical studies on political participation is that political participation is directly related to socioeconomic status (SES). As Nie and his colleagues point out,

> . . . studies report strong relationships between aggregate socio-economic measures such as per capita income, median level of education, and percentage of the population in urban areas, on one hand, and aggregate measures of political participation such as voting turnout on the other. Simultaneously, scholars conducting surveys of individual political participation consistently have reported that an individual's social status, education, and organizational memberships strongly affect the likelihood of his engaging in various types of political activity.[2]

Indeed, the fact that lower-class individuals are less likely to participate in politics has been amply documented by numerous studies in the United States and in cross-cultural research.[3] The lower classes, moreover, appear to be more severely underrepresented in the United States than in any other Western democracy.[4]

Reasons why the lower-class individual does not generally participate in politics have been documented amply. The primary reason is perhaps the "social situation" in which he finds himself. Lower-class status by definition implies lack of financial resources, lack of education, and engagement in low status occupations in generally highly authoritarian and hierarchical environments. These objective life conditions lead, in turn, to subjective perceptions of one's environment, and (more importantly) to subjective evaluations of one's capacity to deal with that environment. This is embodied in a generalized feeling of lack of control over one's life or in the lack of a sense of general personal efficacy.[5]

The absence of a feeling of self-efficacy on the part of the lower-class individual is related intimately to his propensity for political passivity. It is accepted that personal feelings of self-competence underlie in many respects the individual's propensity to participate in politics. As Lester Milbrath suggests, "Persons who feel more effective in their everyday tasks and challenges are more likely to participate in politics."[6] The relationship between one's experience in nonpolitical situations and a propensity to participate in politics, moreover, has been documented extensively in cross-cultural research. As Gabriel Almond and Sidney Verba suggest in *The Civic Culture*,

> If in most social situations the individual finds himself subservient to some authority figure, it is likely that he will expect such an authority relationship in the political sphere. On the other hand, if outside the political sphere he has the opportunities to participate in a wide range of social decisions, he will probably expect to be able to participate in political decisions as well. Furthermore, participation in nonpolitical decision making may give one the skills needed to engage in political participation . . . [7]

It is also generally accepted that the lower-class individual generally subsists in an authoritarian environment. As Carole Pateman puts it, "It is almost part of the definition of a low status occupation that the individual has little scope for the exercise of initiative or control over his job and working conditions, plays no part in decision making in the enterprise and is told what to do by his organizational superiors."[8] Quoting G. Knupfer, Pateman continues, "the commonly found lack of effort to control their environment by lower SES groups may arise from 'deeply ingrained habits of doing what one is told.' Economic underprivilege is thus linked to psychological underprivilege and engenders a lack of self-confidence which increases the unwillingness of the lower status person to participate. . . . "[9]

Lack of self-competence in the work sphere may also be linked to other spheres in the life of the lower-class individual. The more authoritarian nature of the family structure of the lower-class person could be linked to the effect of the low-status occupations of the fathers. "Fathers whose work gives them little autonomy, and who are controlled by others, exercising no control themselves, are found to be more aggressive and severe."[10] Added to authoritarian home and work environments, the cumulative lack of propensity of the lower SES individual to participate in politics is further accentuated by his lack of education. Education, as a horizon expanding experience, often fosters a sense of self-competence and consistently has been linked to participant orientations in most empirical studies.[11]

The lower-SES individual's consistent exposure to authoritarian environments inevitably leads to the acquisition of authoritarian orientations toward the political system, a theme made famous by

Seymour Martin Lipset in his studies on "working class authoritarianism."[12] As he said, "The gradual realization that extremist and intolerant movements in modern society are more likely to be based on the lower classes than on the middle and upper classes has posed a tragic dilemma for those intellectuals who once believed the proletariat necessarily to be a force for liberty, racial equality, and social progress."[13]

While the interrelated set of reasons why the lower classes are not active political participants is generally understood, the obvious conclusions that these causes may be amenable to change through structural changes, particularly changes in the work environment, generally have not been drawn.[14] This is because of the particular conception of democracy to which these theorists have adhered.[15] A clear statement of this conception of democracy comes from Robert A. Dahl:

> We must conclude that the classic assumptions about the need for citizen participation in democracy were, at the very least, inadequate. If one regards political equality in the making of decisions as a kind of limit to be achieved, then it is axiomatic that this limit could be arrived at with the complete participation of every adult citizen. Nevertheless, what we call democracy—that is, a system of decision making in which the leaders are more or less responsive to the preferences of the non-leaders—does seem to operate within a relatively low level of citizen participation. Hence it is inaccurate to say that one of the **necessary conditions** for democracy is extensive citizen participation.[16]

When democracy is defined as the existing Anglo-American empirical reality instead of as a goal-oriented system where each individual has the opportunity to develop his capabilities to the fullest extent,[17] the low level of political participation among the lower classes is not considered a problem. On the contrary, apathy is considered to be "functional" for systemic stability; the question of whether or how it is "functional" for the lower classes is also of no concern. This prevalent research orientation has led to two outcomes relevant to this book: (1) the acceptance of given patterns of political participation as the desirable norm has led to a neglect of research on possible means of altering such patterns and (2) the focus on systemic stability has fostered a tendency to view any efforts to alter existing participation levels, particularly in regard to the lower classes, as threatening stability and as possibly conducive to "mass society."[18]

Also, most studies on political participation and, hence, most of the best available empirical data on political participation could be faulted for the narrow way in which "political participation" is construed. Most studies have focused consistently on electoral participation, that is, on voting, elections, and political parties.[19] In an increasingly bureaucratized age, this emphasis could be mislaid. As continuing research notes,[20] the focus of power in the United States has been shifting away from the representative legislative spheres to the executive branches of government. Concomitantly, as administrative agencies increasingly become the relevant political arena the focus of interest articulation and of demands for representation has been shifting away from electoral and legislative politics to the administrative sphere.[21] As Edgar Litt, taking a historical perspective, puts it,

> White immigrant politics emphasized the representative nature of political life while contemporary Negro politics most fundamentally raises the issue of distribution in a society where the Federal government is the key to the distribution of values.[22]

Empirical studies on political participation, focusing as they have on a narrow and possibly increasingly anachronistic definition of politics, largely have failed to keep up with the shift in both decision-making power and demand articulation away from electoral and legislative politics and toward administrative politics.

## STUDIES ON POLITICAL SOCIALIZATION: THE DETERMINISTIC BIAS

In regard to studies on political socialization, it could be posited that this particular body of literature has been imbued with a strong dose of determinism. The most basic assumption underlying most political socialization studies is that overall orientations toward the political system (that is, cognitive, affective, and evaluative) are acquired at an early age. This overriding assumption is evidenced by the fact that, although many studies do point to the necessity of studying adult socialization processes, the bulk of research has been focused on preadult agents of political socialization, for example, family, school, peer groups, and mass media. As one of the most distinguished students of political socialization, Fred Greenstein, reports, the majority of political socialization studies have been devoted to (1) the study of children's political orientations and (2) the study of the acquisition of prevailing norms.[23] A review of one bibliography on political socialization further demonstrates this research emphasis: of nearly 1,000 entries, only approximately 3 percent are related even remotely to adult socialization.[24]

The assumption that early acquisition of values and orientations toward the political system remains stable over time is not based on sound empirical evidence, as David Marsh aptly points out.[25] Longitudinal studies needed to test this assumption are notably lacking. Moreover, what evidence does exist does not suggest that basic personality traits or attitudes remain very stable during an individual's life cycle.[26] In this respect, it is clear that "the constancy of early socialized attitudes and behavior over the lifetime of an individual must be treated as a researchable question rather than as a premise."[27]

A shift in research priorities in the socialization literature is necessary not only for the sake of scientific validity but also, from a more normative viewpoint, for the sake of exploring the prospects for human malleability of the environment. Operating as it does on the basis of a largely empirically untested assumption, the political socialization literature has been prey to an overemphasis on the environmental causes determining attitudes and behavior, paying little attention to the reverse side of the coin—how can man reshape and mold his environment.

In view of the lack of longitudinal evidence on attitudinal stability over the life cycle, a shift in research priorities should be made to toward an emphasis on the adult socialization processes. As Orville Brim points out, "the socialization that an individual receives in childhood cannot be adequate as preparation for the tasks demanded of him in later years."[28] Brim's statement appears particularly applicable to technologically advanced societies such as in the United States where, as many have suggested, the rate of change is growing in exponential rather than arithmetic progression.[29]

In summary of this section, a brief review of studies on political participation and political socialization has suggested that by and large these studies have not been concerned with the questions posed in this book: that is, by means of what forces and processes can the political participation level of generally inactive lower-status adults be raised? On the one hand, the assumptions underlying most studies of political participation militate against even posing the question, while the assumptions made in political socialization studies similarly direct attention away from it by emphasizing the ineradicable nature of socialized patterns of behavior. Now this book turns to a discussion of more recent studies of political participation, which do suggest how class inequalities in levels of political participation can be redressed. A review of the characteristics of the standard political participation model begins the discussion, alternative models or paths to political participation follow.

## POLITICAL PARTICIPATION: THE STANDARD SES MODEL AND "ENABLING ANTECEDENTS"

The causes and antecedents of political participation represent a highly complex phenomenon composed of many interrelated and interacting variables. Indeed, a voluminous amount of research has searched for these causes and antecedents.[30] Yet, one still does not know precisely the ordering and causal connections among these variables.[31] At the risk of oversimplification, it could be suggested that there has been overall agreement that involvement in politics is a function of a number of "enabling antecedents."[32] That is, an individual's propensity to participate in politics is largely a function of previous attitudes and cognitions, which may be developed in nonpolitical situations.[33]

Among these "enabling antecedents," the following ones are usually considered to be most important. In terms of cognitions the individual, at a minimum, must be aware that government affects him and must be exposed to political stimuli.[34] In terms of attitudes, political efficacy (generally construed as a special case of general social competence or the feeling that the environment can be manipulated and controlled) often is construed as a key antecedent.[35] Added to political efficacy, sense of civic duty to participate and social trust also have received a great deal of attention as enabling antecedents for political participation.[36]

Although, as mentioned, the interrelationships among these variables and their ordering has yet to be fully specified, the correlation between a particular set of attitudes and political participation generally is accepted by most observers.[37] This may be graphically abstracted as follows:

enabling attitudes and cognitions ⟶ political participation

However, as we have already discussed, these enabling antecedents in the form of particular attitudes and cognitions are not randomly distributed throughout society; rather, they tend to be clustered in the middle and upper classes. As Verba and Nie put it, "Political participation is predominantly the activity of the wealthier, better educated citizen with higher status occupations. Those who need the beneficial outcomes of participation the least—who are already advantaged in social and economic terms—participate the most."[38]

In this respect, the causal path must be restructured to include the importance of socioeconomic status, or graphically,

high SES ⟶ enabling attitudes and cognitions ⟶ political participation

Given the strong relationship established in the literature between high SES and the formation of attitudes conducive to participation, the most common prescription offered until recently to upgrade the level of participation of the lower classes (when any prescription was offered at all[39]) has been through the medium of economic development and upward social mobility.[40] A parallel approach advanced by some attacks the problem of poverty in a similar fashion by declaring that it is economic, hence offering economic remedies such as guaranteed income programs for a resolution.[41]

The general logic of this argument is that as economic development progresses, the system of class stratification is altered and society begins to acquire a more diamond-shaped structure, rather than a pyramidal one. As more people enter the middle and upper socioeconomic strata, they become exposed to those stimuli that create "enabling antecedents" of political participation. Ultimately, rates of political participation are increased. Although this strategy may be effective in the long run, it is obvious that, as Nie, Powell, and Prewitt point out, " . . . major changes in the class structure involving occupation, education, and income patterns are extremely difficult to bring about,"[42] and, one should add, take a great deal of time.

Moreover, it is possible that the political structure is more malleable and easily adaptable to change than the socioeconomic structure. In Participation in America, Verba and Nie report some data that bear directly on this point. Posing the question of whether access to political participation is more equal than access to social or economic benefits, they compare differences between blacks (a group whose members are disproportionately found in the lower class) and whites in both arenas. Specifically, they ask the question of "Whether the degree of association between racial status and economic status is greater than that between racial status and political participation."[43] They conclude that "the data do clearly suggest that opportunities for political participation are more equally distributed between the races than are social or economic benefits."[44]

If the political structure were more malleable than the socioeconomic structure, by what means could the lower class bypass the processes that lead those with higher status to participate? Research by Nie, Powell, and Prewitt and Verba and Nie suggests that there may be two alternative routes whereby the participation of the lower class individual may be increased _independently_ of socioeconomic status. The first is through organizational involvement, the second is through group consciousness.[45] Each will be discussed in turn.

## ALTERNATIVE ROUTES TO POLITICAL PARTICIPATION: ORGANIZATIONAL INVOLVEMENT AND GROUP CONSCIOUSNESS

### Organizational Involvement

In their reanalysis of the Almond and Verba data on five Western democracies,[46] Nie, Powell, and Prewitt found that organizational involvement provides an alternative route to political participation and that it operates independently of any intervening or "enabling" attitudinal variables.[47] The pattern discovered is "of overwhelming strength and consistency . . . " and, moreover, "it holds true in all five countries and remains the case in spite of various manipulations of the data, alteration of the order of the intervening variables, changing the number of the intervening variables and the like."[48] Contrasted with the socioeconomic enabling attitudes model (model I), the organizational involvement as an alternative route to political participation model (model II) may be abstracted graphically as follows:

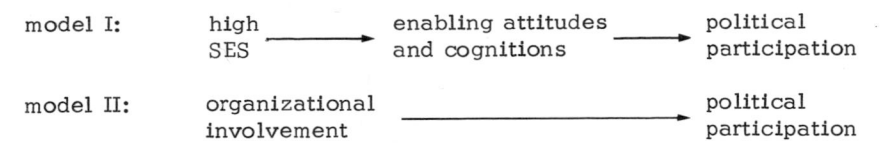

model I:   high SES  →  enabling attitudes and cognitions  →  political participation

model II:  organizational involvement  →  political participation

This finding at its face value is not strikingly novel. Other researchers have pointed consistently to the importance of voluntary associations in determining rates of political participation.[49] What is novel in the findings themselves is that the relationship between organizational involvement and political participation was found to operate so directly and independently of other factors. What is most prominently novel in Nie, Powell, and Prewitt's study, however, is that the implications posed by these findings are fully considered which, as argued earlier, generally has not been the case in previous studies of political participation. In the authors' words, "Organizational involvement may represent an alternative channel of political participation for socially disadvantaged groups—the rural peasant, the industrial laborer, the disadvantaged black may become politically active through his organizational involvement even though he may otherwise lack the status resources for political participation."[50]

Nie, Powell, and Prewitt further suggest that, in view of the importance of organizational involvement as an independent precursor to participation and in view of the likely malleability of the organizational structure, "deliberate government policies can increase the number of citizens who are politically active."[51]

This book, in effect, seeks to explore whether this is so. It seeks to explore whether deliberate government policies to increase citizen participation—in the form of advisory councils—can indeed serve as a bypassing mechanism, whereby individuals not predisposed to participate in politics as a function of their low socioeconomic status can become active participants. Moreover, a major purpose of this book lies in exploring in more detail the operation of the organizational involvement-political participation model. Specifically, the author wishes to explore whether organizational involvement (in the form of advisory council membership) is related to the acquisition of "participant" orientations and to the acquisition of political skills. This factor is in addition to testing the relationship between organizational involvement and political participation. Efforts are also made to specify more clearly under what conditions the operation of the organizational involvement-political participation model is likely to be hindered or facilitated.

Data derived from different research contexts tends to support the operation of the organizational involvement-political participation model posited by Nie, Powell, Prewitt, and Verba. Studies of migrant urban lower classes in Latin America[52] and studies on "industrial democracy"[53] also suggest that organizational involvement represents an independent alternative route to political participation. In his study of urban squatters in government settlements in Chile and Peru, for example, Daniel Goldrich finds that " . . . adults, previously inexperienced and uninvolved in politics, learn to engage in and sustain complex political demand making, under certain circumstances. The most important of these tend to be a sense of acute needs, a perception of a strategy of action adequate to meeting the needs, and the availability of an organization to channel the action."[54]

The initial politicization of the "poblador," however, is not consistently sustained after the more acute demands for housing have been met, that is, after the initial issues over which collective action had been forged have been won. Only among the poblador activists who are affiliated with FRAP, the leftist coalition party, does maintenance of a collective orientation toward problem solving occur and a transition in focus to other problem areas take place.[55] This finding raises some interesting questions for analysis in this book. That is, it raises some questions about the durability of the organizational involvement-political participation model. It suggests that organizational involvement may result in sporadic rather than in enduring propensities to participate in politics. This possibility is tested here by exploring: (1) whether those who evidence a degree of politicization as a result of the advisory council experience are likely to remain politicized and (2) whether the advisory council experience is conducive to the acquisition of those "enabling attitudes" for participation (usually associated with the SES model) and to the acquisition of a capability to affect government, hence possibly fostering a more enduring tendency to participate in political life.

Empirical evidence obtained in studies on industrial democracy also tends to support, in general terms, the operation of the organizational involvement-political participation model. Individual participation in decision making within the work organization has been related tentatively to an increased propensity for participation in social and political activities.[56] Even though involvement in the work organization does not represent a strictly analogous situation to the organizational involvement posited in the model,[57] attention is called to these studies for two reasons. First, this kind of research raises the possibility of altering the structure of political participation through the democratization of work organizations—a possibility which generally has been overlooked by political scientists. Secondly, tentative findings from studies on industrial democracy have posited some interesting relationships between attitude formation and participation within the organization, which parallel some of the concerns of this study. These may be summarized as follows: participation in "lower-level" decisions (decisions that affect the individual's own job in contrast with decisions that affect the enterprise as a whole, or "higher-level" decisions) appears to foster a sense of self-competence, which in turn tends to (1) have spill-over effects manifested as a desire to participate in higher-level decision making and (2) spill over as a propensity to participate in social and political spheres outside the organizational context.[58] Research on industrial democracy thus suggests a step-by-step enlargement of spheres of competence, that is, self-competence in one sphere tends to spill over into a desire and propensity to participate in another broader sphere, and so on.

In conclusion to this section, one could pose the question of what prospects does organizational involvement as an alternative route to political participation offer for correcting the unequal distribution of political participation among social classes in the United States? On this key question, Verba and Nie suggest that one must distinguish between <u>actuality</u> and <u>potentiality</u>. Organizational involvement as an alternative route to political participation, in actuality, operates in a paradoxical manner in the United States. At the <u>individual</u> level, it serves as a compensatory mechanism by bypassing those processes associated with higher status and attitude formation, which lead to participation, and gives the individual lower-class member a significant "boost" in participation. In this sense, at the individual level, organizational involvement closes the gap between the high- and low-status individual.

However, at the <u>group</u> level in the United States,[59] organizational involvement results overall in the opposite effect; it actually works to increase the disparity between upper- and lower-status groups. This is so because of the fact that upper-class individuals are overwhelmingly more active in organizations than lower-class individuals. Verba and Nie estimate that 59 percent of the upper class is likely to belong to organizations, contrasted with 22 percent of the lower class.[60] When one adds the "boosting" effects or organizational membership to other characteristics of the upper class that make it "participant prone," organizational involvement clearly serves to increase political inequality between the lower and upper classes.

The distinction drawn between the <u>actual</u> and <u>potential</u> effects of the organizational involvement-political participation model at the group level highlights even more prominently the need to undertake research on government strategies aimed at increasing citizen participation. The expansion of citizen involvement in the form of advisory councils, neighborhood corporations, and the like, if sufficiently widespread and if involving sufficiently large numbers of individuals, ultimately could bridge the political inequality gap not only at the <u>individual</u> level but also at the <u>group</u> level.

### Group Consciousness

Group consciousness could represent a second alternative route to political participation and a mechanism that "may substitute for the higher social status which impels citizens into political activity."[61] Verba and Nie consider the possible operation of this model in the context of the black population, a group that undeniably has exhibited the development of self-awareness throughout the 1950s and the 1960s.[62] Verba and Nie distinguish between "aware" blacks and "unaware" blacks on the basis of the number of times that black respondents referred to race in a series of questions about the groups in conflict within the community; and on the problems they faced in personal life, in the community, and in the nation.[63] Subsequently, they compare the rates of political participation of blacks and whites controlling for social status and group consciousness. The results obtained are striking. "Blacks who do not mention race [that is, unaware blacks] participate substantially less than the average white. But those who mention race— once or more—participate a bit above the average white. Consciousness of race as a problem or a basis for conflict appears to bring those blacks who are conscious up to a level of participation equivalent to that of whites."[64] Moreover, when blacks and whites are matched on SES variables, the average black is found to participate at a rate higher than the average white, and the group conscious black is found to participate at "a rate far exceeding that of the average white."[65]

The role that group consciousness plays in raising the level of participation among blacks as evidenced by the Verba and Nie data raises a number of interesting questions for analysis in this book.

The Mexican-American people, the second largest minority group in the United States,[66] have been undergoing a similar cultural reawakening in the last decade. Embodied in the Chicano movement,[67] the growth of self-awareness among the Mexican-American population has been manifested in multiple ways throughout the Southwest. Farm worker strikes and boycotts in California,[68] efforts to reclaim formerly Mexican lands in New Mexico,[69] Mexican-American electoral takeovers in Texas cities,[70] radical protest action in the form of marches and demonstrations and school walkouts in East Los Angeles,[71] the emergence of an ethnic party movement throughout the Southwest,[72] and increased community grass roots organization in all southwestern states[73] are but a few examples of this growth in ethnic awareness.

The growth of ethnic consciousness among the population under study poses some difficulties for this analysis of the politicizing effects of involvement in advisory councils in the East Los Angeles community. One, in effect, is faced with a situation where both alternative routes to political participation (that is, organizational involvement and group consciousness) could be operative. The difficulties of isolating or separating the effects of one variable (involvement in advisory councils) from the other (group consciousness) are accentuated further by the fact that both probably are intertwined. The presence of ethnic awareness and the availability of organizational channels well might work to reinforce one another. On the one hand, group consciousness as an alternative route to increased political participation will, it would seem (at some stage), be embodied in organized action. On the other hand, organizational involvement could work either to create or solidify sentiments of group consciousness. This seems particularly true of organizational involvement in an environmental setting experiencing a growth in self-awareness.

In essence, if this empirical investigation of the attitudes and behavior of advisory council members in East Los Angeles reveals that they are becoming politicized, at least three equally valid explanations for this politicization could be posited logically: (1) politicization is a result of organizational involvement, (2) politicization is a result of group consciousness, (3) politicization is a result of both.

In this book, organizational involvement in advisory councils is looked upon as the major explanatory variable (the independent variable), which leads to politicization (the dependent variable). Other plausible "rival hypotheses," however, must be investigated.[74] As Selwyn Becker put it, "If the researcher claims that his treatment produced an effect, it is the researcher's responsibility to demonstrate that more parsimonious explanations would not suffice and <u>that other treatments known to have produced similar effects did not produce them in the case under consideration</u>"[75] (emphasis added). The major "rival hypothesis" to be explored in this study as an alternative explanation for increased politicization is group consciousness.[76] A subsequent section in this chapter explains the research strategy utilized to distinguish between those effects that can be attributed to organizational involvement and those that could be attributed to group consciousness. Efforts also are made to explore the interrelationship between these two factors. What follows is a discussion of the major hypotheses to be investigated.

## MAJOR HYPOTHESES TO BE EXPLORED AND OPERATIONALIZATION OF KEY VARIABLES

The central purpose of this book, as has been outlined, is to explore whether involvement in advisory councils is a politicizing experience. The primary focus of attention thus lies in exploring the effects of the advisory council experience (the independent variable) on the individual member's political orientations and behavior (the dependent variables). Having ascertained what effects accrue at the _individual_ level, the study explores the potential effects that changes in individuals could have at the _group_ level by exploring whether individual members are likely to remain politicized and become active community leaders. Finally, the major rival explanation for increased politicization—group consciousness—is explored. The data on the basis of which these relationships are tested consist of personal interviews with a random sample of advisory council members in East Los Angeles.[77] (The research strategy followed is explained in a subsequent section of this chapter; data collection procedures are specified in Chapter 3.)

In broad terms, politicization can be viewed as a process ranging on a continuum from a lack of perception of the relevance of government to one's life to active participation in politics.[78] Stages or dimensions along this continuum are the following: (1) the individual's awareness of and psychological involvement in poltics, (2) his image of himself as a passive or active agent in it, (3) his capabilities or lack of capabilities to affect government, and (4) his direct participation in politics.[79] These dimensions may be summarized as (1) propensity to affect government (cognitions and attitudes), (2) capabilities to affect government (political skills and political information), and (3) actual behavior (political participation). This study is interested in exploring how involvement in advisory councils affects these three dimensions. After determining whether individual politicization occurs and what dimensions of politicization are affected, the likelihood of sustained politicization is explored, as well as an attempt to speculate about the type of leadership likely to emerge. The relationships explored are abstracted graphically in Figure 2.1 and are explicated below.

FIGURE 2.1

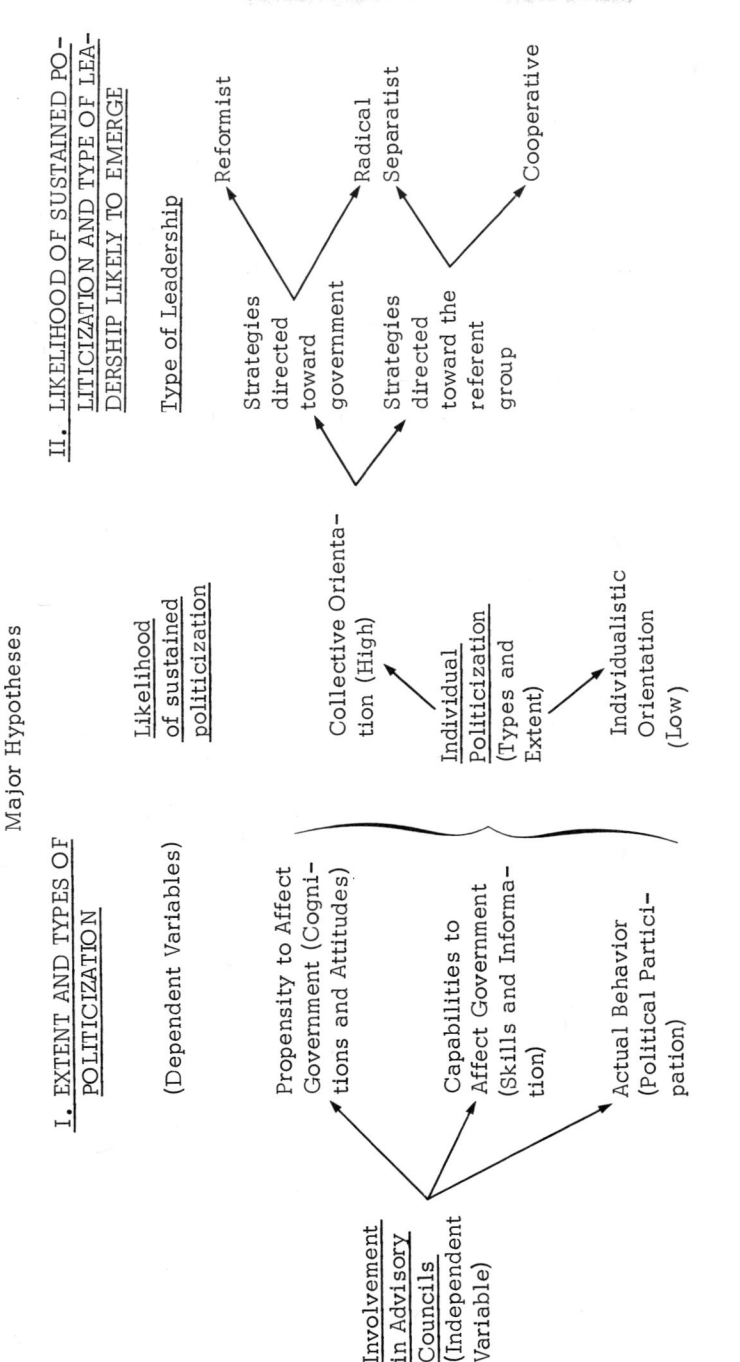

Major Hypotheses

I. EXTENT AND TYPES OF POLITICIZATION

(Dependent Variables)

- Propensity to Affect Government (Cognitions and Attitudes)
- Capabilities to Affect Government (Skills and Information)
- Actual Behavior (Political Participation)

Involvement in Advisory Councils (Independent Variable)

Likelihood of sustained politicization

- Collective Orientation (High)
- Individual Politicization (Types and Extent)
- Individualistic Orientation (Low)

II. LIKELIHOOD OF SUSTAINED POLITICIZATION AND TYPE OF LEADERSHIP LIKELY TO EMERGE

Type of Leadership

- Strategies directed toward government
  - Reformist
  - Radical Separatist
- Strategies directed toward the referent group
  - Radical Separatist
  - Cooperative

Source: Compiled by the author.

## Extent and Types of Politicization

### Hypothesis 1: Development of Propensity to Affect Government

> Involvement in advisory councils leads to changes in the members' cognitive and evaluative orientations toward government and in changes in their image of themselves as active actors in the political system.

Cognitions about Politics and Government. Awareness of the impact of governmental activities on one's life is the minimum precondition for politicization. It is obvious that a "parochial" citizen, one who "tends to be unaware or only dimly aware of the political system"[80] will not be likely to participate in politics. This dimension is tapped by distinguishing between the impact of local and national levels of government on one's life, because a number of studies have found that citizens are differentially cognitively oriented to these two levels of government.[81] Questions tapping this dimension are as follows:*
"About how much effect do you think that the activities of the local government have on your day to day life? Do they have a great effect, some effect, or none?" (Q.85)[82] The question is later repeated with the national government as the referent (Q.95).[83] An effort to obtain a "before" and "after" measure is made with the follow-up question (for both national and local referents): "Did you feel the same way before you were an advisory council member?" The cognitive dimension is bolstered additionally with questions tapping awareness of and exposure to politics and public affairs.[84]

Because advisory councils, unlike other organizations such as political parties, are primarily locally based and deal with local problems, one would expect to find a higher rate of cognition of the impact of local government on one's life than of the national government. This is hypothesized, however, for diffuse cognitions only; one expects higher cognitions rates for specific national outputs, such as the War on Poverty, whose impact may be recognized more readily.[85]

Two additional dimensions of the "propensity to affect government" are an evaluative orientation toward government activities (generally referred to as political trust) and the image that an individual has of himself as an active or passive political actor (political efficacy). The trust dimension generally refers to one's perception of the necessity for influence, political efficacy refers to one's perception of his ability to influence.[86] The relationship between these two

---

*Throughout this chapter, numbers in parentheses refer to the questions in the Appendix.

variables (trust and efficacy) has been a matter of considerable debate in the literature. William Gamson hypothesizes that low trust (perception of a need to influence) combined with high efficacy (perceived ability to influence) can produce a high propensity toward radical political activity.[87] Others have found political trust to be unrelated to political involvement,[88] while, as previously discussed, most studies consistently have found political efficacy to be strongly related to political involvement.[89] Both measures are included for purposes of further clarifying their relationship (or lack thereof). These are operationalized below.

Evaluative Orientations Toward Government and Politics. Evaluative orientations are tapped by the following questions—again distinguishing between national and local referents: "In general, do you think that your local (national) government is run the way it should be, or not run the way it should be?" (Q.86, Q.96).[90] Follow-up questions tap (1) the reasons for the evaluation and (2) a "before" and "after" measure in the form of "Did you feel the same way before you were an advisory council member?" Additional items tap evaluative orientations toward both local and national governments in terms of specific outputs, that is, the War on Poverty as a national output, and evaluation of school outputs at the local level.[91] Again, given the fact that advisory councils deal primarily with local problems, one expects to find a higher incidence of positive or negative evaluations of the local government than of the national government (versus "don't know" or "no response" answers).

Perceived Ability to Influence. Perceived ability to influence (political efficacy) is measured in two ways: (1) by use of the four-item Survey Research Center (SRC) political efficacy scale replicated in numerous studies,[92] and (2) by a more discriminating measure that differentiates between local and national referents. The latter reads, "Some people tell us there is nothing they can do to affect what the local (national) government does. Other people say they can influence what gets decided in this community (in Washington) if they want to. How about you? Do you feel you can affect what the local (national) government does or not?" (Q.87, Q.97). If "yes" or "depends," "How can you have this effect?"; if "no," "Why not?"; and subsequently, "Did you feel the same way before you were an advisory council member?"[93]

As in the previous sections, because of the locally centered activity of the advisory councils, one expects to find higher rates of political efficacy toward the local government than toward the national government. In addition, "strategies respondent would use to affect government" (that is, "How can you have this effect?") should provide a clue as to whether political efficacy is "collectively" oriented (for example, "organize" or "unite") or "individualistically" oriented (such as, "write letters" or "personal petition"). This dimension becomes important in ascertaining whether politicization is sustained and is further explicated below in the section on sustained politicization.

A final dimension of the "propensity to affect" government is a horizontal (oriented toward other citizens) rather than vertical measure (related to government). This is "social trust" operationally defined as the SRC three-item "trust in people" scale.[94] Social trust has been related to politically relevant trust,[95] to a propensity to engage in cooperative activity with others,[96] to faith in the qualifications of voters and the responsiveness of legislators, to a lack of fear of unrestricted freedom of speech, and to an unwillingness to use the state as a repressive instrument.[97] This scale has been included for two reasons: (1) it further examines a propensity to engage in collective action as tapped by the political efficacy items, and (2) related as it is to "democratic" orientations, it allows one to test whether the advisory council experience can help foster such democratic attitudes.

The measurement of cognitive and evaluative orientations toward government, of political efficacy, and of social trust should provide an index of "propensity to affect government" or, in other words, an index of a "latent" tendency to participate in politics. This is an important dimension to examine in the context of the advisory councils, for as was explained earlier, the organizational involvement-political participation model generally assumes that no intervening variables come between organizational involvement and political participation. To add to the understanding of the organizational involvement model, those "enabling orientations" variables, which are much in evidence in the SES standard model, will be explored. The presence of such attitudinal factors could be indicative of a more enduring relationship between organizational involvement and political participation. Additionally, testing this relationship in the context of the Mexican-American population of East Los Angeles hopefully will further the understanding of possible variations in attitudinal changes according to culture or ethnicity.

Hypothesis 2: Development of Capabilities to Affect Government

> Involvement in advisory councils leads to the development of capabilities to affect government in the form of political skills and political knowledge.

Hypothesis 1 deals with the question "<u>would</u> they try to affect government?" This hypothesis deals with the question of "do they <u>know how</u> to affect government?" This seems to be a particularly crucial question to explore in our research context. The poor are typically viewed as unknowledgeable about "access" points in the political system, as unaware of who to see or where to go to get things done, as unable to deal with public bureaucracies, and as lacking minimal organizational skills. Moreover, the development of organizational capabilities and the knowledge to affect government bears particular relevance to the Mexican-American community. Studies on Mexican-Americans often have pointed to a lack of effective organizational capabilities. Organizations and leaders in Mexican-American communities often have been unstable, single issue-oriented, and conflict ridden. As issues become resolved or are superseded by other issues, organizations can lose support and be disbanded.[98] Research on the political capabilities developed by advisory council participants is thus important, for it may augur better prospects for the development of politically knowledgeable and more stable and effective community organizations.

In addition, it would seem that advisory councils could provide an excellent setting where political skills could be learned. Unlike other voluntary organizations, advisory councils are involved intimately in the operation of public agencies and consequently could expose their members to various aspects of administrative and governmental activities. It is likely that advisory council members can learn a variety of skills; for example, they could learn about the internal workings of a particular administrative agency, or about the interrelationship among agencies and among different levels of government, or about where to go to get things done, or about problems of funding and program support.

Development of "capabilities to affect government" is operationalized in terms of acquisition of political skills and level of political knowledge. Acquisition of political skills as a result of the advisory council experience is tapped through the use of both open-ended and forced-choice items. These are as follows: (Q.26) "In the course of your experience as a council member, would you say that you learned any new things, that is, were there any new things that one had to learn in order to get things done?" (If yes), "What kinds of new things would you say you learned?" Later in the questionnaire (Q.31), knowledge about a wide variety of political skills is solicited with the following question: "Some people tell us that they have learned many new things on the advisory council. Others tell us that they haven't learned anything at all. How about you? Looking at this list (HAND RESPONDENT A CARD) please tell me (1) whether you are familiar with any of these things or not, and (2) if you are, whether you learned any of them as a result of your experience on the advisory council?"(1. Roberts' Rules of Order; 2. How to run a meeting; 3. How to persuade people to your own point of view; 4. How things get done in this particular agency; 5. How different government agencies work; 6. How different community groups work; 7. Who has the power in this community; 8. How to lobby in favor of legislation; 9. How to write a proposal for funding; 10. How to get community support for a new program; 11. How to contact public officials; 12. How to organize a protest march; 13. How to get something reported in the newspapers, radio, or TV; 14. How to get out a newsletter; 15. How to quiet a riot.)[99]

As is apparent, this question taps a variety of political skills—skills relating directly to organizational abilities (items 1, 2, 3, 10, 12), skills related to knowledge about the functioning of public bureaucracies and community groups (items 4, 5, 6, 7), and skills related to access points in the political system (items 8, 9, 11, 13, 14). It should be noted, however, that these questions only tap "perceived ability to do these things," not actual behavior.[100]

"Political knowledge" is tapped through knowledge of War on Poverty programs,[101] knowledge of organizations in the community (ranging from long-standing to newly established and from conservatively oriented to radical),[102] and through knowledge of protests, marches, and demonstrations that have taken place in the East Los Angeles community in the last few years.[103]

### Hypothesis 3: Development of Political Participation Behavior

> Involvement in advisory councils leads to changes in the members' patterns of political participation in the direction of increased activeness.

The previous two hypotheses explored underlying propensities and capabilities to participate; here actual political _behavior_ is explored. This is, of course, an important question for analysis for a number of reasons. First, it tests whether the organizational involvement-political participation model operates in the organizational context of advisory councils, thus allowing us to make some empirically grounded conclusions about whether a government strategy to increase rates of political participation does work. As explained in Chapter 1, empirical data on this question are notably lacking. Second, if hypothesis 1 is not found to be invalidated on empirical testing—that is, changes in attitudinal propensities to participate actually occur—it is important to test whether these "latent" tendencies become "manifest" in actual behavior. A great deal of survey research often assumes a relationship between changes in attitudes and subsequent behavioral changes, but this relationship has not been sufficiently tested empirically. In fact, a number of studies in which this relationship has been tested reveal slight inverse relationships between attitude change and self-reported behavior.[104] Finally, the testing of this relationship is necessary for purposes of determining whether emergence of indigenous leadership is a likely consequence of the advisory council experience.

Political participation behavior is tapped in a number of ways. First, a _subjective evaluation_ of changes in levels of political activity oriented toward the community level is solicited from the respondent through the following probes: (Q. 28) "How would you describe the extent of your involvement in community affairs _before_ you joined the council?" (deeply involved, somewhat involved, almost not involved, completely not involved); and (Q. 29) "As a result of your experience on the advisory council, would you say that you have become more involved in community affairs, less involved, or did the advisory council experience make no difference?" (more involved, less involved, no difference, unable to judge).

These "subjective" evaluations of decrease or increase in political activity as a result of the advisory council experience are bolstered by more "objective" indicators of political activity. These explore different types of political activity: (1) local community centered, (2) electoral, and (3) protest activity. In terms of local community-centered participation, immediately following the respondent's subjective evaluation of behavioral changes (if positive) the following questions are asked: "Since you became an advisory council member have you joined any community organizations?" (Q. 29A); (if yes) "Which ones?", and "Since you became an advisory council member have you become more active in organizations you already belong to?" (Q. 29C).[105] Other community-centered political activity is tapped in terms of membership in other organizations (Q. 80), in specifically religious organizations (Q. 79), in community organizations mentioned by the interviewer ranging from radical to conservative (these include explicitly political organizations such as Democratic and Republican clubs and a third party movement, La Raza Unida party) (Q. 88), and in other advisory councils (Q. 32). Time referents (that is, when joined) and extent of activeness within the organization are solicited for all memberships reported.[106]

In terms of locally oriented political activity, then, multiple measures hopefully will demonstrate accurately the extent of the respondent's community-oriented political activity before and after involvement in the advisory councils.

Other political activity measures tapped are: (1) <u>electoral</u> in terms of voting (Q. 91A, B, C, D), membership in political clubs (Democratic and Republican), and membership in La Raza Unida party (Q. 88); and (2) <u>radical political activity</u> in terms of participation in protests, marches, and demonstrations (Q. 68B).

A final item taps the respondent's "intention to be active in community affairs" after leaving the council (Q. 30). This item is included following the suggestion made in a previous study on advisory councils that members reported intentions to become more active in community affairs but had not done so yet because of the time-consuming nature of their activities on the council.[107]

It should be noted that the measures of political participation used in this study are skewed in terms of determining the extent of participation in community affairs rather than in electoral politics (although voting measures, partisan affiliation, and membership in political clubs and movements are solicited).[108] This is in contrast with most previous studies on political participation.[109]

The assumptions underlying this particular choice of indicators are based on the following reasons. First, local levels of government are viewed as more politically relevant to the poor because (1) it is at this level that service programs for the poor are delivered and (2) because of their numerical minority on a national basis, the poor generally have articulated their interests and demands (when they have actually done so) at the local rather than at the national level. Second, the administrative sphere is viewed as more politically relevant to the poor than the legislative or electoral spheres of politics. Government impact on the lives of the poor is most likely felt in administrative contacts, for example, in dealings with welfare, manpower training, and health bureaucracies.[110] Moreover, the organization of the poor, whenever it has occured, has generally been directed toward administrative agencies rather than legislatures or parties. The author is referring here to organizations of the poor such as tenants' associations, welfare rights groups, community development corporations, and neighborhood associations. Third, political parties (involvement in which usually has been used as a major indicator of political participation) may not be particularly useful or responsive to the needs of the poor in general nor particularly relevant as a mobilization mechanism in the specific geographical context studied here. That the political party is "less the vehicle for democratic dialogue and polyarchical power than a pressure group with a narrowly defined interest in the pursuit of office, favor, and patronage"[111] seems to be particularly true in relation to the poor and in relation to the War on Poverty. As David Greenstone and Paul Peterson report, poverty groups best have been able to gain some power in "reform" cities where political parties have been weak rather than in machine-dominated cities.[112] Moreover, the way in which political parties have functioned in the specific geographical context we are concerned with (Los Angeles) militates against them becoming mobilizing agents and spokesmen for the poor. For a number of reasons, most prominently changes in party operation brought about by the reform movement and by nonpartisan elections at the local level, political parties have been notably weak in California.[113] Finally, in the view of some segments of the Mexican-American community, the Democratic party (with which the majority of Mexican-Americans traditionally have been affiliated) has not been particularly responsive to the needs and demands of East Los Angeles residents. Democratic party unresponsiveness has been particularly evident in its lack of support of efforts to redistrict East Los Angeles to ensure the election of ethnic representatives and by the rise of a counterparty among the more militant segments of the population in the form of the La Raza Unida party.

### Likelihood of Sustained Politicization and Type of Leaders Likely to Emerge

Propositions explored in this section are contingent on the empirical results obtained on the hypotheses elaborated above. If, indeed, one finds that the advisory council experience leads to the politicization of <u>individual</u> members, one would wish to speculate further about potential effects that may ensue at the <u>group</u> or community level. That is, is it likely that a governmental policy to increase citizen participation through the creation of advisory councils can be a vehicle to redress class inequalities in rates of political participation at the group level as well as at the individual level? This proposition seems to hinge on two main factors: (1) whether the politicization of individual members (if it occurs) is likely to be sustained; and, hence, indigenous leaders are likely to emerge; and (2) whether the strategy of creating advisory councils (if indeed it results in the individual effects hypothesized) proliferates and comes to involve a large number of lower-class citizens.

In regard to the latter factor, the author can only make recommendations about the effectiveness of advisory councils as politicization agents on the basis of the empirical results obtained. In terms of the first factor, however, one can speculate about it on the basis of the available data. It should be noted here that in contrast with the section on the extent of politicization, where a number of hypotheses to be tested empirically were set forth, the propositions discussed in this section are much more tentative and speculative.

<u>Likelihood of Sustained Politicization</u>

One way of assessing whether individual politicization is likely to endure is to see whether those who are politicized exhibit a <u>collective</u> versus <u>individualistic</u> orientation toward the resolution of common problems. To the extent that they reveal a high degree of individualistic orientations, it may be projected that politicization will diminish. On the other hand, among those for whom a collective orientation is evidenced, it is likely that individual politicization will endure. The assumption underlying the creation of this dichotomy is that those exhibiting individualistic orientations are more likely to pursue self-advancement in nonpolitical ways (for example, through better income, jobs, housing, or moving out of the poverty community). On the other hand, those exhibiting collective orientations probably would tend to see self-advancement as related to group advancement and would tend to pursue political strategies to obtain socioeconomic benefits for the groups as a whole.[114]

"Collective" and "individualistic" orientations may be ascertained on the basis of scores on four indicators:

(1) Whose responsibility it is to solve community problems defined as salient by the respondent? (Q. 98B, 98C)

        (government and grass     (the individual and
        roots groups: collective)   his family: individual-
                                             istic)

(2) Mexican-Americans should get together politically. (Q. 99)

       (positive response:       (negative response:
       collective)                    individualistic)

(3) Strategies respondent would pursue to affect government (local, national). (Q. 87A, 97A)

       ("organize" or "unite":    ("personal letters,"
       collective)                   "petitions,"voting":
                                       individualistic)

(4) Sense of community, that is, the extent to which the respondent believes others think the same way he does. (Q. 103)

    Having ascertained the likelihood of sustained politicization, next the type of leadership likely to emerge will be explored.

Type of Leadership Likely to Emerge

    We explore the type of leadership likely to emerge by investigating orientations toward two referents: (1) a vertical referent, or orientations toward government; and (2) a horizontal referent, or orientations toward the group. In regard to the former, the author is interested in speculating whether those who are likely to remain politicized will be inclined to use "reformist" or "within the system" versus "radical" political strategies to attain their ends. In regard to orientations toward the referent group, the author is interested in exploring the likelihood of ethnically "separatist" versus ethnically "cooperative" orientations.

Orientations Toward Government: "Reformist" versus "Radical." Indices of "reformist" and "radical" political orientations are based on four measures.

(1) Perceptions of discrimination against Mexican-Americans in "this community," in "business," and in "politics and government." (Q. 63)

       (low: reformist)           (high: radical)

(2) Evaluations of protests, marches, and demonstrations that have taken place in East Los Angeles in the last few years. (Q. 68C)

       (negative evaluations:    (positive evalua-
       reformist)                      tions: radical)

# INVOLVEMENT IN ADVISORY COUNCILS

(3) Opinions on community organizations mentioned by the interviewer. (Q. 90)[115]

(negative opinion of organizations espousing radical action: reformist)

(positive opinion of organizations espousing radical action: radical)

(4) Preference for strategies that should be pursued to solve problems in the community. (Q. 102)

(preference:
  (a) elect people of Mexican background to office,
  (b) work within the Democratic or Republican parties,
  (c) get people of Mexican background into government jobs: reformist)

(preference:
  (a) join in public street demonstrations,
  (b) riot if necessary,
  (c) form a separate political party for people of Mexican background only:[116] radical)

<u>Orientations Toward the Referent Group: "Separatist" versus "Cooperative."</u> Indicators used to tap "separatist" versus "cooperative" orientations are the three listed.

(1) Evaluation of the desirability of assimilation into American society. (Q. 60, 61)

(good: cooperative)      (bad: separatist)

(2) Desirability of Mexican-Americans getting together politically with other groups. (Q. 100, 101)

(positive: cooperative)      (negative: separatist)

(3) Opinions on community organizations that espouse ethnic separatism. (Q. 90)[117]

(negative: cooperative)      (positive: separatist)

    Analysis of the research questions posed in this section hopefully will yield useful hypotheses regarding the prospects for sustained politicization as well as propositions regarding the type of leadership likely to emerge. These data are reported on in Chapter 7. Next is a discussion of the research strategy adopted to explore the hypotheses elaborated above.

## RESEARCH STRATEGY

### The Need for Evaluative Research

Testing the hypotheses elaborated in the previous two sections requires an evaluative research strategy.[118] Evaluation research may be defined as "research to provide objective, systematic, and comprehensive evidence on the degree to which a program achieves its intended objectives plus the degree to which it produces other unanticipated consequences which, when recognized, would also be regarded as relevant."[119] Moreover, "an essential first condition for evaluating a program's impact is the existence of methods to distinguish between effects of the program and effects of other forces—in short—the ability to isolate what would have happened in the absence of the program."[120]

The primary methodological tool available to fulfill this condition is the use of experimental or quasi-experimental designs.[121] Basically, the use of experimental or quasi-experimental designs involves three requirements: (1) administration of a "before" and an "after" test to a population undergoing the particular treatment; (2) administration of the same "before" and "after" tests to an equivalent population not undergoing the particular treatment, the "control group" (equivalence is obtained by random assignment to the treatment and nontreatment groups); and (3) consideration of "plausible rival hypotheses" as possible alternative explanations for any changes obtained.[122] The design can be abstracted graphically as shown.

$O_1$     X     $O_2$     (treatment group)
    (Treatment)

$A_1$          $A_2$     (equivalent control
(Time 1)    (Time 2)    group)

Although experimental design methodology has long been used with varying degrees of success in a number of disciplines, education and psychology in particular, its application to evaluate broad-scale social action programs is relatively recent. Evaluation requirements of federal programs have called attention to the need for developing adequate evaluative methodology and have highlighted the intrinsic difficulties of adapting laboratory-type experimental designs to the study of social and political activity.

## Problems in Conducting Evaluative Research

Evaluation research of broad-scale social action programs by and large has been relatively unsuccessful. As Joseph Wholey and his associate put it, "The most impressive finding about the evaluation of social programs in the Federal government is that substantial work in this field has been almost non-existent. Few significant studies have been carried out. Most of those carried out have been poorly conceived."[123]

The underdeveloped state of evaluative research in the social sciences is due to many and varied factors, most prominently to the technical, political, and ethical problems inhibiting the application of rigorous experimental methodology. Evaluation requires first that program goals be operationalized in a readily measurable fashion; this is exceedingly difficult to do when program goals have broad aims and take understandardized forms.[124] Second, in broad-aim programs such as Model Cities, it is often difficult to identify clearly the target population (or treatment versus nontreatment groups).[125] Moreover, complex political and ethical problems arise when efforts are made to determine arbitrarily which groups or individuals are to receive the benefits of exposure to a particular program or to be denied those benefits for the sake of establishing equivalent treatment and control groups. Also, in most cases, lack of research funds or lack of foresight obviates conducting baseline studies before a social change is introduced.

Added to these factors are the ethical problems faced by the social scientist conducting evaluative research. As Robert Weiss and Martin Rein put it, "Some of the ethical issues result from the value that data about process have to actors in the situation. The data often can affect the social standings and careers of individuals, as well as the success of the strategies of interest groups."[126] Too close a relationship between social scientists and agency officials not only introduces possible biases in the evaluative process because of personality factors, but more significantly, it raises a host of questions about the proper role and functions of social science research. It clearly evokes long-standing debates over "pure" and "applied" research;[127] and, moreover, it raises the specter of the "loss of autonomy of social science" so cogently pointed out by C. Wright Mills in his The Sociological Imagination.[128]

## Efforts to Approximate a Quasi-Experimental Design

The political and ethical problems posed by evaluative research efforts—serious and complex as they are—lie beyond the scope of this book for they do not directly affect it. The concerns here are the technical problems involved in conducting an essentially evaluative study under imperfect conditions. There is a lack of the basic requirements of pre- and posttests on the population under treatment and similar measures for an equivalent control group. Recognizing that the research will have to be carried out under imperfect conditions and, that given these constraints, any results obtained necessarily will be only suggestive in nature, the author seeks to alleviate the methodological problems presented by combining several variations of the ideal experimental design.[129] The aim here is to approximate the conditions of a quasi-experimental design, and to adopt a research strategy that can be "sufficiently probing to be well worth employing when more efficient probes are unavailable."[130]

The methods used in this study to approximate a quasi-experimental design approach are the following: (1) administration of a "retrospective pretest" to the population under study, (2) construction of a matched control group tested using similar measures, and (3) consideration of the major plausible "rival hypothesis." These methods are outlined below.

Retrospective Pretest

As previously discussed, we attempt to ascertain "before" and "after" referents on the major attitudinal and behavioral indicators tested. The problem of "memory bias" is present in all these "before" and "after" indicators. However, the author does not feel that this will unduly contaminate the data. On the attitudinal variables, "memory bias" tends to "disguise rather than masquerade the effects of X"[131] (that is, involvement in the advisory councils). As Donald Campbell and Julian Stanley put it, " . . . the probable direction of memory bias is to distort the past attitudes into agreement with present ones . . . "[132] (emphasis added). On the behavioral variables, "memory bias" should be less operative. In addition to soliciting subjective self-perceptions of behavioral changes, more objective indicators of the time referents of communally oriented political activity are ascertained.[133]

Construction of a Matched Control Group

As absence of an equivalent control group would detract seriously from the findings of this study, efforts were made to construct a comparable control group. Baseline data were available on a representative sample of the East Los Angeles population tested in 1965. The Mexican-American study project directed by Leo Grebler, Joan Moore, and Ralph Guzman conducted 236 interviews of residents in the East Los Angeles area as part of a larger study on Mexican-Americans in the Southwest.[134] (A large number of the items used in this study in 1965 are replicated in the advisory council member questionnaire for comparative purposes.) Harry P. Pachon and this author conducted a panel study of this population seven years later in 1972.[135] The number of respondents successfully reinterviewed in 1972 totaled 51, or nearly one-fourth the original sample. Using this panel study as a control group, of sorts, the design followed in this study may be abstracted as shown.

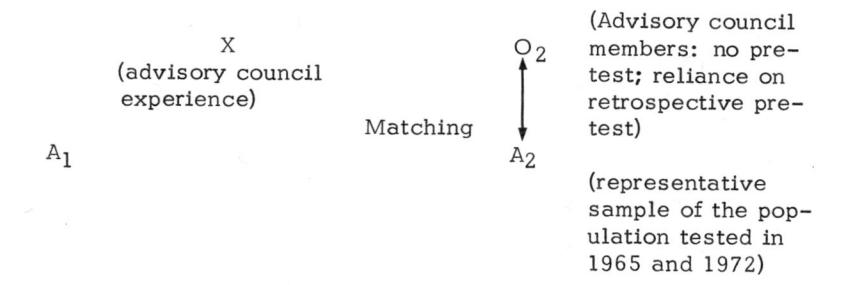

$A_1$  X (advisory council experience)  $O_2$  (Advisory council members: no pretest; reliance on retrospective pretest)

Matching

$A_2$  (representative sample of the population tested in 1965 and 1972)

Matching the $A_2$ respondents with the advisory council members alternatively along (1) socioeconomic, (2) political participation, and (3) ethnicity dimensions and comparing similar measures used in all three studies[136] should work to approximate equivalence. What the panel study does, in effect, is reflect the effects of the environmental changes that have occurred in this population in those seven years,[137] thus allowing for a more precise isolation of those effects which may be attributed to the council experience from those effects attributable to environmental changes.

## Consideration of the Major Plausible Rival Hypothesis

As discussed earlier, the major rival hypothesis to be explored in this study is group consciousness or increased self-awareness as an alternative explanation for any politicization effects obtained. Comparison of advisory council member data with the panel data on the same indicators should work to isolate the effects of each independent variable (that is, advisory council involvement and group consciousness) and possibly should yield useful hypotheses about their interrelationship.

In summary, the research design adopted seeks to approximate the requirements of a quasi-experimental design and hence to isolate more rigorously the effects of the independent variable by the administration of a retrospective pretest, the construction of a comparable control group tested along similar measures, and the consideration of the major rival hypothesis. No claims are made that this design represents a true quasi-experimental design. Nevertheless, the author feels that the degree of precision achieved by this research strategy is superior to that of previous research on advisory councils, which, as was discussed in Chapter 1, consists primarily of largely unsystematic and impressionistic case studies.

What follows is a discussion of major data collection procedures utilized in this study.

NOTES

1. David Marsh, "Political Socialization: The Implicit Assumptions Questioned," British Journal of Political Science 1, no. 4 (October 1971): 455.

2. Norman H. Nie, G. Bingham Powell, Jr., and Kenneth Prewitt, "Social Structure and Political Participation: Developmental Relationships, Part I," American Political Science Review 63, no. 2 (June 1969): 361.

3. See data reported in Gabriel A. Almond and Sidney Verba, The Civic Culture (Boston: Little, Brown and Co., 1965).

4. Norman H. Nie, G. Bingham Powell, Jr., and Kenneth Prewitt, "Social Structure and Political Participation: Developmental Relationships, Part II," American Political Science Review 63 (September 1969): 823.

5. On the importance of self-efficacy for developing feelings of political efficacy, see Lester W. Milbrath, Political Participation: How and Why Do People Get Involved in Politics? (Chicago: Rand McNally, 1965), pp. 56-60.

6. Ibid., p. 59.

7. Almond and Verba, op. cit., pp. 271-272.

8. Carole Pateman, Participation and Democratic Theory (Cambridge: Cambridge University Press, 1970), p. 50.

9. Ibid.

10. Ibid., p. 49.

11. See Almond and Verba, op. cit., Angus Campbell, Phillip Converse, Warren Miller, and Donald Stokes, The American Voter (New York: Wiley, 1960); Angus Campbell, Gerald Gurin, and Warren Miller, The Voter Decides (Evanston, Ill.: Row, Peterson, 1954); and Heinz Eulau, Class and Party in the Eisenhower Years (New York: The Free Press, 1962).

12. Seymour Martin Lipset, Political Man (New York: Doubleday, 1963), pp. 87-127.

13. Ibid., p. 87. The "dilemma" posed by Lipset generally has led to the view that because nondemocratic attitudes are relatively more common among the inactive, any increase in the participation of the inactive is "dangerous," for it may weaken the consensus on the norms of the democratic method. For a clear statement of this view, see Herbert McClosky, "Political Participation," in International Encyclopedia of the Social Sciences, vol. 12, edited by David L. Sills (New York: Macmillan, 1968), p. 259.

14. Moreover, this criticism is applicable even to those theorists who emphasize the social basis of political behavior. Harry

Eckstein, for example, who emphasizes the necessity of congruent authority structures for democratic stability, maintains that " . . . we have every reason to think that economic organizations cannot be organized in a truly democratic manner, at any rate without consequences that no one wants . . . , it is precisely those social relations in which most individuals are engaged most of the time, family life, schools, and jobs, which are the least capable of being democratically organized." Consequently, Eckstein goes on to conclude that given this impossibility and given the necessity for some congruence of authority patterns, for a democratic system to be stable the governmental authority pattern requires a "healthy dose of authoritarianism." See Harry Eckstein, "A Theory of Stable Democracy," in Division and Cohesion of Democracy (Princeton: Princeton University Press, 1966), pp. 237-238, 256. After emphasizing the importance of the individual's participation on the job, in the home, and in the school in determining political attitudes and behavior, Almond and Verba, op. cit., reflect a similar conclusion.

15. The author is referring here to the "process" theory or "democratic elitism" conception of democracy generally espoused by Robert Dahl, Who Governs?: Democracy and Power in an American City (New Haven, Conn.: Yale University Press, 1961); Lipset, op. cit.; Almond and Verba, op. cit.; Eckstein, op. cit.; Milbrath, op. cit.; and Giovanni Sartori, Democratic Theory (Detroit: Wayne State University Press, 1962); among others. For criticisms of this view of democracy, see Peter Bachrach, The Theory of Democratic Elitism: A Critique (Boston: Little, Brown and Co., 1966); Charles A. McCoy and John Playford, Apolitical Politics: A Critique of Behavioralism (New York: T. Crowell, 1968); Henry S. Kariel, The Promise of Politics (Englewood Cliffs, N.J.: Prentice-Hall, 1966); R. J. Pranger, The Eclipse of Citizenship: Power and Participation in Contemporary Politics (New York: Holt Rinehart, Winston, 1968); Pateman, op. cit.; T. B. Bottomore, Elites and Society (London: Penguin, 1967); and Christian Bay, "Politics and Pseudopolitics," American Political Science Review 59, no. 1 (March 1965): 39-51; among others. The past tense is used because it would appear that criticisms leveled at the "process" theory of democracy have had some effect on some of the theorists adhering to this view. See, for example, Robert A. Dahl, After the Revolution?: Authority in a Good Society (New Haven, Conn.: Yale University Press, 1970); and Sidney Verba and Norman H. Nie, Participation in America: Political Democracy and Social Equality (New York: Harper and Row, 1972), both of which reflect a marked shift in research orientation. The latter work is extensively used in this study.

16. Robert A. Dahl, "Hierarchy, Democracy, and Bargaining in Politics and Economics," in Political Behavior: A Reader in Theory and Practice, edited by Heinz Eulau (Glencoe, Ill.: The Free Press of Glencoe, 1956), p. 87.

17. For an elaboration of this alternative view of democracy, see Bachrach, op. cit., chapt. 7.

18. For a classic statement of the dangers of "mass society," see William Kornhauser, *The Politics of Mass Society* (New York: The Free Press, 1959).

19. For a review of this literature, see Milbrath, op. cit.

20. See, for example, Theodore Lowi, "The Public Philosophy: Interest Group Liberalism," *American Political Science Review* 61, no. 1 (March 1967): 5-24; Grant McConnell, *Private Power and American Democracy* (New York: Knopf, 1966); William W. Boyer, *Bureaucracy on Trial* (Indianapolis: Bobbs-Merrill, 1964); and Lewis C. Mainzer, *Political Bureaucracy* (Glenview, Ill.: Scott, Foresman, 1973).

21. Dale Rogers Marshall makes this point in "Public Participation and the Politics of Poverty," in *Race, Change, and Urban Society*, vol. 5, Urban Affairs Annual Reviews, edited by Peter Orleans and William Russell, Jr. (Beverly Hills, Calif.: Sage, 1971), pp. 452-453.

22. Ibid., p. 453.

23. Fred I. Greenstein, "A Note on the Ambiguity of 'Political Socialization': Definitions, Criticisms, and Strategies of Inquiry," *Journal of Politics* 32, no. 4 (November 1970): 971-972.

24. See John S. Jackson, III, "A Political Socialization Bibliography and Survey of Projects in Progress," prepared for the American Political Science Association Committee on Pre-Collegiate Education, September 1972.

25. Marsh, op. cit. See also Donald D. Searing, Joel J. Schwartz, and Alden E. Lind, "The Structuring Principle: Political Socialization and Belief Systems," *American Political Science Review* 67, no. 2 (June 1973): 415-433.

26. See discussion of research by R. D. Taddenham, J. Kagan, and M. Moss, and D. Butler and D. Stokes, and R. J. Benewick et al., in Marsh, op. cit.

27. Kenneth P. Langton makes this point in the first chapter of *Political Socialization* (New York: Oxford Univ. Press, 1969), p. 19. Nevertheless, the remainder of the book is focused primarily on preadult socialization processes.

28. Orville G. Brim, Jr., and Stanton Wheeler, *Socialization after Childhood: Two Essays* (New York: Wiley, 1966), p. 18. It is paradoxical that although this notion has been studied extensively in research on changes in traditional value structures in Third World countries undergoing rapid modernization, it has not been widely recognized in the United States (at least not on the part of political scientists).

29. See, for example, Alvin Toffler's discussion in *Future Shock* (New York: Random House, 1970), part 1.

30. See discussion of this literature in Milbrath, op. cit.

31. For an example, see comments on this question made in Carl P. Hensler, "The Structure of Orientations Toward Government: Involvement, Efficacy, and Evaluation," paper presented at the Sixty-Seventh Annual Meeting of the American Political Science Association, September 7-11, 1971, Chicago.

32. These are Nie, Powell, and Prewitt's terms, op. cit.
33. See Almond and Verba, op. cit.; Milbrath, op. cit.; and Nie, Powell, and Prewitt, "Social Structure and Political Participation: Parts I and II," op. cit.
34. Almond and Verba, op. cit., pp. 45-63.
35. Milbrath, op. cit., pp. 56-60.
36. On "civic duty to participate" see Almond and Verba, op. cit., pp. 117-136; on "social trust" see Morris Rosenberg, "Misanthropy and Political Ideology," American Sociological Review 21, no. 6 (December 1956): 690-694.
37. However, changes in attitudes necessarily do not result in changes in political behavior. This problem is discussed in a subsequent section of this chapter.
38. Sidney Verba and Norman H. Nie, op. cit., p. 150.
39. Nie, Powell, and Prewitt, op. cit., and Verba and Nie, op. cit., depart from this tradition, as will be discussed.
40. See, for example, Philip Cutwright, "National Political Development," in Politics and Social Life, edited by Nelson W. Polsby, Robert A. Dentler, and Paul L. Smith (Boston: Houghton Mifflin Co., 1963), pp. 569-582; and Lipset, op. cit., pp. 27-63.
41. See discussion of this literature in Stephen M. Rose, The Betrayal of the Poor: The Transformation of Community Action (Cambridge: Schenkman, 1972), pp. 70-82.
42. Nie, Powell, and Prewitt, "Social Structure and Political Participation: Part II," op. cit., p. 829.
43. Verba and Nie, op. cit., p. 153.
44. Ibid., p. 156.
45. Two other alternative routes to political participation by the lower classes, "partisan mobilization path" and "parochial participation path," are discussed in Sidney Verba, Bashiruddin Ahmed, and Anil Bhatt, Caste, Race and Politics: A Comparative Study of India and the U.S. (Beverly Hills, Calif.: Sage, 1971).
46. Data collected on Mexico, the United States, Germany, Italy, and Great Britain and reported in Almond and Verba, op. cit.
47. Nie, Powell, and Prewitt, "Social Structure and Political Participation: Part II," op. cit., p. 811.
48. Ibid.
49. See Milbrath, op. cit., pp. 130-133; Almond and Verba, op. cit., pp. 252-264; Robert E. Lane, Political Life (New York: The Free Press of Glencoe, 1959); and Herbert Maccoby, "The Differential Political Activity of Participants in a Voluntary Association," American Sociological Review 23, no. 5 (October 1958): 524.
50. Nie, Powell, and Prewitt, "Social Structure and Political Participation: Part II," op. cit., p. 819.
51. Ibid., p. 826.
52. See, for example, Daniel Goldrich, "Political Organization and the Politicization of the Poblador," Comparative Political Studies

3, no. 2 (July 1970): 176-202; Raymond B. Pratt, "Parties, Neighborhood Associations and the Politicization of the Urban Poor in Latin America: An Exploratory Analysis," Midwest Journal of Political Science 15, no. 3 (August 1971): 495-524; Daniel Goldrich, "Toward the Comparative Study of Politicization in Latin America," in Contemporary Cultures and Societies of Latin America, edited by Dwight B. Heath and Richard N. Adams (New York: Random House, 1965), pp. 361-378; and William Mangin, "Latin American Squatter Settlements: A Problem and a Solution," Latin American Research Review 2, no. 3 (Summer 1967): 65-98.

53. For a review of this literature see Biliana C. S. Ambrecht, "Beyond Bureaucratic Organization: A Case Study of the Yugoslav Experiment in Economic Self-Management," mimeographed, (University of California at Los Angeles, Department of Political Science, 1971); and Pateman, op. cit., pp. 45-85.

54. Goldrich, op. cit., p. 197.

55. Ibid., p. 190.

56. See discussion in Ambrecht, op. cit., and in Pateman, op. cit., pp. 45-67.

57. Primarily because involvement in the work organization is not generally voluntary as it is for other organizations, but generally involuntary (in the sense that particularly for the lower-status person, "perceived ease of movement from the organization" is usually nil). Moreover, although participation within the work organization, in some ways, can be likened to the "active" involvement dimension found by Verba and Nie to correlate with political participation (op. cit., pp. 184-191) , it is a more stringent indicator of activism. It does not refer to how exposed the individual is to the organization through his physical presence at meetings or his involvement in committees or in other organizational tasks that need to be done. Rather, it measures the individual's extent of involvement in actual decision-making processes within the organization.

58. This is discussed in Ambrecht, op. cit., pp. 1-30; and in Pateman, op. cit.

59. This is not necessarily the case in other Western democracies as discussed in Nie, Powell, and Prewitt, "Social Structure and Political Participation: Part II," op. cit., pp. 823-825.

60. Verba and Nie, op. cit., p. 204; conversely 59 percent of the lower class may be classified as nonmembers, while only 22 percent of the upper class are nonmembers.

61. See discussion in ibid., pp. 149-174, and in Verba, Ahmed, and Bhatt, op. cit.

62. See, for example, Lenneal Henderson, "Black Political Life in the U.S.: A Bibliographical Essay," in Black Political Life in the United States, edited by Lenneal Henderson (San Francisco: Chandler, 1972), pp. 253-269; Chuck Stone, "Black Political Power in America," rev. ed. (New York: Delta, 1970); E. V. Essein-Udom, Black Nation-

alism: A Search for Identity in America (Chicago: Dell, 1962); Marvin E. Olsen, "Social and Political Participation of Blacks," American Sociological Review 35, no. 4 (August 1970): 682-696; and James Q. Wilson, "The Changing Political Position of the Negro," in Assuring Freedom to the Free, edited by A. M. Rose (Detroit: Wayne State University Press, 1964), pp. 163-184.

63. Verba and Nie, op. cit., p. 158.

64. Ibid. It should be noted, however, that the modes of participation of blacks and whites are different (see pp. 160-170).

65. Ibid., p. 159.

66. For the best empirical study on Mexican-Americans conducted to date, see Leo Grebler, Joan W. Moore, and Ralph C. Guzman, The Mexican American People: The Nation's Second Largest Minority (New York: The Free Press, 1970).

67. For a statement on the meaning of the Chicano movement, see Armando B. Rendon, Chicano Manifesto: The History and Aspirations of the Second Largest Minority in America (New York: Collier, 1971).

68. See Cesar Chavez, "The Organizer's Tale," Ramparts Magazine 5, no. 2 (July 1966): 43-50.

69. See Joseph P. Love, "La Raza: Mexican Americans in Rebellion," in Mexican Americans in the United States: A Reader, edited by John H. Burma (Cambridge, Mass.: Schenkman, 1970), pp. 459-472.

70. See discussion of the Mexican-American electoral takeover of Crystal City, Texas, in Matt S. Meier and Feliciano Rivera, The Chicanos: A History of Mexican Americans (New York: Hill and Wang, 1972), ch. 15; and in Antonio Camejo, "Texas Chicanos Forge Own Political Power," in Introduction to Chicano Studies: A Reader, edited by Livie Isauro Duran and H. Russell Bernard (New York: Macmillan, 1973), pp. 552-558.

71. For an interpretation of this protest activity, see Antonio Camejo, "Lessons of the Los Angeles Chicano Protest," in Duran and Bernard, op. cit., pp. 510-519; and Charles A. Ericksen, "Uprising in the Barrios," in Burma, op. cit., pp. 289-294.

72. On the most famous electoral gains of the La Raza Unida party, see Camejo, op. cit.

73. See general discussion of this phenomenon in Alfred Cuellar, "Perspectives on Politics," in Duran and Bernard, op. cit., pp. 558-575.

74. Donald T. Campbell and Julian C. Stanley, Experimental and Quasi-Experimental Designs for Research (Chicago: Rand McNally, 1963), p. 36.

75. Selwyn W. Becker, "The Parable of the Pill," Administrative Science Quarterly 15, no. 1 (March 1970): 97. (This is a critique of a study by Robert T. Golembiewski and Stokes B. Carrigan which appears in the same issue.)

76. Among other possibilities, politicization also could be explained by a rise in socioeconomic status in the East Los Angeles com-

munity (which is documented in Chapter 3) or by personality factors. On the importance of personality factors, see Fred Greenstein, Personality and Politics (Chicago: Markham, 1969). In this author's opinion, however, neither of these factors warrants treatment as a major rival hypothesis. As is explained in Chapter 3, although the general SES level of the East Los Angeles community has witnessed a marked increase since 1965, when one takes into consideration the rate of inflation and the increase in socioeconomic indicators in the Los Angeles area as a whole, East Los Angeles still remains an economically underprivileged barrio in contrast with its affluent neighbors in Los Angeles county. In regard to personality factors, it would appear that the design followed in this study (that is, a random sample of the total membership of the universe of advisory councils in the East Los Angeles community) would work to minimize the possible presence of idiosyncratic personality factors. Nevertheless, what could be considered a personality factor is discussed. A second alternative explanation for any politicization results obtained is sought in the factor of "self-selection," or the possibility that council members already could have been active community participants prior to council membership. This possibility is explored in Chapters 4 and 5.

77. A copy of the questionnaire utilized (English version) is available in the Appendix. The Spanish version may be obtained by writing to the author.

78. This definition is adapted from Goldrich, op. cit., pp. 361-362.

79. Adapted from Daniel Goldrich, "The Political Integration of Lower Class Urban Settlements in Chile and Peru," Studies in Comparative International Development, vol. 5 (Beverly Hills, Calif.: Sage, 1967), pp. 1-22.

80. Almond and Verba, op. cit., p. 45.

81. See Hensler, op. cit., and Almond and Verba, op. cit.

82. The full text and placement of all questions cited may be found in the Appendix.

83. The wording of these two questions was suggested by Carl P. Hensler, Department of Political Science, UCLA.

84. They read, (Q. 93) "Talking about politics, do you follow the accounts of political and governmental affairs? Would you say that you follow them regularly, from time to time, or never?"; and (Q. 94) "Do you follow (listen to, read about) public affairs in newspapers (radio, television, magazines) nearly every day, once a week, from time to time, or never?" (These questions are adopted from Almond and Verba, op. cit.)

85. This question reads, (Q. 65) "In the past few years, the federal (national) government has been directing its attention to the problems of the poor through a number of programs usually called the War on Poverty. Some people in this community tell us that they are familiar with these programs, while others tell us that they never

heard of them. How about you? Have you ever heard about any of these programs?" (If heard) "Which programs have you heard about?" (this question is original to this study).

86. See William A. Gamson, Power and Discontent (Homewood, Ill.: Dorsey, 1968), p. 42.

87. Ibid., ch. 8.

88. See Hensler, op. cit.

89. See a review of these studies in Milbrath, op. cit., pp. 56-60.

90. The wording of these questions was suggested by Hensler.

91. National output: following a filter question on whether they had ever heard about the War on Poverty (see Note 85), respondents were asked, (Q. 66) "Some people say that the programs of the War on Poverty have been successful in helping to resolve the problems of the poor, others say that, overall, the War on Poverty has been a failure. What do you think? Why do you say that?", and (Q. 67) "The current administration has recently been cutting a number of programs associated with the War on Poverty. Do you feel that this is a good thing or is it bad?" "Why do you say that?" (these questions are original to this study). Local output: after a question on "In your opinion, what are the main things that children need to be taught in the schools today?", the following evaluative question is asked: (Q.49) "Are the schools in this community teaching these things?"

92. The SRC Political Efficacy scale developed by Campbell, Gurin, and Miller, op. cit., reads, (1) "I don't think public officials care much about what people like me think;" (2) "Voting is the only way that people like me can have any say about how the government runs things;" (3) "People like me don't have any say about what the government does;" (4) "Sometimes politics and government seem so complicated that a person like me can't really understand what is going on." (Q. 81, 82, 83, 84).

93. Suggested by Hensler.

94. Reported in John P. Robinson and Phillip R. Shave, Measures of Social Psychological Attitudes (Ann Arbor, Mich.: Survey Research Center, Institute for Social Research, August 1969), p. 529. The scale reads, (1) "Generally speaking, would you say that most people can be trusted or that you can't be too careful in dealing with people?", (2) "Would you say that most of the time people try to be helpful or that they are mostly just looking out for themselves?", (3) "Do you think that most people would try to take advantage of you if they got the chance, or would they try to be fair?" (Q. 43, 44, 45).

95. Almond and Verba, op. cit., p. 285.

96. On this question, see the political problems posed by the absence of social trust in France; for example, Michel Crozier, The Bureaucratic Phenomenon (Chicago: University of Chicago Press, 1964);

and Henry W. Ehrmann, Politics in France (Boston: Little, Brown and Co., 1972).

97. See Rosenberg, op. cit.

98. See Grebler et al., op. cit., pp. 542-556, and Paul M. Sheldon, "Community Participation and the Emerging Middle Class," in La Raza: Forgotten Americans, edited by Julian Samora (North Bend, Ind.: University of Notre Dame Press, 1966), p. 48. For an opposite view on this question, see Salvador Alvarez, "Mexican American Community Organizations," Voices: Readings from El Grito 4, no. 3 (Spring 1971): 68-77.

99. These questions are original to this study.

100. To insure the authenticity of responses on the forced-choice questions, these are checked against the respondent's open-ended answers.

101. For wording of these questions, see Note 85.

102. The question reads, (Q. 88) "Now I would like to ask you about organizations in the community. Here is a list of organizations which people tell us are around here. Please follow me on the list I give you (HAND RESPONDENT CARD) Please tell me if (1) you never heard of the organization, (2) if you heard of the organization somewhere, or (3) if you belong to it. (GI Forum, LUCHA, PTA, Alianza Hispano Americana, La Raza Unida party, MAPA, Chicano Moratorium, TELACU, Republican clubs, Democratic clubs, PASSO, LULAC, Brown Berets, Chicano Liberation Front, CSO, Neighborhood Legal Aid, MECHA, United Farm Workers).

103. (Q. 68) "Over the past years, do you remember hearing or reading anything about protests, marches, or demonstrations in the Mexican-American community?" (If Yes) "In your opinion, why did these protests, marches, or demonstrations occur?"

104. See a discussion of these studies in Leo Festinger, "Behavioral Support for Opinion Change," Public Opinion Quarterly 28, no. 3 (Fall 1964): 404-417.

105. The extent of the respondent's organizational involvement prior to membership in the advisory council already had been ascertained in Q. 27, "Before you joined the advisory council, were you a member of any community organizations?" (If Yes) "Which ones?"

106. Degree of activeness, however, is not solicited for membership in other advisory councils. For all memberships reported, the following items are tapped: "About how long have you been a member?", "About how often do you attend the meetings?", and "Have you ever been an officer?"

107. Dale Rogers Marshall, The Politics of Participation in Poverty: A Case Study of the Board of Economic and Youth Opportunities Agency of Greater Los Angeles (Richmond, Calif.: University of California Press, 1971).

108. (Questions 91 A, B, C, D; Q. 92; Q. 88, items 5, 9, 10)

109. See above, pp. 41-42.

110. For a description of problems encountered by the poor in dealing with public bureaucracies, see Gideon Sjoberg, Richard A. Brymer, and Buford Farris, "Bureaucracy and the Lower Class," in Blacks and Bureaucracy: Readings in the Problems and Politics of Change, edited by Virginia B. Ermer and John H. Strange (New York: Crowell, 1972), pp. 159-171.

111. Michael Parenti, "Power and Pluralism: A View from the Bottom," Journal of Politics 32, no. 3 (August 1970): 528.

112. David Greenstone and Paul Peterson, "Reformers, Machines, and the War on Poverty," in Cities and Suburbs, edited by Bryan T. Downes (Belmont, Calif.: Wadsworth, 1971), pp. 377-399.

113. On political parties in California, see, for example, James Q. Wilson, "Party Organization: The Search for Power," in The California Governmental Process, edited by Eugene C. Lee (Boston: Little, Brown and Co., 1966), and Oliver P. Williams and Charles Adrian, "The Insulation of Local Politics Under the Non-Partisan Ballot," American Political Science Review 53, no. 4 (December 1959): 1052-1063.

114. On this point, see similar reasoning used in Verba, Ahmed, and Bhatt, op. cit., p. 24; and in Goldrich, "Political Organization and Politicization of the Poblador," op. cit.

115. Organizations considered to be "radical" are La Raza Unida party, Chicano Moratorium, Chicano Liberation Front, and Brown Berets.

116. This is coded as "radical" because a "separate party for people of Mexican background only" is probably embodied in the La Raza Unida party.

117. These are La Raza Unida party, Chicano Liberation Front, and the Brown Berets.

118. On evaluative research, see Joseph S. Wholey, et al., Federal Evaluation Policy: Analyzing the Effects of Public Programs (Washington, D.C.: The Urban Institute, 1970); Charles R. Wright, "Evaluation Research," in International Encyclopedia of the Social Sciences, Vol. 5, edited by David L. Sills (New York: Macmillan, 1968), pp. 197-202; M. Jahoda and E. Barnitz, "The Nature of Evaluation," International Social Science Bulletin 7, no. 3 (1955): 353-364; Edward Suchman, Evaluative Research (New York: Russell Sage, 1967); Howard E. Freeman and Clarence S. Sherwood, "Research in Large Scale Intervention Programs," The Journal of Social Issues 21, no. 1 (January 1965): 11-28; Robert T. Golembiewski and Stokes B. Carrigan, "Planned Change in Organizational Style Based on the Laboratory Approach," Administrative Science Quarterly 15, no. 1 (March 1970): 79-93; Donald T. Campbell, "Reforms as Experiments," American Psychologist 24, no. 4 (April 1969): 409-429; Walter Williams and John H. Evans, "The Politics of Evaluation: The Case of Headstart," Annals of the American Academy of Political and Social Sciences 385 (September 1969): 118-132; and Walter Williams, Social Policy Research and Analysis (New York: Elsevier, 1971).

119. Wright, op. cit., p. 346.
120. Wholey et al., op. cit., p. 92.
121. See discussion in Campbell and Stanley, op. cit.
122. Ibid., p. 36.
123. Wholey et al., op. cit., p. 15.
124. See discussion of this problem in Robert S. Weiss and Martin Rein, "The Evaluation of Broad Aim Programs: Experimental Design, Its Difficulties and an Alternative," Administrative Science Quarterly 15, no. 1 (March 1970): 97-109.
125. Ibid., p. 98.
126. Ibid., p. 197.
127. See discussion in Kenneth M. Dolbeare, "Public Policy Analysis and the Coming Struggle for the Soul of the Post-Behavioral Revolution," in Power and Community: Dissenting Essays in Political Science, edited by Phillip Green and Sanford Levinson (New York: Random House, 1969), pp. 85-111.
128. C. Wright Mills, The Sociological Imagination (London: Oxford University Press, 1959), p. 106.
129. Suggested by Jahoda and Barnitz, op. cit.
130. Campbell and Stanley, op. cit., p. 35.
131. Ibid., p. 66.
132. Ibid.
133. See above, pp. 48-49.
134. Leo Grebler, Joan W. Moore, and Ralph C. Guzman, The Mexican American People: The Nation's Second Largest Minority (New York: The Free Press, 1970).
135. Although the 1972 questionnaire replicates most of the questions asked in 1965, it also includes a large number of items that had not been asked previously, particularly items tapping additional dimensions of political attitudes and behavior.
136. These are marked accordingly in the English version of the questionnaire found in the Appendix.
137. The data of the baseline study (1965) fortuitously coincides with the beginnings of the Chicano movement.

# CHAPTER 3

## DATA COLLECTION PROCEDURES

### DEFINITION OF KEY CONCEPTS

#### The Community

"Community" in this study is defined as those census tracts in Los Angeles County that are found in the contiguous localities of East Los Angeles; Boyle Heights; City Terrace; Belvedere; and census tracts 1997, 1998, and 1999; portions of census tract 1991 in the southern section of Lincoln Heights; and portions of census tracts 2014.02 and 2017 in the southern section of El Sereno.[1] This definition of community has been arrived at according to three criteria: (1) ethnic homogeneity, (2) economic characteristics of the population, and (3) availability of attitudinal and behavioral survey data of the population at two different time periods, 1965 and 1972.

#### Ethnic Homogeneity

Ethnic homogeneity clearly differentiates the area delimited from surrounding communities in the Los Angeles-Long Beach SMSA (standard metropolitan statistical area). Eighty-four percent of the population of this area may be classified as Mexican-American.[2] This figure represents the highest concentration of Mexican-Americans in the Los Angeles-Long Beach SMSA, which in itself contains the largest urban population of Mexican-Americans outside Mexico City.[3] This area is indeed the largest and most ethnically homogenous barrio in the Los Angeles metropolis. It should be noted here that the "ghettoization" of Mexican-Americans in the East Los Angeles area has increased in the last decade, while the overall population of the area has declined in relation to the total population of the Los Angeles-Long Beach SMSA. See Table 3.1.[4]

TABLE 3.1

Total Population and Proportion of Spanish-Surnamed Persons
for Los Angeles-Long Beach SMSA and the East Los Angeles
Community (1960, 1970)

|  | 1960 | 1970 | Percent Change |
|---|---|---|---|
| Los Angeles-Long Beach SMSA | | | |
| Total Population | 6,041,302 | 7,032,075 | +16.4 |
| Percent Spanish-surnamed | 10.4 | 18.3 | + 7.9 |
| East Los Angeles-Boyle Heights | | | |
| Total Population | 192,938 | 188,073 | - 2.5 |
| Percent Spanish-surnamed | 66.1 | 85.0 | +18.9 |
| East Los Angeles-Boyle Heights plus selected tracts | | | |
| Total Population | — | 204,598 | — |
| Percent Spanish-surnamed | — | 84.0 | — |

Source: U.S. Bureau of the Census, U.S. Census of Population and Housing: 1960, Census Tracts, Final Report PHC (1) 82 (Washington, D.C.: U.S. Government Printing Office, 1962) and U.S. Bureau of the Census, Census of Population and Housing: 1970, Census Tracts, Final Report, PHC (1)—117 Los Angeles—Long Beach, Calif. SMSA, Parts 1 and 2 (Washington, D.C.: U.S. Government Printing Office, 1972).

Moreover, this increase in spatial ethnic concentration has been accompanied by a significant increase or resurgence of ethnic political activity. The 1960s in East Los Angeles have witnessed the appearance of the Chicano movement and its attendant emphasis on ethnic mobilization and radical political activity. Grass roots community organization, riots, marches, demonstrations, and clashes with police have all marked this apparent resurgence in ethnic sentiment. To some, this represents a new style in Mexican-American political behavior, a style "which questions and challenges not only the assumptions of other generations of Mexican American political leaders but also some of the most basic assumptions of American politics as well."[5]

The predominance of Mexican-Americans in this community allows one to explore the effects of participation in advisory councils in a different cultural context from that of previous studies, which focused primarily on participation in the black communities. Moreover, the apparent resurgence of ethnic awareness that this community has manifested provides an interesting backdrop against which the interplay

DATA COLLECTION PROCEDURES

between ethnic mobilization and increased governmental accessibility in the form of advisory councils may be explored.

## Economic and Social Characteristics of the Population

East Los Angeles is one of two poverty target areas in Los Angeles County.[6] Although the majority of residents of the area do not fall below the poverty level definition of the Social Security Administration,[7] the economic characteristics of the population clearly set the area apart from its more affluent neighbors in Los Angeles County. Median family income figures for the East Los Angeles area as well as for Los Angeles County as a whole are reported in Table 3.2.

Although the median family income in the East Los Angeles area has increased significantly in the last decade (by 42 percent), this increase compares unfavorably with the overall increase of 55 percent in median family income in Los Angeles County and with the national increase in median income of all urban families (66 percent).[8] In addition, the differences in family income between residents in East Los Angeles and Los Angeles County are accentuated further by differences in family size. Large families are relatively common among persons of Spanish surname. In 1960, for example, 24 percent of the Spanish surname families in California consisted of six or more family members. This compared with 10 percent having six or more members among all white families in the state and 19 percent among all nonwhite families.[9]

TABLE 3.2

Median Family Income for Los Angeles-Long Beach SMSA
and East Los Angeles Community (1960, 1970)

|  | 1960 | 1970 | Percent Change |
|---|---|---|---|
| Los Angeles-Long Beach | 7,078 | 10,972 | +55 |
| East Los Angeles-Boyle Heights | 5,094 | 7,250 | +42 |
| East Los Angeles-Boyle Heights plus selected tracts | — | 7,333 | — |

Source: U.S. Bureau of the Census, U.S. Censuses of Population and Housing: 1960, Census Tracts, Final Report PHC (1) 82 (Washington, D.C.: U.S. Government Printing Office, 1962), and U.S. Bureau of the Census, Census of Population and Housing: 1970, Census Tracts, Final Report PHC (1)—117 Los Angeles-Long Beach, Calif. SMSA, Parts 1 and 2 (Washington, D.C.: U.S. Government Printing Office). Figures have been compiled by the author.

A variety of other socioeconomic indicators clearly define the East Los Angeles area as economically deprived in relation to Los Angeles County. The percentage of families below the poverty level for the area delimited is 19.1 percent,[10] as compared with 8.2 percent for the county as a whole. The percentage of unemployed males aged 16 and over in the civilian labor force is approximately 7.1 percent as compared with 6.0 percent for the county as a whole.[11]

The median number of years of school completed for residents of the area in 1970 is estimated at 8.4[12] as compared with 12.4 for the county as a whole. Moreover, the proportion of high school dropouts in the area in 1970, estimated at 28.5 percent,[13] sharply contrasts with the county's proportion of 13.5 percent.

All these factors—low income, high unemployment, and low level of educational achievement have qualified East Los Angeles as a poverty target area for the major federal programs of the 1960s, the CAP and Model Cities,[14] as well as for California state programs aimed at providing services for low income communities.[15] In this respect the East Los Angeles community has been subject to the whole variety of government strategies to eliminate poverty undertaken in the 1960s. Hence, it provides an excellent laboratory for the study of the effects of one such strategy: "maximum feasible participation."

Availability of Panel Data for a Sample of the Population

Panel data are available for a sample of the population residing in East Los Angeles, Boyle Heights, City Terrace, and Belvedere (that is, 91.9 percent of the area delimited). As previously mentioned, the Mexican-American study project directed by Grebler, Moore, and Guzman interviewed 236 respondents residing in this area in 1965. Pachon and this author conducted a follow-up of this study seven years later and were able to locate and reinterview 51 of the original respondents, or close to one-fourth the original sample. As discussed in Chapter 2, this panel study will be used as a control group in an attempt to distinguish between changes that may be due to the independent variable under study (that is, involvement in advisory councils) and changes that may be due to environmental factors (that is, increased ethnic awareness and ethnic mobilization).[16]

The area encompassing East Los Angeles proper, Boyle Heights, City Terrace, Belvedere, and selected census tracts in southern Lincoln Heights and El Sereno is defined as the "community" in this study because it represents an economically deprived Mexican-American barrio, one which has been subject to the multiple currents that have traversed poverty communities across the country in the 1960s: a variety of government programs to eliminate poverty, as well as an apparent rise in ethnic consciousness, grass roots organization, and radical political activity.

DATA COLLECTION PROCEDURES 65

## Advisory Councils to Public Agencies

"Public" agencies are defined as those agencies that are clearly part of the governmental structure or are primarily dependent on governmental (versus private) funds for their support. This classification is meant to encompass all levels of government (city, county, state and federal) and includes agencies such as schools, health centers, departments of social services, and commissions on human relations.
"Advisory councils" are defined as councils or committees composed of citizens that have been created, either by the agencies themselves or through community impetus, to advise and provide community input into the operation of agencies.[17] This definition excludes "boards of directors" or "governing boards," which are committees empowered actually to run particular agencies.[18]

## THE UNIVERSE OF ADVISORY COUNCILS

At the outset of the study, an extensive telephone survey of all public agencies in the area was made to determine how many agencies had operative advisory councils. As no comprehensive agency listing of the area in question was available, a number of directories were compiled hopefully to produce an all-inclusive listing of agencies.[19] Approximately 180 agencies were contacted to determine (1) existence of an advisory council and length of time in operation, (2) name of agency official responsible for the council and/or name of advisory council chairman, (3) location and frequency of meetings, and (4) availability of minutes.[20] It was found that 70 agencies had operative advisory councils.[21] The total number of councils may be categorized according to the level of government of the agency and according to the functional service area. (See Table 3.3).

It is apparent from these breakdowns that, although advisory councils are operative in agencies at all levels of government and in most policy areas, city and federal levels of government, (94 percent of the total) and educational agencies, (64 percent of the total) are involved most heavily in the practice of creating advisory councils. Moreoever, the influence of the federal government in fostering the practice of citizen participation in advisory councils becomes even more apparent when one considers that, in addition to the 27 agencies administered directly by the federal government, (1) 36 city-administered schools have created citizen advisory councils following federal regulations as specified in Title 1,[22] and (2) two other city-administered agencies[23] consist of special programs funded by the federal government and administered by federal requirements.

TABLE 3.3

Advisory Councils: Breakdown by Government Level and Service Area

| | |
|---|---:|
| Government Level | |
|   Federal[a] | 27 |
|   State of California | 1 |
|   Los Angeles County | 3 |
|   Los Angeles City[b] | 39 |
|   Total | 70 |
| Service Area | |
|   Health-welfare | 4 |
|   Multifunctional service centers | 8 |
|   Legal aid | 3 |
|   Manpower training | 5 |
|   Senior citizens | 2 |
|   Community training and leadership—cultural | 4 |
|   Public housing | 1 |
|   Education | |
|     Preschool | 4 |
|     Elementary | 27 |
|     Junior high | 3 |
|     High school | 6 |
|     Posthigh school | 1 |
|     Special education programs | 2 |
|   Total | 70 |

[a] EYOA (Economic and Youth Opportunities Agency) delegate agencies, 10; Model Cities delegate agencies, 10; federal miscellaneous, 7.

[b] School advisory councils, 36; others, 3.

Source: Compiled by the author.

No other empirical data on all the councils were available. However, impressionistic evidence gathered on the basis of contacts with agency officials, advisory council chairmen, and personal observation suggests that the majority of councils have been created fairly recently (that is, within one to five years of the study) and that frequency of meetings varies from a maximum of once a week to a minimum of once a month. Other characteristics of the councils, for example, recruitment patterns, purposes, functions, perceived power configurations, and such, are reported in subsequent chapters on the basis of responses to the interviews with advisory council members.

## MEMBERSHIP OF THE ADVISORY COUNCILS

Once the universe of advisory councils was identified, the next research stage entailed the collection of membership lists from each advisory council to compile a master list of all members of all councils on the basis of which a random sample could be drawn.[24]

The collection of these membership lists proved to be the most difficult and time-consuming aspect of this study.[25] The problems encountered are worth mentioning for other scholars undertaking similar studies. The original approach followed was to employ Chicano research assistants to contact each advisory council chairman personally to explain the purposes and scope of the project and to obtain membership lists. The first problem encountered lies in the fact that poverty communities have been overstudied (or at least they feel they have been). In the opinion of many people in the East Los Angeles community, the poor already have been oversubjected to survey studies without any tangible, positive benefits accruing to their participation in these studies.[26] This attitude raises a number of thorny ethical and practical problems for the researcher.

Ethical problems arise because it is indeed difficult to justify the "invasion of privacy" character of survey research and the absence of readily tangible benefits accruing to the research process in the name of some lofty goal such as scientific inquiry. This type of goal is neither readily understandable nor readily acceptable to the leadership of poverty communities, which is primarily interested in tangible program results. Moreover, this type of attitude is beginning to create a number of practical problems for the survey researcher. A new trend in conducting survey research in poverty communities appears to be that vocal segments of these communities are beginning to exert some controls over the research process. These controls seem to be exerted in two major ways: (1) "bargaining" with the survey research institutes over the kinds of research or the kinds of questions that are acceptable or not acceptable (for example, demanding that certain questions be dropped and certain other questions of more interest to community leaders be added); and (2) insisting that research institutes train and employ residents of the area as part of their research staff.[27] From this author's value perspective, this is a desirable trend which can be interpreted as a positive assertion of community control. Nevertheless, it intimates bad auguries for future survey research studies of poverty communities.

A second problem encountered lies in the increased militancy and ethnic separatism characterizing some segments of the Mexican-American community of East Los Angeles. For some of these individuals, survey research of the type conducted here is a manifestation of "Anglo status quo-oriented social science," which is neither relevant nor useful to the cause of the Chicano. To alleviate this problem, the author stressed the potential long-range usefulness of the study findings, made her services available to community organizations needing advice on research techniques, and offered to send a summary of research findings to all who expressed an interest. Additionally, only Chicano bilingual research assistants and interviewers were used in the study.[28]

The final problem besetting the compilation of membership lists[29] was the fact that a number of advisory council chairmen proved to be highly reluctant to take the responsibility of releasing the names and addresses of the advisory council members without obtaining the permission of all council members or, in some cases, of agency officials. This procedure, of course, caused an extraordinary amount of delay. Whether the reluctance of the chairmen could be construed as a manifestation of the generalized hostility to survey research present in the community or whether it was primarily a manifestation of positional insecurity could not be ascertained. Given this difficulty, the personal approach directed at the chairmen was supplanted by a more formal approach directed at agency officials. This approach proved to be much more fruitful; many responded favorably and promptly. Finally, membership lists were obtained for 61 of the 70 advisory councils, or 85 percent of the total.

## COMPOSITION OF THE ADVISORY COUNCILS

Membership in the 61 advisory councils for which lists were obtained totaled 1,520 individuals. Council size ranged from 5 to 105 members,[30] average size being 25 members.[31]

Membership in the advisory councils consisted generally of three types of individuals: (1) community representatives, (2) agency representatives, and (3) professionals. It should be noted that this breakdown follows the general pattern established by the CAP, where at least one-third of the membership had to be "representative of the poor." However, no set proportion of "community" versus agency and professional representatives was found to prevail in the East Los Angeles councils. Rather this proportion varied from council to council from a low of 15 percent to a high of 95 percent of "community" representatives. The average proportion of community representatives in all councils was 70 percent.

Because this study focuses on the possible effects of participation on community people (that is, laymen or nonprofessional types), it was decided to delete the agency and professional people from the population. The underlying assumption made was that, given the higher socioeconomic status of the professionals and the position of agency representatives, these two groups probably already possessed a high level of political efficacy and skills.

DATA COLLECTION PROCEDURES 69

Definition of "community" representatives was accomplished in several ways. In some cases, the distinctions already had been established by the agencies themselves; recruitment was strictly based along proportional lines. In other cases, advisory council chairmen or agency officials were asked to differentiate between community representatives and agency representatives and professionals.[32] Finally, in a number of cases, the author had to make the choice. In the latter case, the criteria used were the following: (1) all individuals without a stated agency or professional affiliation were chosen, and (2) individuals affiliated with grass roots community groups were included. Composition of the advisory councils is broken down in Table 3.4.

It should be noted here that the proportion of community representatives in these councils (71 percent) is much larger than that found in the two major community participation programs, CAP and Model Cities, where the proportion of community representation usually hovers around the one-third point.[33] This supports the proposition made in Chapter 1 that the process of citizen participation in advisory councils has grown beyond the boundaries and guidelines specified by the CAP and Model Cities programs.

TABLE 3.4

Composition of Advisory Council Membership
By Type of Representation

|  | Number | Percent |
|---|---|---|
| Community representatives | 1,076 | 71 |
| Other (agency and professional) | 444 | 29 |
| Total | 1,520 | 100 |

Source: Compiled by the author.

Membership Overlap

Previous studies of Community Action councils[34] as well as personal direct observation of a number of councils in the East Los Angeles area[35] had suggested that the membership of some councils is composed of "super-activists" and overinvolved individuals who spend an inordinate amount of time going to meetings of different organizations and councils.[36] An effort to test this particular proposition was made by checking for membership overlap in the advisory councils.[37] The extent of membership overlap identified is surprisingly low and does not appear to support the contention that an activist elite dominates the membership of the advisory councils. Among the community representatives, approximately 5.4 percent belonged to more than one council; but among the agency and professional representatives, the proportion of membership overlap was slightly higher, or 7.2 percent. These are surprisingly low proportions, particularly in regard to the agency and professional representatives. Agency people often are required to represent the agency at a number of community organizations and councils, while professional people, because of their expertise and social status, are usually in great demand in low income communities.

## Other Selected Characteristics of Advisory Council Members

General socioeconomic data (such as education, income, or occupation) were not available for the total membership of the advisory councils.[38] Ethnically, the majority of advisory council members are Mexican-American, in tune with the general make-up of the population. Membership breakdowns by sex are reported in Table 3.5.

TABLE 3.5

Sex of Advisory Council Members by Type of Member

|  | Male | Female | Total |
|---|---|---|---|
| Community representatives |  |  |  |
| School advisory councils | 213 (32) | 461 (68) | 673 |
| Other advisory councils | 160 (40) | 243 (60) | 403 |
| Total community | 373 (35) | 704 (65) | 1,076 |
| Agency and professionals (all advisory councils)* | 260 (63) | 153 (37) | 413 |
| Total membership | 633 (42.5) | 857 (57.5) | 1,489 |

*Sex breakdown figures were not available for 31 agency and professional representatives active in school advisory councils. Percentages are given in parentheses.
Source: Compiled by the author.

While the overall sex breakdown for the total membership of the advisory councils differs only slightly from the sex ratio found in the population as a whole (that is, females, all ages, 52 percent of the population; males, all ages, 48 percent),[39] the predominance of females among the community representatives (65 percent) and particularly among the community representatives in the school advisory councils (68 percent) is noteworthy. In the traditional machismo-oriented Mexican culture, the women usually have been relegated exclusively to the role of mother and wife—to "making frijoles, tortillas, 'limpiando la casa, cuidando los ninos'"—as a young Chicana activist put it.[40] Viewed in this cultural perspective, this author doubts that the high proportion of women on the councils can be attributed exclusively to the fact that women usually have more free time available or, in the case of school advisory council participation, that women traditionally have been more involved in school-related activities than men. Rather, the overrepresentation of women in the advisory councils raises some interesting questions about the underlying causes of this involvement, as well as about community perceptions of this participation.

On the one hand, it is possible that female overrepresentation may be intertwined with the Chicano movement. Chicano liberation could have also fostered Chicana liberation. As Armando Rendon put it,

> Chicanas today are far different from their grandmothers and even their mothers in certain aspects as a result of the explosion of the small universe which once enveloped the Chicano community. The woman of the Chicano revolt believes that Chicano liberation must also include Chicana liberation. Thus within the overall Chicano movement toward self-determination and creation of a new identity, a struggle is going on between our men and women. It is not a mortal struggle nor a divisive struggle, because the women are saying that they want to be recognized by the Chicano Macho as a companion in the Revolution. . . . [41]

The evidence available on this question, however, is conflicting. On the one hand, ample impressionistic evidence tends to suggest that Mexican-American communities are undergoing a true cultural revolution and moving away from deeply ingrained sex roles and notions about the proper place of men and women in society.[42] As one community influential put it, "The women are the real grass roots leaders in East Los Angeles. It is they who are in the forefront of the movement demanding increased citizen participation. This is a trend which is increasingly causing family friction between husband and wife, oftentimes leading to divorce or separation."[43] On the other hand, the few questionnaire data that we have available on this question do not indicate that perceptions of sex roles have undergone changes in the past seven years.[44] Further research on this question is clearly needed.

Overrepresentation of women on the councils also raises interesting questions regarding communitywide perceptions of participation in advisory councils. It is possible that—because of female domination—advisory councils could be viewed by the general population as innocuous "women's clubs." Although no direct data on this question are available, this possibility is not supported by other relevant data. Respondents in the second wave of the panel study (1972) were asked cognitive and evaluative questions about advisory councils operative in the community.[45] As is reported in Chapter 4, high cognition rates and favorable evaluations of the councils are prevalent in the general population.

## DRAWING THE SAMPLE

Selection of members to be interviewed from the total population of 1,076 community representatives was accomplished by means of a simple random sampling technique.[46] After all the names of members were arranged alphabetically in a master file, names were drawn using tables of random numbers. A sample of 120 names was originally drawn with the expectation that approximately 75 to 100 interviews would be obtained. The 75 to 100 desired sample size figure was arrived at for the following reasons: (1) 75 to 100 constitutes between 7 and 10 percent of the population, (2) consideration of the resources available, and (3) the expectation that most of the advisory councils (N = 61) would be represented. Response rates obtained are reported in a subsequent section of this chapter.

## QUESTIONNAIRE DESIGN

### Criteria for Selection of Items

The questionnaire administered to a random sample of advisory council members was designed with two major criteria in mind: comparability and flexibility. To allow for adequate comparisons to other populations, particularly to the panel study, a large number of items utilized in previous studies were replicated. The items replicated are generally of the "structured" variety,[47] and many consist of scales and indices that have been extensively tested. Unstructured or "free-response" questions also were utilized extensively in an effort to insure flexibility. Given the wide variety of advisory councils included in the sample and the researcher's limited knowledge about the possible range of responses to particular probes, it was felt that on some topics[48] structured questions would be premature, possibly forcing subjects to give misleading responses.

# DATA COLLECTION PROCEDURES

Approximately one-third of the items utilized are original to the study; these deal primarily with questions idiosyncratic to the study, for example, related to the advisory councils and to the War on Poverty. Another third are items used in both waves of the panel study of the population (1965 and 1972); these include many items and scales previously tested in other studies. Finally, another third consists of items asked in the 1972 panel study alone.[49] The latter, written by Pachon and this author, are tailored to tap political attitudes and events in the Mexican-American community of East Los Angeles not previously asked in 1965. Particularly, there are items designed to explore the extent of ethnic mobilization or group consciousness.[50] Among these, whenever possible, standard scales and items were utilized.

## Spanish Version

As it was projected that close to half the sample would probably prefer to be interviewed in Spanish rather than in English because of language difficulties, a Spanish version of the questionnaire was created. On the items replicated from the Mexican-American study project of 1965 the available translations were utilized. On the items used exclusively in the advisory council questionnaire or those asked only in the 1972 panel study, the following translation procedures were used. First, the questionnaire was translated by advanced graduate students in Spanish to insure correctness in syntax and grammar. Then, a group of fluent bilingual Mexican-American students were asked to evaluate the "equivalence"[51] of the Spanish version taking into account the idiosyncratic nature of the Spanish generally spoken in the barrio. Whenever appropriate, the Spanish version was "Mexican-Americanized."

## Pretesting

It was felt that an extensive pretest of the questionnaire was unnecessary because, as mentioned, the questionnaire replicates a number of questions already tested in both waves of the panel study as well as in other studies.[52] Nevertheless, a small pretest was taken ($N = 10$) to test for (1) possible ambiguity, misperception, and loading of items never used previously,[53] (2) the sequence of questions, and (3) interview length. After the pretest, appropriate changes in wording, sequence, and length were made. The questionnaire finally adopted took between 50 minutes to three hours to administer, median time of interview being one hour and thirty minutes.

## CONDUCTING THE FIELD WORK

### Selection and Training of Interviewers

Eight bilingual Mexican-American interviewers, all students at Loyola Marymount University, were employed to conduct the personal interviews. Because most of them had not had previous interviewing experience, extensive briefing sessions were held. These sessions stressed interviewing approaches and strategies and knowledge and practical understanding of the content of the questionnaire. Moreover, efforts to insure high morale constantly were made by involving the students in the theoretical aspects of the study as well as in all research stages of the project.[54]

### Interviewing Procedures

Each respondent in the original sample drawn (N = 120) was sent a letter in both English and Spanish requesting his or her participation in the project. These letters stressed the potential long-range usefulness of the study as well as guaranteed the anonymity of responses.

Subsequently, interviewers were instructed to telephone each respondent selected to arrange for a convenient interview time, or to go to the respondent's residence if the respondent lacked a telephone. If a correct telephone number was available, interviewers were instructed to call back at least five times at different times of the day. If no telephone was available, interviewers were instructed to visit the respondent's home at least three times during different periods of the day.

The major problem encountered during this stage was that a large number of respondents could not be located. This problem was probably due to the fact that some of the advisory council membership lists obtained were dated;[55] hence a number of people had moved since the compilation of the lists.

To insure that a sufficiently large number of completed interviews could be obtained, additional names (N = 19) were drawn at random from the master file of names. After approximately four weeks of field work (in June of 1973), 80 interviews were completed. A 15 percent random sample of completed interviews was then verified by the author.[56] If systematic error were suspected, all the questionnaires from particular interviewers were verified. Replacement and refusal rates as well as replacements by type of lack of availability are reported in Tables 3.6 and 3.7.

DATA COLLECTION PROCEDURES 75

TABLE 3.6

Replacement and Refusal Rates

| Completed Interviews | Total Sample Drawn | Replacement | | Refusal* | |
|---|---|---|---|---|---|
| | | Number | Percent | Number | Percent |
| 80 | 139 | 43 | 30.9 | 16 | 11.5 |

*Major reasons cited for refusal were lack of time and interest and hostility to surveys.
Source: Compiled by the author.

Forty councils or 66.6 percent of the total number of councils for which lists were available were represented in the sample interviewed.[57] Of the sample interviewed, 67.5 percent consists of respondents who are members of school advisory councils, and 32.5 percent consists of respondents who are members of other advisory councils. This proportion closely reflects the ratio between school advisory council members and other advisory council members found in the total advisory council population[58] (that is, 62.5 percent are members of school councils, and 37.4 percent are members of other advisory councils). The male/female ratio in the sample interviewed also closely reflects the sex ratio in the advisory council population as a whole (that is, sample: 36.2 percent male, 63.7 percent female; population: 35 percent male, 65 percent female).

TABLE 3.7

Replacements by Type of Lack of Availability

| Total Replacements | Moved[a] | | Call Back[b] | | Other[c] | |
|---|---|---|---|---|---|---|
| | Number | Percent | Number | Percent | Number | Percent |
| 43 | 25 | 58.1 | 14 | 32.5 | 4 | 9.3 |

[a]Moved: moved, left no forwarding address.
[b]Call back: call back a minimum of three times if respondent lacked phone, a minimum of five times if respondent had phone.
[c]Other: two on vacation, one died, one sick.
Source: Compiled by the author.

## ANALYSIS OF THE DATA

The questionnaire data were analyzed with the aid of the University of California at Los Angeles (UCLA) IBM 360-91 computer using the programs available in the Statistical Package for the Social Sciences (SPSS).[59] The analysis of the survey data is presented in Chapters 4 through 7.

Chapter 4 consists of a description of the advisory councils and of their membership and addresses itself to the question of the "representative nature of the advisory council membership. The appropriateness of using the 1972 panel study as a control group of sorts without the introduction of standard SES controls is also established.

In Chapter 5, the major hypotheses posed in this study are explored. The first part of the chapter establishes the extent to which advisory council members are more politicized than could be expected on the basis of SES status alone. It compares the significance of differences on politicization measures between members of the advisory councils and panel respondents. The second part of the chapter explores the organizational and member-related correlates of politicization in an effort to ascertain under what conditions politicization is likely to be facilitated and who is most affected by the organizational experience.

In Chapter 6, the alternative hypothesis, group consciousness, is explored by analyzing the environmental changes that have occurred since 1965. The interaction between the effects of organizational involvement and those of group consciousness also is analyzed. Finally, Chapter 7 consists of a speculative analysis of the prospects for sustained politicization and of the type of leadership group likely to emerge.

## NOTES

1. The East Los Angeles, Belvedere, and City Terrace localities (reported in aggregated census figures under the heading "East Los Angeles") represent 51.3 percent of the area delimited; Boyle Heights represents 40.6 percent, and the selected census tracts from El Sereno and Lincoln Heights represent 8.1 percent of the area delimited. Although other localities are included in this definition of "community," the author refers to this study as a "case study of East Los Angeles" for the sake of expediency as well as because East Los Angeles represents the core of the area delimited.

2. Defined in the 1970 census materials as "Persons of Spanish Language," and "Other Persons of Spanish Surname." For problems in census identification of Mexican-Americans, see Anthony Gary Dworkin, "A City Founded: A People Lost," in <u>Introduction to Chicano Studies</u>: <u>A Reader</u>, edited by Livie Isauro Duran and H. Russell Bernard (New York: Macmillan, 1973), p. 408.

## DATA COLLECTION PROCEDURES

3. Ibid., p. 407.

4. These data as well as other census data reported in this chapter may be found in the 1960 and 1970 census reports. See U.S. Bureau of the Census, <u>Census of the Population: 1970, General Population Characteristics</u>, Final Report PC (1)-B6 California; <u>General Social and Economic Characteristics</u>, Final Report PC (1)-C6 California; <u>Detailed Characteristics</u>, Final Report PC (1)-D6 California, Section 1; <u>Census Tracts,</u> Final Report PHC (1)-117 Los Angeles-Long Beach, Calif. SMSA (Washington, D.C.: U.S. Government Printing Office, 1972). For 1960, see U.S. Bureau of the Census, <u>U.S. Census of the Population 1960, Subject Reports</u>. <u>Persons of Spanish Surname</u>, Final Report PC (2)-1B (Washington, D.C.: U.S. Government Printing Office, 1963), and <u>U.S. Census of the Population, 1960</u>, vol. 1 <u>Characteristics of the Population</u> Part 6 California (Washington, D.C.: U.S. Government Printing Office, 1963).

5. Alfredo Cuellar, "Perspectives on Politics," in Duran and Bernard op. cit., p. 560.

6. The other is a predominantly black area, south central Los Angeles.

7. The poverty level established in 1969 was $3,700 for a nonfarm family of four. See Dorothy Buckton James, <u>Poverty, Politics and Change</u> (Englewood Cliffs, N.J.: Prentice Hall, 1972), p. 5.

8. The national median income of all urban families was $6,166 in 1960 and $10,226 in 1970. Figures derived from: U.S. Bureau of the Census, <u>U.S. Census of the Population: 1960</u>, vol. 1, <u>Characteristics of the Population</u>, Part 1 U.S. Summary (Washington, D.C.: U.S. Government Printing Office, 1964), and U.S. Bureau of the Census, <u>Census of the Population: 1970, Detailed Characteristics</u>, Final Report PC (1)-D1 U.S. Summary (Washington, D.C.: U.S. Government Printing Office, 1971).

9. California, Department of Industrial Relations, Division of Fair Employment Practices, "Negroes and Mexican Americans in South and East Los Angeles: An Analysis of a Special U.S. Census Survey of November 1965," San Francisco, California, July 1966 (figures for 1970 were not available).

10. These are 1970 census figures. The proportion of families below the poverty line is slightly higher for the Boyle Heights-East Los Angeles population (91.9 percent of the area delimited), that is, 19.4 percent. This represents a decrease of 4.2 percent from 1960. ("Negroes and Mexican Americans in South and East Los Angeles," op. cit., p. 32).

11. This figure represents a slight decrease since 1965 (7.7 percent) and a more significant decrease since 1960 (8.5 percent). ("Negroes and Mexican Americans in South and East Los Angeles," op. cit., p. 29).

12. This figure represents an average median for all the census tracts in the area. Reported aggregated statistics for East Los Angeles represent a similar median, 8.8.

13. Reported aggregated percentages for East Los Angeles proper are 30 percent; the 28.5 percent figure has been arrived at by adding weighted percentages for each census tract.

14. The Los Angeles East-Northeast Model Cities program, however, does not include the whole East Los Angeles area, as defined in this study (see Note 16).

15. The East Los Angeles State Service Center, located in the heart of the East Los Angeles area, is one of six statewide service centers created after the Watts riots of 1965 "to bring into low income communities combined state, county, federal, and private services heretofore scattered throughout civic center complexes and most often inaccessible to many due to language and transportation difficulties." Source: mimeographed statement of purpose, East Los Angeles State Service Center (no date).

16. It should be pointed out here that the definition of the "community" used in this study differs slightly from that used in the panel study. The northern boundary of the "community" in this study has been drawn approximately ten blocks north of the northern boundary specified in the panel study to include census tracts 1997, 1998, 1999, and portions of tracts 1991, 2014.02, and 2017 in the southern portions of Lincoln Heights and El Sereno. The major reason for this minor change is that these additional census tracts (particularly those in the southern portion of Lincoln Heights) include the hub of Model Cities activity and many of the advisory councils associated with Model Cities or with its delegate agencies. As the boundaries of Model Cities' jurisdiction encompass a large part of the community under study (all of Boyle Heights), it was felt that the additional advisory councils located in this area should be included in this study because their activities (1) involve many residents in the community under study, and (2) they affect, through their program outputs, a large portion of the community under study.

17. "Community councils," "resident councils," "community boards," and "resident boards," are synonyms.

18. A number of these "governing boards" were identified, particularly in agencies connected with Model Cities programs.

19. Eight agency directories were compiled. They are the following:

(1) "Associations, Organizations, and Agencies Serving the Poor in Los Angeles County Stressing Grass Roots Organizations," Los Angeles Urban Coalition, November 18, 1970.
(2) "Directory of Health, Welfare, Vocational, and Recreational Services in Los Angeles County," 1971 Edition.
(3) Paul Bullock, "Directory of Organizations in South and East Los Angeles," Institute of Industrial Relations, UCLA, June 1971.
(4) "Mexican American Community Organizations," on KRLA 100, no date.

## DATA COLLECTION PROCEDURES

(5) "Directory of Services for Senior Citizens," Gerontology Center, University of Southern California, University Park, Los Angeles, 1971 Edition.
(6) "Agency Listing of the East Central Area," compiled by the East Central Area Welfare Planning Council, Los Angeles, 1971 Edition.
(7) Listing of EYOA Delegate Agencies, Economic and Youth Opportunities Agency, mimeograph (no date).
(8) Listing of Model Cities Delegate Agencies, East-Northeast Model Cities Program, mimeograph (no date).

Although total coverage cannot be guaranteed due to the lack of availability of a comprehensive listing, the short lifespan of some agencies, and the dates of publication of the directories, every effort was expended to obtain an all-inclusive listing.

20. All this information could not be procured for all advisory councils identified. A number of agency officials proved to be uncooperative and did not provide any information beyond the presence or absence of an advisory council.

21. It is interesting to note that a few agencies (two to three), which had had advisory councils had eliminated them; and a similar number were in the process of creating them. Also, a small number of officials (two to three) refused to provide any information by saying that "the advisory council is a delicate subject around this office," or by suggesting that the particular agency "did not need an advisory council."

22. Title I of the Elementary and Secondary Education Act of 1965, Public Law 89-10. Title I requires the creation of target school parent advisory councils (Section 2.1.2). Revised 1971 Title I guidelines require that representatives from parent groups must comprise at least 75 percent of the membership.

23. These are the East Los Angeles Skill Center and the East Los Angeles Occupational Center.

24. At the outset, it was also planned to interview each of the 70 advisory council chairmen to build a data bank on the advisory councils in the area on such indicators as council purposes, activities, recruitment patterns, size, length of time in operation, frequency of meetings, and perceived effectiveness. In addition, other materials such as council minutes and by-laws were to be collected. The major purpose of this endeavor had been to provide an independent check on the responses reported by advisory council members in their interviews and to build additional information on the councils not directly solicited in the interviews with advisory council members. Unfortunately, this task proved to be exceedingly costly and time consuming and was abandoned because it was not considered to be of central concern to the study. However, a number of interviews with advisory council chairmen were completed (N = 11). Whenever appropriate, the results of these interviews will be mentioned in subsequent data analysis chapters, only for illustrative purposes.

25. It took approximately six months' time of three research assistants working on a part-time basis.

26. For a general discussion of this problem, see Joan W. Moore, "Political and Ethical Problems in a Large Scale Study of a Minority Community," in Ethics, Politics, and Social Research, edited by Gideon Sjoberg (Cambridge, Mass.: Schenkman Publishing Co., 1967), pp. 225-244; Eric Josephson, "Resistance to Community Surveys," Social Problems 18, no. 1 (Summer 1970): 117-129; and Joan W. Moore, "Social Constraints on Sociological Knowledge: Academics and Research Concerning Minorities," Social Problems 21, no. 1 (Summer 1973): 65-77.

27. Panel discussion on "Survey Research in Minority Communities," Annual Meeting of the Pacific Chapter of the American Association of Public Opinion Research, February 2-4, 1973, Los Angeles.

28. With the exception of four interviews conducted by bilingual Latin Americans.

29. Access to the names of members of school advisory councils was procured through the approval of the central committee on Research and Evaluation of the Los Angeles City Board of Education.

30. The East Los Angeles Health Center Advisory Council was composed of 105 members. This, however, represents an extreme case in the sense that membership in this council was defined solely in terms of attendance at meetings—105 different people had come to at least one meeting. This method of defining membership was the exception rather than the rule.

31. Taking into account this average size figure and considering the councils for which lists could not be obtained (N = 10), a gross estimate of the total number of advisory council participants in the East Los Angeles area is 1,895, or close to 1 percent of the population.

32. It is interesting to note the hesitation expressed by a number of advisory council chairmen when asked to point out "low income community people." Queries as to "who is a 'community representative'?", "someone who lives in the community?", "someone who lives outside yet is very involved?", or "agency people can be very active community people" were raised constantly.

33. In the case of Model Cities, no set figure has been established: it is up to the discretion of local authorities administering the program.

34. See Chapter 1, p. 10.

35. As previously mentioned, the author spent approximately one year as a participant observer in a number of councils in the area. Among the councils observed were the Model Cities Resident Council, the East Los Angeles State Service Center Advisory Council, and the East Los Angeles Health Center Advisory Council. For methods employed in participant observation, see Howard S. Becker and Blanche Geer, "Participant Observation and Interviewing," Human Organizations 16, no. 3 (Fall 1957): 28-32; Morris Schwartz and Charlotte G.

Schwartz, "Problems in Participant Observation," American Journal of Sociology 60, no. 4 (January 1955): 343-353; Florence R. Kluckhohn, "The Participant Observer Technique in Small Communities," American Journal of Sociology 46, no. 3 (November 1940): 331-343; and Arthur J. Vidich, "Participant Observation and the Collection and Interpretation of Data," American Journal of Sociology 60, no. 4 (January 1955): 354-360.

36. This is also the conclusion reached by some studies in cross-cultural research on participation at the community level in socialist countries; see Albert Meister, Socialisme et Autogestion (Paris: Seuil, 1965). The author is indebted to Joan W. Moore, University of Southern California, for suggesting that this possibility be investigated.

37. Procedures for determining membership overlap were as follows: all names in each category (that is, community, agency representatives, and professionals) were listed on separate cards and arranged alphabetically in a master file. The addresses of those identified as belonging to more than one council were then checked to insure that it was the same person. Finally, proportions were computed.

38. Socioeconomic data on the sample interviewed are reported in the next chapter.

39. These are 1970 census figures.

40. Quoted in Armando Rendon, "Chicano Culture in a Gabacho World," in Duran and Bernard, op. cit., p. 358.

41. Ibid.

42. Ibid. See, for example, the numerous examples cited there. My own personal experience as a participant observer in the advisory councils also confirms the presence of this trend. Moreover, among Mexican-American student groups in the universities (MECHA), Chicanas are beginning to demand that women be represented in positions of power on a proportional representation basis.

43. Personal interview with a high-level Los Angeles Board of Education official who was in charge of coordinating all school advisory councils in the area and who was also highly active in community affairs. This community influential further noted that although women seem to be extremely active in community affairs, women also seem to be afraid to engage in political activity beyond a certain threshold, that is, in "higher level decision making." The specific example he cited related to female participation in school councils. He suggested that although women were clearly the leaders in presenting demands to the schools and in relating to local agencies and to community grass roots groups, when it came to presenting demands or proposals to influential people or agencies outside of the community, for example, Los Angeles Board of Education, they showed timidity and reluctance.

44. Respondents in all three samples (council, and panel for 1965 and 1972) were asked the following sex stereotype questions: "People have different ideas about how family members should act toward each other. Will you please tell me whether you agree or disagree with the following statements (Q. 42):

(1) having children is the most important thing that can be done by a married woman;
(2) a husband ought to have complete control over the family's income;
(3) a father should take care of the children when the mother wants some time to herself."

No significant differences between men and women nor changes over time were evidenced on these questions.

45. Questions read (panel study, 1972), "Some government agencies in this area have formed community advisory councils in order to get advice from community people in administering their programs. Some examples are school advisory councils, the Model Cities Resident Council, the Ferris Clinic Community Council, the East Los Angeles State Service Center Advisory Council, etc. Are there any advisory councils in this area that you have heard about?" (If Yes) "Can you please tell me which ones are you familiar with? Have you ever attended any meetings of the _____ advisory council? Do you belong to the _____ advisory council? What is your opinion of the advisory councils you've mentioned? Do you think that they are good for the community, make no difference for the community, or are bad for the community? Why do you say that?"

46. For an explanation of this technique, see Hubert M. Blalock, Social Statistics (New York: McGraw Hill, 1960), pp. 392-397; and Leslie Kish, "Selection of the Sample," in Research Methods in the Behavioral Sciences, edited by Leo Festinger and Daniel Katz (New York: Holt, Rinehart and Winston, 1965), pp. 175-239. Because the main interest here was in being able to generalize about "members of advisory councils" rather than about the advisory councils themselves, alternative sampling methods considered, that is, stratified or quota sampling, were rejected.

47. For a discussion of the merits of "structured" versus "unstructured" questions, see Charles H. Backstrom and Gerald D. Hursh, Survey Research (Evanston, Ill.: Northwestern University Press, 1963), pp. 72-84.

48. Particularly on topics related to the activities of the advisory councils.

49. Those items in the advisory council questionnaire that are replicated from the 1965 and 1972 waves of the panel study are marked accordingly in the English version questionnaire found in the Appendix.

50. On tailoring items for specific target populations, see Survey Research Center, A Manual for Coders (Ann Arbor, Mich: Institute for Social Research, 1955), pp. 3-14. See also Stanley Payne, The Art of Asking Questions (Princeton: Princeton University Press, 1951), pp. 228-238.

51. On the problem of language equivalence in cross-cultural research, see Susan Erwin and Robert T. Bowen, "Translation Problems

in International Surveys," Public Opinion Quarterly 16 Special Issue (Winter 1952-1953): 595-604.

52. Also, available resources did not allow for extensive pre-testing.

53. For a discussion of wording problems, see Backstrom and Hursch, op. cit., pp. 84-107.

54. In this stage, the suggestions made in ibid., pp. 128-149, were followed closely.

55. A few were as old as 1970.

56. For verification procedures used, see Backstrom and Hursch, op. cit., pp. 149-152.

57. The 40 councils represented consist of 24 school advisory councils (out of a possible total of 35) and 16 "other" advisory councils (out of a possible total of 26).

58. The reader should recall that "total" refers to the 1,076 people who have been classified as "community" representatives.

59. See Norman H. Nie, Dale H. Brent, and C. Hadlai Hull, Statistical Package for the Social Sciences (New York: McGraw Hill, 1970).

CHAPTER

# 4

## THE ADVISORY COUNCILS AND THEIR MEMBERSHIP

The purposes of this chapter are, first, to describe selected characteristics of the advisory councils as reported by the random sample of advisory council members interviewed and, second, to describe the socioeconomic and demographic characteristics of the council members. The description of the organizational setting aims, on the one hand, at furthering social science knowledge about the activities of advisory councils in different functional areas and at different levels of government, knowledge of which, as discussed in Chapter 1, is rather sparse. A brief review of the organizational setting is further necessary for the purposes of identifying those council-related variables that could be of relevance in the analysis of individual politicization in subsequent chapters.

The second part of the chapter, description of the socioeconomic and demographic characteristics of the advisory council members, aims at contributing information to the debate over the "representative" nature of advisory council members in low-income communities. As previously discussed, many studies of CAP and Model Cities advisory councils have pointed consistently to the "unrepresentative" character of the membership of community advisory councils. It is hoped that this analysis of the characteristics of a sample of members selected at random and representing a wide variety of councils in one community will contribute useful data to this debate. The description of socioeconomic and demographic characteristics of the council sample is also necessary for purposes of exploring its equivalence to the 1972 panel study, which will be used as a control group of sorts.

### DESCRIPTIVE ANALYSIS OF THE ADVISORY COUNCILS

Throughout this section, the reader should bear in mind that even though 40 different advisory councils are represented in the sample interviewed, 60 percent of these (N = 24) represent a similar type of advisory council (school advisory councils), and the remaining 40 percent (N = 16) represents a wide variety of "other" councils (such as, health, Model Cities, manpower training, senior citizens, legal aid).[1] Because the advisory councils in the "other" category generally are represented by only one or two respondents, it is difficult to report on the characteristics of advisory councils controlling for either the functional service area or the level of government involved. Instead, the analysis is limited to an overall description of all the councils, occasionally distinguishing between "school" and "other" councils when differences between these two types emerge. The major council characteristics focused upon in this section are length of time in operation, functions, activities, strategies used to accomplish goals, internal operation, effectiveness, and impact on the community.

### Length of Time in Operation

Half the members interviewed were not aware of how long their respective councils had been in operation. Median number of years councils have been in operation (for those reporting) is 2.8, ranging from three months to seven years. All the councils were still in operation notwithstanding recent program cutbacks. The median number of years respondents have been on the council is 1.7.

### Recruitment Patterns

The three major recruitment patterns identified among the 40 councils represented are the following: (1) respondents were asked to join, (2) respondents volunteered, and (3) respondents were elected.

Of those asked to join the council (40 percent), half were asked to join by agency officials; and 40 percent were asked to join by personal acquaintances on the council, friends, neighbors, or by community influentials.[2] Among those reporting that they volunteered to participate on the council (30 percent), most reported hearing about the council from information notices distributed by the agencies or from open meetings, friends, and neighbors. Of those who report being elected to the council (23 percent), the majority reported being nominated at open meetings of the council and elected by secret ballot. Only one respondent reported campaigning in the community for election.

When asked why they joined the council, 31 percent mentioned various reasons related to wishing to help the community in general or in a particular policy area; a similar proportion expressed a desire to learn how a particular agency was being run or a program implemented;

another 12 percent expressed a wish to become involved in community affairs. The remainder reported either that they had joined because there was insufficient particpation or because of self-interest (the latter, for example, in the case of parents joining the advisory council of their children's school).

The majority of members (68 percent) reported that before joining the council they had not known what they would be expected to do as council members. After joining, most of the members conceived their role primarily in service rather than in representative terms, for example, to voice their own opinions, attend meetings, engage in study and research, point to specific problems, suggest solutions, and generally help in whatever needs to be done.

The recruitment patterns identified in the East Los Angeles councils seem to be highly informal and sharply contrast with the more formalized procedures established by the CAP programs (that is, campaigning and community elections). Particularly in the case of the school councils, the recruitment pattern followed seems to be one whereby the agency widely advertises the council throughout the community coupled with personal, word-of-mouth contacts. It would appear that, in this respect, membership does not require great initiative on the part of the community resident (initiative in the sense of expending a great deal of time and effort). Councils are advertised and people join, although, of course, some interest has to be present.

## Functions of the Councils

The most often mentioned purpose of the councils was improvement of a particular area of policy, for example, education, to make it more in tune with community needs and wants. A second category most often mentioned was improvement in the operation of the agency itself in terms of planning and implementing new programs or overseeing the budget and the curriculum (the latter in the case of the schools). A third most often mentioned category was what could be construed as a representation function, that is, advise the agency of community needs and wants. Other functions mentioned concerned a communication function, informing the community of the activities of the agency, helping the community in general, and uniting the community. Only a small proportion of respondents (6.3 percent) suggested that the council did not have any functions. It should be added here that, in terms of this negative response (council does not have any purpose), 12.9 percent of the respondents from the "other" councils offered this response while only 3.6 percent of the school representatives did so. This is a discrepancy that will be further illustrated on responses to other items. It suggests that the school councils tend generally to receive more positive evaluations than other councils.

## Council Activities—Present and Past

The most often mentioned category among numerous council activities listed by respondents[3] was initiating or working on particular programs. Examples ranged from overseeing the implementation of bilingual education programs, to working on improvement of police-community relations, to establishing rehabilitation programs for alcoholic and narcotic offenders. These answers tended to be highly specific and detailed and frequently reflected a great deal of satisfaction about program accomplishments. In the words of a female member of a health advisory council, "The clinic on . . . would not be there if it hadn't been for the council's efforts."

A second most often mentioned category (related to the first) was working on the overall improvement of a particular policy area to make it more in tune with the needs and wants of the East Los Angeles community. Other activities mentioned by the respondents included involvement in the selection or removal of agency personnel, involvement in making and overseeing the budget and obtaining new funding for agency programs, involvement in community affairs outside the boundaries of the particular agency (for example, fighting to stop urban renewal), and working on enhancing the communication and relations between agencies and the community.

Only a small proportion of the total responses offered on the councils' present and past activities (7 percent of all responses) suggested that the councils had not done anything, or "not much" had been accomplished. In this respect, members of "other" advisory councils tended to report negative responses more frequently than members of school councils. This was particularly true of respondents associated with Model Cities programs (N = 6). These respondents consistently reported negative evaluations of the councils on most items. Charges of the type "the advisory council is a sham" and charges of corruption and self-interested behavior on the part of both agency and community representatives on the Model Cities councils abounded among these respondents.

In terms of future plans of the councils, the types of planned activities suggested closely parallel those mentioned in regard to present and past activities; the only difference being that a great deal of uncertainty was expressed due to possible program and agency cutbacks.

When one considers the type of activities in which the councils have been engaged, it seems reasonable to suggest that activities such as planning and implementing programs, involvement in recruitment, planning budgets, and writing funding proposals could all be "learning" experiences for the advisory council members. This is, of course, one of the main concerns of this study: that is, do advisory council members learn politically relevant skills on the council?

Although this question is explored in detail in the next chapter, it seems reasonable to conclude here that this brief review of activities undertaken by the councils does suggest that the organizational setting of the advisory councils may be potentially conducive to the acquisition of politically relevant skills.

## Council Strategies

Following probes on council activities, members were asked how the council went about accomplishing a particular activity, that is, what strategies were employed. Responses to this question are of interest, for they provide further indications of what potential skills may be learned on the council. Total responses[4] to this question can be broken down as follows: 22 percent of the responses indicated that the council had accomplished a particular goal by making the community aware of a problem and by generating support; 16 percent indicated that the goal had been accomplished through internal council organization (for example, committee formation, research, and discussion); 13 percent suggested strategies that involved writing proposals or allocation of funds; 11 percent suggested that the goal had been attained through pressure, complaints, or protests on officials or agencies outside the agency in question; 9 percent by pressure or protest on the agency itself; and 5 percent by changes in personnel. It seems apparent that the type of strategies mentioned also could be construed as potentially useful experiences in learning organizational skills and in learning about the operation of public agencies and about potential access points in the political system.

## Unsuccessful Projects

When asked whether any projects undertaken by the council had not been successful, almost half the members (49 percent) reported instances of unsuccessful projects. Reasons cited for lack of success are interesting, for they do not reveal perceptions of lack of power as the fundamental reason for lack of success (as could be expected judging from previous studies of CAP councils). Overall, only 3 percent of members reporting unsuccessful projects cite lack of power on the part of the council as a major reason for failure. The most often mentioned category (19 percent) of all responses is insufficient participation or involvement on the part of the community. In addition, close to 9 percent blamed agency officials for obstructing passage or implementation of specific programs.

In general terms, members from "other" advisory councils tended to point more readily to lack of power reasons (8.3 percent) and to external circumstances reasons (25 percent) than the school advisory council members. Yet the small numbers involved (one respondent in the first case and three respondents in the second case) preclude drawing conclusions about differences between councils on this question.

### Internal Operation of the Councils

In regard to the internal operation of the councils, two major areas were probed, (1) council-agency relations and (2) perceived power configurations within the council. Regarding the relationship between councils and agencies, 50 percent of the respondents reported that the relationship is generally good; 34 percent reported that there are occasional problems, and 6 percent reported that the relationship is generally bad. A clear difference does emerge on this question between members of school and 'other' councils. Fifty-six percent of members from the "other" councils reported either occasional or perennial problems with their relationship to the agencies, as compared with 36 percent of members of school advisory councils. Similarly, a larger proportion of members from "other" councils (22 percent) reported that their agency generally has not been open to suggestions and proposals made by the councils (78 percent).

An effort to explore the internal power configurations of the councils was made with the following question: "In general, how do things get done on the council, that is, are there some people who seem to have more influence than others, or does everyone seem to have equal influence?" Overall, 56 percent of members report that some people seem to have more influence, compared with 36 percent who report that everyone has equal influence. Again, a distinction should be drawn between types of councils on this question. Members of "other" advisory councils tended to point to agency officials and to professionals as being more influential in larger proportions than school advisory council members, who generally tended to point to better educated or more articulate fellow community council members as being more influential.

### Overall Evaluation of the Councils

Questioned as to how well the council was fulfilling its purposes, overall, 65 percent of members offered a positive response (very well and moderately well); 31 percent responded negatively (not very well and not at all well). Differences between councils are again evident in this summary evaluation of council effectiveness: 44 percent of members from "other" councils report negative responses, as contrasted with 25 percent of members of school councils. Among those evaluating the performance of the councils favorably, most justified their evaluation by citing specific examples of council-agency cooperation in program development or implementation, improvement in particular areas of policy, and furthering community interest and involvement. Among those evaluating the councils negatively, close to half the members from both school and "other" councils reported disappointment with council performance by suggesting that "nothing ever gets done," "most of the time is spent arguing at meetings," and the like.

When questioned about how council effectiveness could be improved, it is interesting to note that overall most members (63 percent) offered suggestions related to improving either the performance or the intensity of involvement of the membership rather than calling for more decision-making power or for more receptive agency officials. Among these, 45 percent called for greater participation and involvement on the part of community members and 18 percent called for better and more dedicated leadership on the councils (more hard-working community representatives). Overall, only 10 percent suggested a necessity for more decision-making power, and 4 percent called for more receptive agency officials. Paradoxically, no significant differences emerged between members of schools and "other" councils on this question.

## Effects on the Community

Asked whether the activities of the council have had any effect on the community, the majority of members (81 percent) responded affirmatively; no differences were evidenced between different types of councils on this assessment. Affirmative responses were justified in terms of two broad categories: (1) fostering greater community awareness of problems, greater involvement of community people (particularly Spanish-speaking ones), and fostering greater community unity; and (2) in terms of improvement in particular policy areas and in the operation of particular agencies. Data gathered on the East Los Angeles population in the 1972 wave of the panel study seem to support the council members' perceptions that advisory councils have had some effect on the community. Cognition of advisory councils among the 51 respondents reinterviewed in 1972 is fairly high; 41.2 percent report that they have heard about some advisory council in the community. This compares favorably with cognition of long-standing Mexican-American community organizations, such as the Community Service Organizations (CSO) and the GI Forum (25.5 percent for the former and 35.3 percent for the latter), and with cognition of newer community organizations, which have attained notoriety and extensive coverage in the media, such as the Brown Berets and the

Chicano Liberation Front (47.1 percent and 41.2 percent, respectively). Moreover, among those who have heard of advisory councils, the overwhelming majority (76 percent) report favorably on these as "good for the community."

## Conclusions

On the basis of this brief review of selected council characteristics, three conclusions seem to be warranted.

(1) The informal recruitment patterns identified suggest that council membership does not require a great deal of self-initiative and effort on the part of the community resident. This leads us to hypothesize that the mechanism of "self-selection" may not be overly operative in the East Los Angeles councils. That is, although it is expected that the councils do attract a large number of people who are already active in community affairs, it would also seem that the apparent ease of definition of membership would work to attract community residents previously uninvolved in community affairs. The operation of the "self-selection" mechanism is explored at the end of this chapter.

(2) The type of activities undertaken by the councils and the type of strategies pursued suggest that the organizational setting of the councils may be conducive to the acquisition of politically relevant skills.

(3) Although the overall evaluation of council activities, accomplishments, and impact on the community is generally positive, significant differences do emerge between school and "other" council members, particularly in regard to perceptions of council purposes, reports of council activities, perceptions of causes of program failure, reports of council-agency relations, and summary evaluations of the councils. School council members are consistently more satisfied with council performance than members of "other" councils. Though an exploration of the causes of these differential perceptions lies beyond the scope of this study and poses an interesting subject for further research, its potential effects on individual politicization are explored in Chapter 5. (The possible impact of other council characteristics identified above—for example, length of time in operation, recruitment patterns, functions, activities, strategies, lack of success, internal operation, overall evaluation, and effects on the community— is also explored in the next chapter.)

We turn now to a discussion of selected characteristics of the advisory council members, focusing particularly on their similarity (or lack thereof) to the general population and to the respondents of the 1972 panel study.

"REPRESENTATIVENESS" OF ADVISORY COUNCIL MEMBERS:
A COMPARISON WITH THE GENERAL POPULATION AND
WITH THE 1972 PANEL STUDY

Socioeconomic Indicators

Advisory council members, by and large, appear to be representative of the East Los Angeles adult population on major socioeconomic variables, such as family income and education.[5] Moreover, a high degree of fit exists between the council and panel samples on these variables. Comparative statistics on family income for all three groups are noted in Table 4.1.

TABLE 4.1

Distribution of Family Income for Council and
Panel Respondents and East Los Angeles Population
(in percent)

|  | Advisory Council Members | Panel | Population* |
|---|---|---|---|
| Low (under $5,000) | 35 | 31 | 30 |
| Medium ($5,000 to $10,000) | 31 | 33 | 41 |
| High (over $10,000) | 34 | 36 | 30 |
| Median family income | $6,500 | $7,214 | $7,333 |

*Includes the whole area delimited: East Los Angeles, Boyle Heights, plus additional census tracts in El Sereno and Lincoln Heights.

Source: East Los Angeles population data, U.S. Bureau of the Census, Census of the Population and Housing: 1970, Census Tracts, Final Report PHC (1)-117 Los Angeles-Long Beach, Calif., SMSA (Washington, D.C.: U.S. Government Printing Office, 1972). Figures have been aggregated by the author.

As is readily apparent from these figures, family income of advisory council members fits remarkably well with family income of panel respondents and tends to parallel, in general terms, the distribution of family income in the population as a whole. The major difference between council members and the general population is that family income among the advisory council members tends to be slightly more skewed toward the lower and higher ends of the income continuum, thus possibly accounting for the lower median income. Although the fit between council members and the general population is obviously not perfect, it is readily apparent that advisory council members do not tend to be drawn from the higher-income strata disproportionately to the population. On the contrary, when one considers other income-related characteristics, such as proportion of families below the poverty level and family size, council members turn out to be drawn from the lower socioeconomic strata in greater proportion than either the panel respondents or the general population and the proportion of families below the poverty level (under 4,000) for council and panel respondents and the East Los Angeles Population is as shown below.

| Council | Panel | East Los Angeles Population |
|---|---|---|
| 21.6 percent | 18 percent | 19.1 percent |

The median family size for council and panel respondents and the East Los Angeles population is as shown.

| Council | Panel | East Los Angeles Population |
|---|---|---|
| 4.9 | 3.0 | 3.54 |

The comparatively low median family size for panel respondents possibly could be accounted for by the fact that the median age of panel respondents is 48.5; consequently, some of their children probably have left home already. (In 1965, median family size for the same respondents was 4.6). Median family size for the general population is defined as the census category "number of persons per household."

TABLE 4.2

Education: Years of School Completed for Council and Panel Respondents and East Los Angeles Population (in percent)

|  | Council | Panel | East Los Angeles Population |
|---|---|---|---|
| Low (less than 8 years) | 39 | 30 | 52 |
| Medium (8 to 12 years) | 43 | 53 | 40 |
| High (more than 12 years) | 19 | 16 | 8 |
| Median years of school completed | 10.1 | 10.1 | 8.8 |

Source: East Los Angeles population data, U.S. Bureau of the Census, Census of the Population and Housing: 1970, Census Tracts, Final Report PHC (1)-117 Los Angeles-Long Beach, Calif., SMSA (Washington, D.C.: U.S. Government Printing Office, 1971). Figures have been aggregated by the author.

In regard to education (defined as number of years of school completed), the fit between the council and panel samples is also close. However, both samples tend to be somewhat better educated than the general population. Comparative statistics for all three groups are noted in Table 4.2.

Demographic Indicators

The overwhelming majority of individuals in all three groups may be classified as being of Mexican descent. Most respondents in both samples as well as individuals in the general population have been born in the United States (62 percent of council members, 60 percent of panel respondents, and 71 percent of the general population).

In terms of residential mobility, it is difficult to make comparisons among all three groups. The 1970 census indicates that 73 percent of the East Los Angeles population had resided in the Los Angeles SMSA in 1965. This compares closely with the 83 percent of council respondents who report living in the area for more than five years. The panel respondents, on the other hand, tend to represent a more residentially stable group. Obviously, all have lived in the community more than seven years, as they originally were interviewed in 1965.

In regard to citizenship status (an important variable to consider in a study of political attitudes and behavior among Mexican-Americans) the proportion of citizens in the council and panel samples is almost identical (74 percent and 75 percent, respectively). Although no citizenship statistics are readily available for the population as a whole, it would appear that the proportion of citizens in both samples may be higher than that in the population. Among the 236 respondents interviewed in East Los Angeles in 1965 by the Mexican-American study project, 61 percent were found to be citizens.[6]

In terms of sex, as it had already been indicated, the proportion of women in the advisory council sample is higher than that in the population. However, the sex ratio in the council sample is almost identical to that of the panel sample (64 percent female, 36 percent male in the former; and 65 percent female and 35 percent male in the latter).

The high degree of congruence between the council and panel samples is further highlighted when one considers additional variables for which no general population data are available. Both groups are predominantly Catholic (approximately 85 percent in each sample); in both samples, half the respondents appear to be more at ease when speaking Spanish, as tapped by the language chosen for the interview. Both groups evidence highly similar predispositions in terms of Spanish or English media preference. Both groups also predominantly vote Democrat, and both groups are almost equally likely to be registered voters.[7]

On the basis of this brief review of socioeconomic and demographic variables, two conclusions seem to be warranted. First, in broad terms, the council sample is fairly representative of the attributes of the general population as a whole. Although slightly more poor, somewhat better educated, slightly more stable, and somewhat more female, the fit between the two groups appears to be sufficiently close to warrant making this conclusion. At least on the basis of socioeconomic and demographic data, this appears to contradict previous findings of the "unrepresentative" nature of advisory council members in low-income communities.

Second, the fit between the panel and council samples on all attribute variables, with the exception of residential mobility and age, is remarkably close. These findings warrant the use of the panel study as a control group of sorts in the analysis of politicization without controlling for standard SES variables. However, notwithstanding the close affinity of the two samples on socioeconomic and demographic data, a potential difference between the two samples remains what might be called a "self-selection" variable, that is, the possibility that although council members come from similar SES backgrounds as panel respondents, they may have been active community participants before joining the councils. As the possible operation of a "self-selection" factor would necessitate the introduction of controls in the comparison of council members with the panel sample, the nature of the "self-selection" factor is briefly discussed.

## THE OPERATION OF "SELF-SELECTION": EXTENT AND CORRELATES

Given the absence of an appropriate pretest, in an effort to determine the member's extent of involvement in community affairs before joining the council, previous involvement was tapped through the following recall self-perception item: "How would you describe the extent of your involvement in community affairs before you joined the council, that is, were you deeply involved, somewhat involved, almost not involved, or completely not involved?"

On the basis of responses to this item and on a continuum of "extent of previous involvement," 23 percent of council members may be classified as "high" (that is, responding "deeply" involved), 30 percent as medium ("somewhat" involved), and 46 percent as "low" ("almost not involved" and "completely not involved"). These figures, it would seem, support the suggestion made earlier that the informal recruitment patterns of the councils tend to result in attracting individuals who are already involved in community affairs as well as individuals who are not involved. Almost half the sample has not been involved previously in community affairs.

An effort to determine what factors are associated with previous involvement was made by exploring the association of previous involvement with several council-related variables, which were thought to be possibly relevant (type of council, mode of recruitment, and reasons for joining the council) and with possibly relevant member-related variables (family income, education, citizenship status, sex, age, length of time in the community, language spoken in the home, and language of interview).[8]

Analysis of these variables reveals, first, that previous involvement is related significantly to type of council ($p = 0.05$), as can be seen in Table 4.3. School councils are more likely to attract previously inactive individuals than "other" types of councils. In terms of other council variables probed (mode of recruitment and reasons for joining), no association was found. Those who have been involved previously and those who have not appear to follow similar recruitment paths and join for similar reasons.

TABLE 4.3

Members' Previous Involvement by Type of Council
(in percent)

| Previous Involvement | Type of Council | |
| --- | --- | --- |
|  | School | Other |
| High | 18 | 36 |
| Medium | 28 | 36 |
| Low | 56 | 28 |
| | (N = 79) | |
| | $X^2 = 5.95$ ($p = 0.05$) | |

Source: Compiled by the author.

In regard to member-related variables, two particular factors were found to be related significantly to levels of previous involvement: education and preference of language. Individuals who are better educated are more likely to have been involved in community affairs, as are individuals who are fluent in English. (Relative frequencies for both categories are illustrated in Tables 4.4 and 4.5). Although the association between higher levels of education and higher previous involvement is, of course, to be expected, the association between preference of language and previous involvement calls attention to another obstacle to political participation in low-income Mexican-American communities: lack of fluency in English by some segments of the population, particularly among those who are older or more recent immigrants. As Leo Grebler and his associates point out, "Mexican Americans appear to have diverged substantially from the usual pattern of dissolution of old-country language use over succeeding generations in the U.S. . . . Spanish is the most persistent of all

TABLE 4.4

Members' Previous Involvement by Language of Interview
(in percent)

| Previous Involvement | Language of Interview | |
|---|---|---|
| | Spanish | English |
| High | 13 | 33 |
| Medium | 23 | 38 |
| Low | 64 | 30 |

(N = 79)
$X^2 = 9.61$ (p = 0.008)

Source: Compiled by the author.

foreign languages and the one with the greatest prospects of survival. . . ."[9] Notwithstanding efforts to involve predominantly Spanish-speaking individuals in community affairs through such techniques as holding meetings in both English and Spanish, monolingualism remains a serious obstacle to political participation in communities where English is the predominant transactional language.

This brief review of the extent and correlates of previous involvement suggests that those who claimed that poverty councils are composed of the "vivid poor and the noisy poor and the terribly participatory poor" were, at best, only partially correct. As has been seen, close to one-half the sample has had little or no experience in community affairs; while another third, according to their own estimation, has been only "somewhat" involved. On the other hand, it has been

TABLE 4.5

Members' Previous Involvement by Education
(in percent)

| Previous Involvement | Education | | |
|---|---|---|---|
| | Low | Medium | High |
| High | 11 | 44 | 44 |
| Medium | 26 | 39 | 20 |
| Low | 68 | 36 | 28 |

(N = 79)
$X^2 = 16.4$ (p = 0.002)

Source: Compiled by the author.

seen that members of those councils that have been studied most extensively (those in the "other" category) are more likely to have been active in community affairs. Yet, considering that only 36 percent of members of these councils are previous activists, the claim that poverty councils attracted only the "terribly participatory poor" does seem to be a gross exaggeration.

Nevertheless, the fact that, overall, close to a third of the advisory council sample is composed of previous activists does raise the possibility of the operation of a "self-selection" factor. "Self-selection" is thus posited as a second alternative plausible explanation, which may account for any differences found between council members and panel respondents on politicization measures. This alternative explanatory hypothesis is explored at the end of Chapter 5. What follows is an analysis of the major questions posed in this study.

## NOTES

1. Refer to Table 3.2, p. 63 for a complete breakdown.
2. The remaining 10 percent was indeterminable.
3. These data are reported adding up first, second, and third mentions.
4. Also adding first, second, and third mentions.
5. The qualification "adult" population is made because the median age of advisory council members is 40 years old, but the overall median for the general population is much lower given the large family size generally characterizing Mexican-American communities (see data discussed in Chapter 3). Also, occupation is not included as a major socioeconomic variable for comparison because the occupational questions, unfortunately, were not phrased identically for both the council and panel samples.
6. It is possible however, that this percentage has gone up since 1965.
7. Sixty-one percent of council members and 67 percent of the panel respondents are registered voters.
8. "Language spoken in the home" and "language of interview" are construed as measures that tap the respondent's potential capacity to deal effectively in community affairs through his ability to communicate in English. (The assumption being that those respondents who only are able to communicate in Spanish face serious obstacles in becoming involved in community affairs.)
9. Leo Grebler, Joan W. Moore, and Ralph C. Guzman, The Mexican American People (New York: The Free Press, 1970), pp. 423-442.

CHAPTER

# 5

## THE POLITICIZATION OF ADVISORY COUNCIL MEMBERS

    This chapter explores the major concern of this study: is involvement in advisory councils a politicizing experience? Is it conducive to the development of a propensity to affect government, to the acquisition of political capabilities, and to an increase in rates of political participation? The strategy utilized to test these hypotheses in the first part of this chapter is twofold. First, it will be established to what extent advisory council members differ from individuals of similar socioeconomic status in the community under study on measures of politicization. This is done by comparing the significance of differences on politicization measures between members of advisory councils and members of the general population as represented by respondents of the 1972 panel study. As discussed earlier, these two groups are sufficiently similar in terms of socioeconomic and demographic characteristics to warrant such a comparison. The major method employed to determine the significance of differences between the two samples is the chi square test for two independent samples.[1] As it is established to what extent and on what measures of politicization advisory council members differ from individuals of similar SES status in the same community, simultaneously it will be explored to what extent higher levels of politicization can be attributed tentatively to council involvement by relying on the members' reported self-perceptions of political attitudinal and behavioral changes as a result of the council experience.
    The second part of this chapter explores the correlates of politicization, that is, those factors that tend to be most highly associated with high levels of politicization. The purposes of this analysis are (1) to contribute to the understanding of organizational involvement as an alternative route to political participation by exploring selected organizational conditions associated with high levels of politicization, and (2) to explore what type of individual appears to be most affected by the organizational experience by focusing on the association between high levels of politicization and member-related variables.

## THE DEVELOPMENT OF POLITICIZATION

### Propensity to Affect Government

The first dimension of politicization to be explored is the propensity or tendency to affect government, which, as previously discussed, is defined in terms of the following orientations: (1) awareness of the impact of government on one's life or cognitions about government, (2) evaluations of governmental activities, (3) perceived ability to influence government, and (4) supportive attitudinal orientations in the form of "activity and passivity" and "social trust." Each orientation is discussed in turn.

### Cognitions About Politics and Government

It should be recalled that awareness of the impact of government on one's life is operationalized by the following measures, which distinguish between national and local referents: "About how much effect do you think that the activities of the national (local) government have on your day to day life? Do they have a great effect, some effect, or none?" A comparison of the differences between the two populations on cognitions about the local government is noted in Table 5.1.[2]

As is apparent from Table 5.1, the chi square test for two independent samples reveals that in regard to awareness of the impact of the local government on one's life, the two populations differ with respect to the relative frequency with which group members fall in several categories ($p = 0.01$). Eighty-eight percent of council members perceive the local government as having an impact on their lives, as compared with 60 percent of panel respondents.

TABLE 5.1

Awareness of the Impact of the Local Government
Among Council and Panel Respondents
(in percent)

|  | Council | Panel |
|---|---|---|
| Great effect | 35 | 23 |
| Some effect | 53 | 37 |
| None | 8 | 23 |
| Don't know | 5 | 16 |
|  | (N = 78) | (N = 43) |
|  | $X^2 = 11.42$ ($p = 0.01$) | |

Source: Compiled by the author.

TABLE 5.2

Awareness of the Impact of the National Government
Among Council and Panel Respondents
(in percent)

|  | Council | Panel |
|---|---|---|
| Great effect | 45 | 31 |
| Some effect | 31 | 31 |
| None | 9 | 23 |
| Don't know | 15 | 15 |
|  | (N = 78) | (N = 48) |
|  | $X^2 = 5.33$ $(p > 0.05)$ | |

Source: Compiled by the author.

In an effort to ascertain whether cognitive orientations toward the local government had changed since membership in the council, respondents were asked "Did you feel the same way before you were an advisory council member?" It should be recalled that this type of attitudinal recall item is not a powerful measure of previous attitudes. In fact, "the probable direction of "memory bias" is to distort the past attitudes into agreement with present ones."[3] Nevertheless, 23 percent of the respondents replied negatively to this probe: leading one to believe that their attitudes had changed during the council experience. Moreover, among those reporting a change, the direction of change is overwhelmingly in the direction of increased awareness of the local government's impact.[4]

In regard to cognitive orientations toward the national government, although a larger proportion of council respondents (76 percent) perceives the national government as having some or great impact on their lives than panel respondents (62 percent), the differences between the two groups are not statistically significant, as may be seen in Table 5.2.

Twenty-one percent of council respondents report that their cognitive orientations toward government are different than they had been prior to membership. The direction of change, however, is not as clearcut as in the case of the local government. Seventy-one percent of those who report changes in cognitive orientations toward the national government have become more aware of the impact of the national government, compared with 94 percent who have become more aware of the local government among those reporting changes.

In Chapter 2 it was hypothesized that the level of cognition of government's impact would tend to be higher in reference to the local government than toward the national government. At first glance, the data bears out this expectation, supporting arguments made in other studies in favor of distinguishing between national and local referents rather than exploring orientations toward the unspecified general referent "government;"[5] 88 percent of council respondents perceive the local government as having "great" or "some" effect on their lives, versus 76 percent reporting similar perceptions about the national government. However, when one considers solely those respondents reporting that the national government and local government affect them greatly, the national government emerges as having more impact (45 percent versus 35 percent). This is possibly due to an awareness of the proliferation of the federal government's intervention during the 1960s, particularly in regard to poverty programs. This is supported by data on cognitions about the War on Poverty. Eighty-two percent of the council members report having heard about the War on Poverty, and the overwhelming majority of these are able to mention specific programs.

Evaluative Orientations Toward Government

As previously discussed, evaluative orientations toward the local and national governments were tapped in terms of a diffuse evaluation in the form of "In general, do you think your local (national) government is run the way it should be?", and in terms of evaluations of specific national and local outputs—that is, the War on Poverty as a national output and evaluation of school outputs at the local level.

An analysis of the diffuse evaluative orientation measures (see Table 5.3) reveals that a high level of discontent exists among both council and panel respondents. Fifty-five percent of council members and 48 percent of panel respondents report dissatisfaction with the way the local government is run. As is readily apparent from Table 5.3, the two groups are not significantly different on this question. In terms of the national government, however, there is a significant difference between the two groups ($p = 0.05$). Panel respondents are more likely either to view the national government more favorably than council respondents or to report that they don't know.

It was suggested earlier that a higher incidence of substantive responses (that is, positive or negative) than "don't know" or "no response" answers would characterize evaluations of the local versus the national government among council respondents. The data do not bear out this expectation: evaluations of local and national governments are almost identical and predominantly negative. Reasons cited for negative evaluations of both local and national government are also similar. Most respondents either refer to the fact that government does not help and that problems remain unsolved or cite some manifestation of corruption. References to Watergate as justifications for negative evaluations of the federal government were numerous.

An effort to determine whether evaluative orientations toward government change during the council experience was made by asking

TABLE 5.3

Evaluation of Local and National Government Among
Council and Panel Respondents
(in percent)

|  | Local | | National | |
| --- | --- | --- | --- | --- |
|  | Council | Panel | Council | Panel |
| Run the way it should be | 13 | 19 | 13 | 16 |
| In between | 18 | 12 | 55 | 48 |
| Not run the way it should be | 55 | 48 | 56 | 30 |
| Don't know | 14 | 21 | 14 | 30 |
|  | (N = 77) | (N = 42) | (N = 78) | (N = 43) |
|  | $X^2 = 2.40$ | | $X^2 = 8.53$ | |
|  | ($p > 0.05$) | | ($p = 0.05$) | |

Source: Compiled by the author.

the respondents whether they felt the same way before joinging the council. Among the 19 percent who report changes in evaluative orientations toward the local government and among the 17 percent who report changes in evaluations of the national government, the overwhelming majority report either that the local and national government are not run well or are run "in between." In this respect, it would seem that council membership and attendant exposure to governmental affairs increases rather than decreases negativism toward government or, in other words, fosters a realization that things are not as they should be.

Evaluation of specific local and national outputs (that is, the War on Poverty at the national level and school outputs at the local level) are also somewhat negative, but less so than the more diffuse orientations. This finding is of interest, for it suggests that negative evaluations of government may be based on generalized and preconceived notions about the overall responsiveness of government to the lower classes and to the particular ethnic group (hence possibly reflecting a sense of frustration with the lack of socioeconomic advancement), rather than on consideration of specific outputs. Breakdowns of evaluations of the success of War on Poverty programs among council respondents are noted in Table 5.4.[6]

TABLE 5.4

Evaluation of War on Poverty Programs
Among Council Respondents
(in percent)

| | |
|---|---|
| Overall success | 18.8 |
| Part success, part failure | 41.2 |
| Overall failure | 17.5 |
| Don't know | 5.0 |
| | (N = 80) |

Source: Compiled by the author.

Among those who evaluate the War on Poverty either as an overall failure or as a partial failure, major reasons cited for this evaluation are poor administration, abuses of the program (such as "welfare chiseling"), and the fact that it did not help a sufficient number of people or it did not help "in the right way." However, even though the War on Poverty does not rate highly among our respondents, when asked to evaluate recent program cutbacks, 53 percent of the advisory council members evaluate these as "bad" or "very bad." Major reasons cited for negative evaluations of the cuts were that the poor will suffer and that many good programs will be ended, thus thwarting the attendant rise in hopes and expectations.

Evaluation of a local output for which measures are available for both groups are also somewhat negative. When asked their opinions about the operation of schools in the community, 38 percent of council respondents and 26 percent of panel respondents answered unfavorably. No statistically significant differences were evidenced between the two groups on this question.

Overall, it would appear that both council and panel members generally are similarly dissatisfied with government at both national and local levels. Moreover, dissatisfaction seems to increase rather than decrease as a result of council membership. Whether this should be interpreted as an increase in the political sophistication of council members in the sense that they become aware that government is not receptive to the interests of low-income individuals or whether it should be interpreted in the sense that the council setting is not conducive to the acquisition of political trust is debatable and largely dependent, it would seem, on the perspective of the observer. This question is further explored in a subsequent section of this chapter.

Perceived Ability to Influence Government

The reader should recall that perceived ability to influence government (political efficacy) was measured in two ways: (1) by use of the SRC political efficacy four-item scale, which is cast in somewhat vague terms as to subject and referent; and (2) by a more direct and more specific measure as to subject and referent in the form of, "Some people tell us that there is nothing they can do to affect what the local (national) government does. Other people say that they can influence what gets decided in this community (in Washington) if they want to. How about you? Do you feel that you can affect what the local (national) government does or not?"

The differential results obtained through the use of these two types of measures are striking and seem to cast doubts as to the validity of the more vague and indirect SRC scale for the particular population under study. On the one hand, on the basis of results obtained with the SRC scale probe, one would have to conclude that the advisory council members are highly inefficacious; but on the other hand, diametrically opposite conclusions are reached through the use of what, on face validity, would seem to be the more direct measure. Results obtained on the different political efficacy measures are abstracted below in Tables 5.5 and 5.6.

As can be readily seen from Tables 5.5 and 5.6, diametrically divergent results are obtained through the use of the different measures.

TABLE 5.5

Political Efficacy Among Council and Panel Respondents
As Measured by the SRC Political Efficacy Scale
(in percent)
(positive responses: low efficacy; negative responses:
high efficacy)

|  | Council | Panel |
|---|---|---|
| 1. Public officials don't care about what people like me think. | | |
| Agree | 68 | 59 |
| Disagree | 32 | 41 |
|  | (N = 73) | (N = 37) |
|  | $X^2 = 0.531$ ($p > 0.05$) | |
| 2. Voting is the only way that people like me can have any say about how the government runs things. | | |
| Agree | 64 | 78 |
| Disagree | 36 | 22 |
|  | (N = 77) | (N = 41) |
|  | $X^2 = 1.95$ ($p > 0.05$) | |
| 3. People like me don't have any say about what the government does. | | |
| Agree | 49 | 56 |
| Disagree | 51 | 44 |
|  | (N = 76) | (N = 41) |
|  | $X^2 = 0.326$ ($p > 0.05$) | |
| 4. Sometimes politics and government seem so complicated that a person like me can't really understand what's going on. | | |
| Agree | 86 | 89 |
| Disagree | 14 | 11 |
|  | (N = 76) | (N = 45) |
|  | $X^2 = 0.062$ ($p > 0.05$) | |

Source: Compiled by the author.

TABLE 5.6

Political Efficacy Toward the Local and National
Government Among Council and Panel Respondents
["Do you feel you can affect what the local (national) government does?"]
(in percent)

|  | Local | | National | |
| --- | --- | --- | --- | --- |
|  | Council | Panel | Council | Panel |
| Yes | 60 | 21 | 46 | 21 |
| Sometimes, it depends | 8 | 21 | 12 | 17 |
| No | 29 | 37 | 37 | 38 |
| Don't know | 2 | 21 | 5 | 24 |
|  | (N = 78) | (N = 43) | (N = 78) | (N = 42) |
|  | $X^2 = 23.97$ ($p = 0.001$) | | $X^2 = 13.16$ ($p = 0.001$) | |

Source: Compiled by the author.

The applicability of the SRC political efficacy scale to the particular population under study must be questioned when one considers the following findings. First, items 1 and 3 are not correlated with item 4 when using alternatively Spearman's rho, and Kendall's tau or Pearson r correlation coefficients.[7] Secondly, when all the politicization measures (including the SRC political efficacy scale) were factor analyzed,[8] the four items of the SRC scale loaded on three separate factors. The more direct efficacy measures, on the other hand, were intercorrelated highly and together formed a distinct and separate factor when factor analyzed.[9] It is not within the bounds of this study to resolve these discrepancies; but these findings do raise some interesting methodological questions for further study and research, especially in regard to the applicability of standard scales to particular subpopulations.

Considering then, what in the author's view are the more direct and empirically more powerful measures (presented in Table 5.6), one finds that council members score significantly higher on political efficacy both toward the national and local governments than panel respondents (at the 0.01 significance level in the former case and at the 0.001 level in the latter).

Exploring whether changes in self-images as political actors change during the council experience, one sees that 22 percent of members report changes in their ability to affect the local government and 16 percent report similar changes in regard to the national government. The direction of these changes is overwhelmingly in the direction of perceptions of _increased_ ability to affect government (100 percent in the case of national government, 94 percent in regard to local government).

Comparing rates of political efficacy toward different levels of government among council respondents, the data support a previously made suggestion that council members feel more efficacious toward the local than toward the national government (68 percent versus 58 percent). This is probably due to the fact that most council members have had more experience in dealing with local affairs than in national ones, although their awareness of the impact of the national government on their lives is great.

Reasons cited for perceptions of their ability to influence both local and national governments are of interest, for they provide an indication of the likelihood of sustained politicization—a question to be discussed fully in Chapter 7. When respondents who report being able to affect both the national and local governments are asked, "How can you have this effect?," over half mention some type of collective action, such as "organize," "unite the community," "join community organizations," or "demonstrate," versus individualistically oriented responses such as "vote," "write letters," or "send petitions."

## Supportive Attitudes: "Passivity-Activity" and "Social Trust"

Two final dimensions to be explored in an effort to ascertain whether advisory council members are likely to exhibit a "propensity to affect government" are a "passivity-activity" scale[10] and the SRC "trust in people" scale. Conceptually, these are considered primarily as supportive attitudinal orientations to the more direct politicization measures of government's impact on one's life: evaluation of government activities and perceived personal ability to influence government.

"Passivity-activity" is generally cast as a belief or lack thereof in the potential mastery over one's environment.[11] Conceptually, it is related to self-efficacy or to the belief that the environment is pliable and open to change through one's own design. It is also related to present or future orientations and to the ability (or lack thereof) to defer present gratification to attain some future goal. It is in the latter sense that "passivity" has been construed as a major obstacle to change in the condition of the poor by "culture of poverty" theorists.[12] According to these theorists, the major causes of poverty lie not in oppressive social conditions nor in the lack of economic opportunity, but rather lie in the poor themselves—in their lack of personal efficacy and in their inability to defer instantaneous gratification and look toward the future.[13]

The differences between council and panel respondents on all items of the "passivity-activity" dimension are statistically significant at the 0.05 level or better. As may be seen in Table 5.7, council members are consistently more self-efficacious and future-oriented than panel respondents.

The strong future orientations evidenced in the responses of the council members on the "passivity-activity" scale are further supported by additional attitudinal data. By and large, council members appear to be highly optimistic about the future. When asked to situate their past, present, and future life conditions on the Cantril ladder[14] (which ranges from 1 to 10, 10 being the "best possible life" and 1 being the "worst possible life"), most respondents place their present life situation at a higher level than five years ago and further place their living condition five years hence at almost the top level of the ladder. Comparative figures (abstracted in Table 5.8) best illustrate this point.

Not only do council members exhibit a high level of optimism about their future in both comparative and absolute terms,[15] but they also tend to view their own future in more optimistic terms than the future of the community.[16] (Overall, they place the community at 4.2 five years ago, 4.7 at present, and 7.0 five years hence.[17]) Taking into account that council members are _more_ economically underprivileged than the general East Los Angeles population (as measured by median family income[18]), the comparatively higher level of optimism that characterizes perceptions of their own future lives is a further indication of their relatively high sense of mastery over the environment.

TABLE 5.7

"Passivity-Activity" Orientations Among
Council and Panel Respondents
(in percent)
(Positive responses: passivity; negative responses: activity)

|  | Council | Panel |
|---|---|---|
| 1. Making plans only brings unhappiness because the plans are hard to fulfill. | | |
| Agree | 24 | 49 |
| Disagree | 76 | 51 |
|  | (N = 72) | (N = 41) |
|  | $X^2 = 6.41$ (p = 0.02) | |
| 2. It doesn't make much difference if the people elect one or another candidate, for nothing will change. | | |
| Agree | 29 | 50 |
| Disagree | 71 | 50 |
|  | (N = 68) | (N = 42) |
|  | $X^2 = 3.86$ (p = 0.05) | |
| 3. With things as they are today, an intelligent person ought to think only about the present without worrying about what is going to happen tomorrow. | | |
| Agree | 14 | 36 |
| Disagree | 86 | 64 |
|  | (N = 78) | (N = 45) |
|  | $X^2 = 6.46$ (p = 0.02) | |
| 4. The secret of happiness is not expecting too much out of life and being content with what comes your way. | | |
| Agree | 33 | 64 |
| Disagree | 67 | 36 |
|  | (N = 73) | (N = 44) |
|  | $X^2 = 9.31$ (p = 0.01) | |

Source: Compiled by the author.

TABLE 5.8

Perceptions of Past, Present, and Future Life Situations
Among Council and Panel Respondents
(median levels)

|  | Council | Panel |
|---|---|---|
|  | (best) | (best) |
| Future | 9.5 | 7.7 |
| Present | 6.8 | 5.3 |
| Past | 4.5 | 4.5 |
|  | (worst) | (worst) |

Source: Compiled by the author.

Other indications of future-oriented attitudes lie in the council members' heavy emphasis on education[19] when asked their opinions on occupational advice and when expressing their future hopes for themselves and their families. Their great concern with education is found in other questioning as well and is almost all-pervasive. A high degree of concern with education, however, is not idiosyncratic to the council members; it also pervades the panel respondents' answers to a variety of probes. The almost overwhelming and consistent concern with education in both samples clearly belies cultural stereotypic notions of the Mexican-American as somewhat passive and present-oriented and as somehow not greatly interested in education.

A final attitudinal dimension to be considered is a horizontal (related to other people) rather than a vertical (related to government) measure. This is social trust operationally defined as the SRC "trust in people" scale. Social trust is often considered both as a prerequisite and as a by-product of group affiliation.[20] It is a prerequisite in the sense that "the art of associating together"[21] requires, at a minimum, that people perceive a necessity for coming together and a belief that joining together may be worthwhile. It is a by-product in the sense that group affiliation generally can breed a realization that association is worthwhile, hence prompting a propensity toward further association.

The results obtained on this particular dimension are surprising, for they reveal that council members (those who are more organizationally involved) are less trustful than those who are less organizationally involved (the panel).[22] The differences between the two populations, however, are small and statistically insignificant as may be seen in Table 5.9.

The low level of social trust among council respondents is open to divergent interpretations. On the one hand, it could reflect the possibility that the organizational involvement - political participation

TABLE 5.9

"Trust In People" Among Council and Panel Respondents
(in percent)

|  | Council | Panel |
|---|---|---|
| 1. Generally speaking, would you say that most people can be trusted, or that you can't be too careful in dealing with people? | | |
| Trust | 38 | 52 |
| Distrust | 62 | 48 |
|  | (N = 73) | (N = 42) |
|  | $X^2 = 1.60$ | $(p > 0.05)$ |
| 2. Would you say that most of the time people try to be helpful or that you can't be too careful in dealing with people? | | |
| Trust | 42 | 57 |
| Distrust | 58 | 43 |
|  | (N = 69) | (N = 44) |
|  | $X^2 = 1.79$ | $(p > 0.05)$ |
| 3. Do you think that most people would try to take advantage of you if they got the chance, or would they try to be fair? | | |
| Trust | 45 | 51 |
| Distrust | 55 | 49 |
|  | (N = 64) | (N = 39) |
|  | $X^2 = 1.48$ | $(p > 0.05)$ |

Source: Compiled by the author.

model not only operates independently of SES status and of its attendant "enabling antecedents" but also does not result in the acquisition of this particular enabling orientation. In the view of Nie and his associates, this raises a host of questions about the possibly undemocratic nature of the type of participation engendered by the organizational involvement model.[23] This possibility seems to be negated when one considers the relationship between "trust in people" and the extent of the respondent's involvement in community affairs before joining the council. Those who rate "high" and "medium" on the extent of their previous community activity are almost twice as likely to express trust in other people than those who were uninvolved previously.[24]

Although this finding supports the power of organizational involvement in general as a facilitator for the acquisition of social trust, it nevertheless leaves unanswered questions about whether the particular organizational setting of the advisory councils works to increase or to decrease the member's level of social trust. The latter is a difficult question to explore given the absence of retrospective pretests on the social trust scale, for there is no way of identifying previous levels of social trust. Nevertheless, anticipating subsequent discussions, other data appear to indicate that the council experience, paradoxically, could work to both increase and decrease social trust. On the one hand, as is reported in the next section, the council experience seems to breed an increased capability for cooperative activity. On the other hand, however, the council experience could breed a negative orientation toward government as a result of frustrating experiences encountered in accomplishing council goals. Negativism toward government and public officials, in turn, possibly could breed a generalized sense of mistrust. This notion is further discussed in a subsequent section of this chapter.

## Conclusions

The previous discussion has sought to explore whether the advisory council experience is conducive to changes in the members' cognitive and evaluative orientations toward government and in their self-images as political actors by following a two-pronged approach. On the one hand, the author has focused on the extent to which council members differ from individuals of similar SES status in the same community on particular attitudinal measures of politicization. In this respect, it has been shown that, compared with panel respondents, council members exhibit higher levels of awareness of government's impact on their lives, higher levels of political efficacy toward government, and higher levels of personal efficacy and future-oriented attitudes, fairly equal levels of dissatisfaction with government performance at both national and local levels, and a lower level of social trust.

Second, the author has sought to explore to what extent higher levels of politicization could be attributed tentatively to the council experience by focusing on the somewhat imprecise measures of the members' own recollections of their previous attitudes before joining the council. In this respect, it has been shown that on each orientation approximately one-fifth of the respondents report changes occuring subsequent to council membership. These changes, moreover, are overwhelmingly in the direction of increased politicization.

The kind of information presented to test the development of a "propensity to affect government" is not sufficiently precise to allow drawing definite conclusions about a causal connection between council membership and the attitudinal dimension of politicization. As has been observed repeatedly, this kind of precision cannot be obtained in a study of this nature—hindered as it is by the lack of an appropriate pretest. Thus considering the data presented as primarily suggestive in character, it may be concluded on the basis of the comparison with a similar population and on the basis of the members' own perceptions that the council experience appears to be conducive to the acquisition of particular attitudinal propensities to affect government at both national and local levels. A more precise elaboration of this suggestion awaits future studies able to utilize more rigorous experimental designs.

## Capabilities to Affect Government

One of the major dimensions of politicization of interest in this study is whether advisory council membership is conducive to the acquisition of capabilities to affect government in the form of political skills and political information. As has been discussed, learning "the rules of the game" and learning where to go to get things done appears to be a salient subject for analysis in regard to low-income individuals— typically viewed as politically unknowledgeable and unsophisticated and as unable to deal with the public bureaucracies that closely and directly affect their daily lives. Moreover, the organizational setting of the advisory councils appears to be highly conducive to the learning of politically relevant skills. As was concluded in the discussion of the activities of the advisory councils (in Chapter 4), activities such as planning and implementing programs, planning budgets and writing funding proposals could all be potentially useful learning experiences for the advisory council member.

### Political Skills

These data, by and large, support the expectation that advisory council members learn politically relevant skills as a result of the advisory council experience. When asked whether in the course of their experience as advisory council members, they had learned "any new things," the majority of members (76 percent) responded affirmatively. An analysis of the open-ended explanatory responses to this question is of interest, for they closely parallel the type of responses elicited on a subsequent closed-ended measure.

When members were asked what kinds of things they had learned, approximately one-third of the responses referred to some type of organizational skill in terms of enhancement of personal effectiveness in dealing with people or more directly in terms of coordination, parliamentary procedures, or committee formation. Some of these responses are quoted at length to provide the reader with a feeling for the member's own perception of his learning experience:

"I learned how to work with others to find solutions to problems" (male, 36 years old, member of a retarded children's association council);

"how to deal with decisions and make the council see my view, and how to make contacts" (female, 68 years old, Model Cities council);

"I learned how to be a politician" (female, 40 years old, educational advisory council);

"how meetings are run and that the council has a lot of potential strength" (female, 26 years old, school advisory council);

"lots of things: how to express myself better, how to work with others . . . too many to mention all of them" (female, 35 years old, Headstart Advisory council);

"learned by observation the importance of proposals, parliamentary procedure, and the importance and need for community representation" (female, 44 years old, Community Development Corporation council);

"how to organize committees" (female, 23 years old, school advisory council);

"to work with people of different backgrounds and with different ideas" (male, 42 years old, immigration advisory council).

Another 40 percent of the responses referred to learning about the operation of public agencies and community groups. The following responses were typical:

"how the Board of Education works in conjunction with the community and who to go to to get something done" (male, 48 years old, school advisory council);

"I got involved in community affairs and learned how children are taught in the schools" (female, 53 years old, school advisory council);

"had to learn everything; didn't know what it was all about when I joined—learned how the school functions and about appropriations" (male, 35 years old, school advisory council);

> "I learned how the teachers are organized and how the principal sits in his office and how the money gets wasted on things that aren't needed" (male, 25 years old, school advisory council).

A final 30 percent of the responses dealt with what could be construed generally as skills related to access points in the system, for example, learning the rules of the game, who to contact, and where to go to get something done. Again, typical responses of this nature are as follows:

> "as a member of the council, I've met important people and learned what goes on in other agencies and groups. And I've also learned how parents can go to the Board of Education and get things done" (female, 32 years old, school advisory council);

> "to understand legal matters better" (male, 21 years old, Center for Law and Justice advisory council);

> "how to work with professionals and educators" (male, 40 years old, school advisory council);

> "where to go for your needs and contact top people right away. The thing is to know how to go about it" (female, 42 years old, school advisory council);

> "how the system worked and what we could and couldn't do" (female, 48 years old, school advisory council);

> "how to write up a budget proposal" (female, 32 years old, school advisory council);

> "how to get a law passed" (woman, 45 years old, legal aid advisory council);

> "to fight verbally, regardless of position, especially with those who have pull and with higher ups" (male, 40 years old, school advisory council).

In addition to the open-ended measure tapping "things learned" as a result of the advisory council experience, later on in the interview closed-ended measures were tapped through the following probe: "Some people tell us that they have learned many new things on the advisory council. Others tell us that they haven't learned anything at all. How about you? Looking at this list (HAND RESPONDENT A CARD) please tell me (1) whether you are familiar with any of these things or not; and (2) if you are, whether you learned any of them as a result of the council."[25] Table 5.10 abstracts the responses to this probe, grouping them by type of skill learned; within each category these are rank-ordered.

The finding that generally between one-fourth to one-half of the advisory council members report learning particular skills on the councils is corroborated further by the more informal interviews that the author conducted with advisory council chairmen at the outset of this study.[26] The chairmen also were asked whether they thought the membership "learned new things on the council." Some of these responses are worth quoting again to provide the reader with the flavor of the nature of responses elicited. Consider, for example, the statement of the chairman of a Headstart advisory council, a middle-aged woman.

> Being a member of the council, gives the parent a sense of responsibility, a feeling of self-worth. Instead of just sitting at home, the parent comes to realize that there's a new world of opportunity . . . the council gives them a feeling of belonging. . . . Some parents begin participating in other community groups, and as the children move on to other schools, they become active participants in the elementary school, the high school, and so on. . . . Membership in the council definitely seems to have a carry over effect in terms of participation in other groups.

Then there is the commentary of the chairman of a neighborhood services council, a man in his middle thirties.

> The members have become aware of the many federal and state laws which govern the delivery of services. . . . On the whole, however, the council has made them very bitter because they have to go through a lot of "red tape" in order to help get services for the people.

And, there is the statement from the chairman of a mental health advisory council.

> A change in attitudes has occurred. At the beginning everyone was mutually suspicious of one another. Now they have learned to trust one another and are working with a "community oriented mentality."

Judging from some of the commentaries above, it would seem that even those who are embittered and who evaluate council performance

TABLE 5.10

Type of Skills Learned
(in percent)

|  | Learned from Council | Already Knew | Don't Know |
|---|---|---|---|
| Organizational skills | | | |
| 1. How to get community support for a new program | 44 | 31 | 24 |
| 2. How to run a meeting | 39 | 35 | 25 |
| 3. How to persuade people to your own point of view | 33 | 41 | 24 |
| 4. Robert's Rules of Order[a] | 25 | 24 | 50 |
| 5. How to organize a protest march | 14 | 21 | 63 |
| 6. How to quiet a riot | 6 | 18 | 75 |
| Knowledge about the functioning of public bureaucracies and community groups | | | |
| 1. How things get done in this particular agency | 51 | 19 | 26 |
| 2. How community groups work | 46 | 23 | 30 |
| 3. How government agencies work | 45 | 18 | 36 |
| 4. Who has the power in this community | 38 | 26 | 35 |
| Skills related to access points in the political system | | | |
| 1. How to write a proposal for funding[b] | 51 | 14 | 34 |
| 2. How to contact public officials | 34 | 38 | 26 |
| 3. How to lobby in favor of legislation | 30 | 19 | 48 |
| 4. How to get something reported in the newspapers, radio, or TV | 26 | 40 | 32 |
| 5. How to get out a newsletter | 24 | 35 | 40 |

[a]It is possible that the way in which this item was phrased (Robert's Rules of Order) was unintelligible to some respondents thus resulting in a lower rate of cognition. "Parliamentary procedure" may have been more appropriate.

[b]This question may have been equated by some with "writing a budget" (which many respondents mentioned in the open-ended responses).

Source: Compiled by the author.

negatively could be learning some things.[27] This possibility is enhanced when one considers whether the likelihood of learning skills is affected by the type of council the member belongs to. In this respect, we find that 88 percent of members from "other" councils report learning "new things," compared with 73 percent of school council members. Recalling that members from "other" councils generally tend to express more negative views about council performance and are more likely to suggest that the council does not have any power,[28] the fact that they also tend to report learning new things in slightly higher proportions than school council members suggests that the council setting may be conducive to the acquisition of skills, regardless of the members' evaluation of council performance and regardless of the actual decision-making power of the council. This tends to support the assertion made earlier that, whether councils have any power or not, the council experience and the attendant exposure to public affairs can be conducive to the acquisition of politically relevant skills.

The notion that the council setting per se is conducive to skill learning is further supported when one considers the distribution of those reporting that they have learned something according to the extent of their previous involvement. As can be seen in Table 5.11, council members appear to learn new skills regardless of their previous experience in community affairs.

TABLE 5.11

Learned New Things as Member by Extent
of Previous Involvement
(in percent)

| Extent of Previous Involvement | Learned New Things | |
|---|---|---|
| | Yes | No |
| High | 83 | 18 |
| Medium | 71 | 29 |
| Low | 78   (N = 78) | 22 |

Source: Compiled by the author.

Political Knowledge

The reader should recall that a second aspect of the development of "capabilities to affect government" was conceptualized as "political knowledge" and operationalized as knowledge about War on Poverty programs, knowledge of community organizations ranging from long-

TABLE 5.12

Cognition of Community Organizations Among
Panel and Council Respondents
(proportion having heard of the organization)
(in percent)

|  | Council | Panel |
|---|---|---|
| PTA | 95 | 88 |
| La Raza Unida party | 86 | 77 |
| Chicano Moratorium | 83 | 75 |
| United Farm Workers | 83 | 71 |
| MAPA (Mexican-American Political Association) | 79 | 67 |
| Neighborhood Legal Aid | 79 | 49 |
| MECHA (Chicano Student Association) | 75 | 55 |
| Brown Berets | 75 | 47 |
| Chicano Liberation Front | 69 | 41 |
| TELACU (The East Los Angeles Community Union) | 69 | 41 |
| LUCHA (exaddict group) | 63 | 49 |
| Democratic clubs | 55 | 33 |
| Republican clubs | 50 | 31 |
| Alianza Hispano Americana | 49 | 47 |
| GI Forum | 43 | 35 |
| CSO (Community Service Organization) | 40 | 26 |
| LULAC (Leage of United Latin American Citizens) | 29 | 18 |
| PASSO (Political Association of Spanish Speaking Organizations) | 14 | 10 |

Source: Compiled by the author.

standing to newly established and from conservatively oriented to radical, and by knowledge of the protests, marches, and demonstrations that rocked the East Los Angeles community in recent years. The underlying assumption behind exploring this dimension is that council membership and the attendant exposure to public affairs may be conducive to increased awareness of and knowledge about politics and government.

Although no self-perception data are available on this dimension, comparative data on panel respondents indicates that council members tend to be more politically knowledgeable. The differences between the two populations, however, are by and large not statistically significant on this cognitive dimension.[29] Table 5.12 compares cognition rates of community organizations specifically mentioned by the interviewer among council and panel respondents. These are rank ordered.

As can be seen from Table 5.12, cognition rates of community organizations are consistently higher for council respondents. Moreover, when asked whether they were familiar with any other community organizations in addition to the forementioned, 38 percent of council respondents are able to mention other organizations, compared with 12 percent of panel respondents. Finally, 87 percent of council members report having heard about protests, marches, and demonstrations which have taken place in East Los Angeles in the last few years, compared with 74 percent of panel respondents.[30]

Conclusions

Evaluation of the data presented to explore the hypothesis that advisory council membership is conducive to the acquisition of politically relevant skills and information is, in some ways, difficult. First of all, no comparative data are available for the population on the skill dimension, and, although the comparative data on the information dimension suggest that council members are more politically knowledgeable, the differences between the two populations are not, by and large, statistically significant. Moreover, the skill data presented are only reflective of a perceived ability to do certain things, not of actual behavior.

Notwithstanding these caveats, however, when one considers the close affinity between the open- and closed-ended responses to the skill probes and when one recalls that a review of the council setting revealed its potential as a learning experience, one must conclude tentatively that the council experience appears to be conducive to the acquisition of politically relevant skills and information. A more precise and more behaviorally grounded elaboration of this suggestion must again await future studies.

Although tentative, this finding is nevertheless of importance. The development of a propensity to affect government, the dimension discussed in the previous section, is of importance because it explores the salient question of _whether_ council members are inclined to try to affect government. The skills and information dimension explores their _capability_ to do so. Knowledge of organizational skills, knowing where to go to get things done, and learning the ropes of the system are by no means trivial questions to consider in the case of low-income individuals and in the particular case of Mexican-Americans. If, as has been argued, the policy of creating advisory councils composed of laymen and nonprofessional community representatives survives the War on Poverty programs that fostered it and if the tentative conclusions arrived at in this section are supported by future studies, the potential of advisory councils as a training ground for the development of capabilities to affect government appears great. Hence, these factors augur better prospects for the political organization of low-income communities.

### Development of Political Participation Behavior

The final dimension of politicization to be explored is a behavioral one, that is, is experience in advisory councils conducive to changes in the political behavior patterns of the members in the direction of increased activeness. Here it will be explored whether the changes in attitudes and skill levels tentatively identified in the previous sections are also embodied in actual political participation behavior. As previously discussed (in Chapter 2), this is an important dimension to explore given the hypothesized operation of the organizational involvement model and given the uncertain relation between changes in attitudes and subsequent (or concurrent) changes in behavior.

Considering first comparative data on the level of political activity of both panel and council respondents, one finds that council members are much more likely than panel respondents to participate in a variety of groups and organizations, more likely to be engaged in protest activity, and equally likely to engage in electoral activity in the form of voting. Comparative figures on associational membership are abstracted in Tables 5.13 and 5.14.

It should be noted here that council members appear to be involved heavily in the organizational life of the East Los Angeles community. Among those reporting organizational memberships, 72 percent belong to two organizations, 41 percent to three organizations, and 26 percent

TABLE 5.13

Membership in Organizations Among
Council and Panel Respondents
(in percent)

|  | Council | Panel |
|---|---|---|
| Yes | 74 | 19 |
| No | 26 | 81 |
|  | (N = 78) | (N = 43) |
|  | $X^2 = 29.26$ | (p = 0.001) |

Source: Compiled by the author.

TABLE 5.14

Membership in Religious Organizations Among
Council and Panel Respondents
(in percent)

|  | Council | Panel |
|---|---|---|
| Yes | 28 | 11 |
| No | 72 | 89 |
|  | (N = 78) | (N = 45) |
|  | $X^2 = 3.92$ | (p  0.05) |

Source: Compiled by the author.

to four or more organizations. Moreover, judging from their responses as to frequency of attendance and office holding in various organizations, by and large council members appear to be active members of the organizations to which they belong. The type of organizations council members tend to belong to are also worth noting. Generally, most council members are not active in explicitly political organizations such as political parties or political clubs but rather tend to be engaged predominantly in educational groups and community service organizations. Although not explicitly political, the extent to which some of these educational and community service organizations are

TABLE 5.15

Attendance at Protests, Marches, and Demonstrations
(among council and panel respondents
having heard of these)
(in percent)

|  | Council | Panel |
|---|---|---|
| Yes | 29 | 12 |
| No | 71 | 88 |
|  | (N = 69) | (N = 33) |
|  | $X^2 = 2.65$ | (p = 0.05) |

Source: Compiled by the author.

TABLE 5.16

Evaluation of Protest Activity
(among council and panel respondents
having heard of the protests)
(in percent)

|  | Council | Panel |
|---|---|---|
| Good for the community | 45 | 38 |
| Partly good, partly bad* | 12 | 3 |
| Bad for the community | 32 | 35 |
| Makes no difference | 9 | 15 |
| Don't know | 2 | 9 |
|  | (N = 69) | (N = 34) |

*The major reason put forth for the qualification "partly good and partly bad" among both groups was that, although they generally approved of protest activity, they deplored the violence that occasionally accompanies protests, marches, and demonstrations.

Source: Compiled by the author.

involved in politics should not be underestimated. Many of the organizations mentioned by the council respondents are involved intimately in bargaining with public bureaucracies, in planning and developing service type programs, in lobbying, and in obtaining funding support. This tends to support previously made arguments that definition of political participation behavior solely in terms of electoral activity is somewhat constrictive, overlooking as it does communal involvement.

In regard to more radically oriented political activity, both council and panel respondents were asked whether they attended any protests, marches, or demonstrations that have taken place in the East Los Angles community in the previous last few years to the study. As can be seen in Table 5.16, although council members are more likely to have participated in demonstrations, the differences between the two groups are not statistically significant.

That council respondents are also more likely to evaluate protest activity more favorably is suggested by Table 5.16. This becomes an important dimension to consider when exploring what type of leadership is likely to emerge from among the rank and file of advisory councils. This question is fully explored in Chapter 7.

Finally, in terms of electoral political activity, both groups exhibit similarly high rates of voter registration of voting. Comparative figures are abstracted in Table 5.17.

POLITICIZATION OF MEMBERS

TABLE 5.17

Electoral Behavior Among Council and Panel Respondents
(in percent)

|  | Council | Panel |
|---|---|---|
| Registered to vote | 61 | 65 |
| Voted in last presidential election among those registered to vote | 94 | 100 |

Source: Compiled by the author.

In addition to exploring the differences between council and panel respondents on the political participation dimension, the author also sought to explore the members' own subjective perceptions of changes in their political participation behavior. In this regard, council members were first asked to evaluate the impact of the council experience on their own involvement in community affairs.[31] As can be seen in Table 5.18, the majority of council members perceives that they have become _more_ involved in community affairs as a result of the council experience. Perceptions of increased involvement, moreover, are not related to the member's previous involvement in community affairs; that is, those who had been highly involved in community affairs before joining the council are just as likely to report increased involvement as those who had been previously inactive (see Table 5.19).

In an effort to determine whether perceptions of increased involvement were based on actual behavior changes, those reporting increased levels of involvement were further asked whether they had joined any

TABLE 5.18

Perception of Impact of Council Experience on Own
Involvement in Community Affairs
(in percent)

| | |
|---|---|
| Have become more involved | 64 |
| No difference | 23 |
| Have become less involved | 8 |
| Unable to judge | 6 |
| | (N = 79) |

Source: Compiled by the author.

TABLE 5.19

Perception of Impact of Council Experience on Own
Involvement in Community Affairs by Previous Involvement
(in percent)

| Previous Involvement | Impact of Council | | |
|---|---|---|---|
| | More Involved | Less Involved | No Difference |
| High | 56 | 17 | 28 |
| Medium | 63 | 8 | 29 |
| Low | 68 | 3 | 30 |
| | (N = 50) | (N = 6) $X^2 = 3.42$ (p > 0.05) | (N = 23) |

Source: Compiled by the author.

TABLE 5.20

Joining Community Organizations Subsequent to Council
Membership by Previous Involvement
(in percent)

| Previous Involvement | Joined Organizations | |
|---|---|---|
| | Yes | No |
| High | 25 | 75 |
| Medium | 26 | 74 |
| Low | 32 | 68 |
| | (N = 18) $X^2 = 0.32$ (p > 0.05) | (N = 45) |

Source: Compiled by the author.

community organizations or had become more active in organizations they belonged to since joining the council. Among those reporting increased involvement, 35 percent have joined community organizations,[32] and 37 percent report becoming more active in organizations to which they already belonged. It is interesting to note that joining community organizations after attaining council membership is not related to previous levels of community involvement; the previously active are just as likely to join new organizations as the previously inactive (see Table 5.20).

The fact that perceptions of increased community involvement and changes in behavior patterns are not associated with differential levels of previous community involvement suggests that council membership provides a "boost" in the member's level of political activity regardless of his previous activity or passivity. This notion is reinforced when one recalls that members also report learning new skills on the council regardless of their previous political participation behavior. This suggests that the council experience and the attendant exposure to public affairs could work to activate the previously inactive as well as to further politicize those who are already "participants."

Finally, the prospects for continued political involvement among council members appears to be high. When asked whether they planned to be active in community affairs after leaving the councils, the majority of respondents (73 percent) responded affirmatively. No differences between types of councils were evidenced on this probe.

Conclusions

On the basis of the data presented in this section, it appears reasonable to conclude that the council experience seems to work to increase the level of political participation of the members. Not only do the majority of members perceive that they have become more involved in community affairs, but also approximately one-fourth the members report actual changes in behavior in terms of joining new organizations and in terms of becoming more active in organizations to which they belonged already. Although the proportion of those actually reporting behavioral changes is relatively small, it is by no means negligible when one considers that the majority of respondents have been involved in the councils for a short period of time (median time is 1.7 years).

Also, one must note their generally low income level and large family size. In the latter respect, hard working conditions could hinder the member's ability to be active in a variety of groups and organizations in addition to his council involvement. This possibility was suggested by a number of respondents who answered that although they wanted to become active in other groups, they had not yet done so because of work-related constraints.

Summarizing our findings up to this point, the data presented offer both support for and some modification of organizational involvement model. The reader should recall that the organizational involvement model (as conceptualized by Verba, Nie, and their associates) was found to operate independently of socioeconomic status and of enabling orientations. In essence, political participation in this model was viewed as a direct by-product of organizational involvement, independent of cognitions and evaluations of government and of self-images as political actors. On the one hand, a major part of the analysis above has been to explore whether organizational involvement in the context of advisory councils is indeed associated with higher levels of political participation behavior than would be expected generally from individuals of similar SES status. As the previous discussion has shown, council members exhibit higher rates of political participation behavior than individuals of similar SES status and, additionally, tend to perceive that their involvement in community affairs has increased as a result of their organizational experience. The data presented thus fully support the operation of the organizational involvement model as elaborated by Verba, Nie, and their associates.

Another major purpose of the analysis, however, was to explore in more detail the operation of the organizational involvement model. In addition to testing its relationship to political participation behavior, the author sought to explore whether organizational involvement is also conducive to the acquisition of those "enabling attitudes" for political participation (usually associated with the SES model) and to the acquisition of capabilities to affect government. The underlying assumption behind the latter line of inquiry was that acquisition of "participant" orientations and capabilities would foster a more enduring tendency to participate in political life. In this connection, the reader should recall that research by Goldrich and others in Latin America—while supporting the general operation of organizational involvement as an alternative route to political participation—also raised a number of questions about its durability. The data presented in the first part of this chapter suggest that involvement in advisory councils appears to be conducive to increases in other dimensions of politicization besides political participation: that is, to increases in political awareness, in political efficacy, and in political capabilities. Thus, Verba and Nie's unidimensional model of organizational involvement as an alternative route to political participation should be revised to include other dimensions of politicization.

## THE CORRELATES OF POLITICIZATION

The second part of this chapter further explores the dynamics of organizational involvement as a politicization mechanism by (1) focusing on the organizational correlates of politicization (under what conditions is politicization likely to be hindered or facilitated?) and (2) by exploring what types of individuals appear to be most affected by the organizational experience.

Before undertaking this analysis, however, efforts were made to reduce the large number of politicization variables in this study so far into a smaller number of indices for the sake of more manageable and parsimonious analysis. This was done through factor analysis, which is ideally suited for these purposes.[33] As Fred Kerlinger put it,

> Factor analysis serves the cause of scientific parsimony. Generally speaking, if two tests measure the same thing, the scores obtained from them can be added together. If, on the other hand, the two tests do not measure the same thing, their scores cannot be added together. Factor analysis tells us, in effect, what tests or measures can be added and studied together rather than separately. It thus limits the variables with which the scientist must cope. It also (hopefully) helps the scientist to locate and identify unities or fundamental properties underlying tests and measures.[34]

Several separate factor analyses were made on the politicization data.[35] All politicization variables for which comparative measures for the panel study were available and significant differences between the council and panel samples had been found[36] were first factor analyzed. Subsequently, all the additional politicization variables present only in the council sample were also factor analyzed.

Although the author conceptually had posited three distinct dimensions of politicization (that is, "propensity to affect government," "capabilities to affect government," and "political participation behavior,") the factor analyses revealed that a number of the measures conceptually grouped to define these three dimensions did not form separate factors empirically. More specifically, considering the "propensity to affect government" first, the measures used to define this dimension do not form a separate and distinct factor, but rather four separate factors. These are (1) awareness of government's impact (both national and local), (2) evaluation of government (national, local, and evaluation of school outputs), (3) political efficacy (both national and local), and (4) self-efficacy (all passivity-activity items). Factor loadings for these items are shown in Table 5.21.

In terms of the second dimension—capabilities to affect government in the form of political skills and political information—the relationships among the political skills items were analyzed first. All political skills items were found to be intercorrelated highly with one another at the 0.001 level of significance or better. On the basis of these results, an additive scale consisting of "skills learned from the council" items was constructed. This scale, however, was not correlated sufficiently with the political information items to form a single separate factor. It is interesting to note in this regard that the political knowledge or information items not only did not load on the same factor as the skills items but also did not load on the "awareness of government"

TABLE 5.21

Factor Loadings of Politicization Items

|  | (1) | (2) | (3) | (4) | (5) |
|---|---|---|---|---|---|
| Evaluation of school outputs | 0.36 | 0.008 | -0.12 | 0.13 | 0.11 |
| Evaluation of local government | 0.54 | 0.02 | 0.18 | 0.07 | 0.17 |
| Evaluation of national government | 0.80 | 0.06 | 0.13 | -0.09 | 0.14 |
| Local political efficacy | -0.23 | 0.52 | 0.24 | 0.30 | 0.01 |
| National political efficacy | 0.05 | 0.97 | 0.10 | 0.11 | -0.08 |
| Awareness of local government | 0.17 | -0.05 | 0.56 | 0.14 | -0.18 |
| Awareness of national government | 0.00 | 0.21 | 0.56 | -0.01 | -0.04 |
| Political participation: belong to community organizations | 0.08 | 0.17 | 0.11 | 0.74 | -0.14 |
| Political participation: Voting | -0.06 | -0.06 | -0.00 | 0.26 | 0.35 |
| Making plans brings unhappiness because plans are hard to fulfill | 0.01 | 0.02 | 0.03 | -0.17 | 0.76 |
| It doesn't make any difference who gets elected, nothing changes | -0.04 | -0.08 | -0.30 | -0.15 | 0.72 |
| Ought not to worry about the future | -0.10 | 0.05 | -0.03 | -0.03 | 0.38 |
| Secret of life is not expecting too much | 0.00 | -0.07 | -0.29 | 0.02 | 0.79 |
| Cognition of organizations mentioned by interviewer | 0.09 | -0.19 | 0.05 | -0.11 | 0.57 |
| Involvement in community organizations mentioned by interviewer | -0.01 | 0.02 | -0.02 | 0.12 | 0.09 |

Source: Compiled by the author.

factor. This suggests that diffuse cognitions of the impact of government at both national and local levels are not related necessarily to recognition of specific outputs or to knowledge about particular political events, organizations, and the like.

In terms of the political participation behavior items, the only two items loading together on the same factor were voting and belonging to community organizations.[37] Other political participation behavioral items as well as perceptions of changes in behavior items, which were used exclusively in the council sample, tended to load separately on several different factors.

In summary, on the basis of the results obtained through factor analysis procedures, the original three dimensions of politicization can be reformulated as the following empirically distinct politicization dimensions:

(1)  evaluation of government (EVALUATION);
(2)  awareness of government (AWARENESS);
(3)  mastery over one's destiny (PERSONAL EFFICACY);
(4)  political efficacy (POLITICAL EFFICACY);
(5)  political participation behavior—voting and belonging to community organizations (PARTICIPATION);
(6)  political skills learned from the council (SKILLS); and
(7)  perceptions of changes in political participation behavior (PERCEPTION OF CHANGES).

It should be noted here that the first five dimensions (on which comparative measures are available for the panel study) also were found to be distinct empirically when factor analyzed in the panel sample. (The only exception was that voting did not load together with belonging to community organizations in the panel sample.) It should also be noted that the last dimension (PERCEPTION OF CHANGES) consists of a single measure, that is, evaluation of the impact of the council experience on one's involvement in community affairs. Given that measures of perceptions of behavioral changes did not load together in a conceptually meaningful sense, only this measure has been retained for further analysis.

Once additive indices composed of those items loading together on separate factors were constructed,[38] the author sought to explore the organizational and member-related correlates of each dimension of politicization.

## Organizational Correlates of Politicization

The analysis in this section is primarily exploratory in character, for few hypotheses have been developed on which organizational

conditions are likely to hinder or facilitate the development of politicization. The work of Verba and Nie, however, does suggest two such conditions. Their data analysis reveals that the operation of the organizational model is enhanced when (1) the individual member is active within the organization and (2) when the organizational setting offers opportunities for exposure to specifically political stimuli. The major explanatory factor for these authors is the individual's active involvement within the organization, because "the individual who is a passive member of one or more organizations is no more likely to be active in politics than the individual who belongs to no such association."[39]
In terms of the second variable, exposure to political stimuli within the organization, the authors suggest that when the members are exposed to political discussions in the organization, this form of political stimuli tends to enhance only the active member's involvement in politics. However, when the organizational setting provides exposure to political stimuli in the form of the organization's involvement in community affairs, "passive members are a bit more likely than non-members to be active in politics." As the advisory councils clearly represent an example of organizations that expose their members to political stimuli through "involvement in community affairs," one does not expect individual activeness within the organization to be as key a factor in the development of politicization as is suggested by the Verba and Nie data.

In an effort to determine under what conditions politicization is likely to be enhanced in the particular organizational setting of the advisory councils, the relationship between each dimension of politicization and a wide variety of organizationally related variables was explored. The latter can be divided into two broad categories: (1) variables measuring different council-related conditions and (2) variables measuring the members' own role and activities within the council. Under the first category, council-related conditions, the following variables were examined: (1) type of council; (2) type of activities undertaken by the council; (3) evaluations of council performance in terms of perceptions of unsuccessful projects, perceptions of the council's effect on the community, and overall evaluations of the council; and (4) power configurations within the council in terms of perception of power relations within the council and perceptions of council-agency relationships. In terms of the second broad category, council-member variables, the author sought to explore the relationship between each dimension of politicization and the following variables: (1) how long the respondent had been a member of the council, (2) how the respondent was recruited, (3) reasons for joining the council, (4) the extent of the member's own activeness within the council,[40] and (5) the member's perception of the extent of his own influence within the council.

Before discussing the relationships between each dimension of politicization and the organizationally related variables, it should be noted that the data available to explore what organizational conditions tend to hinder or facilitate the development of politicization are, in some respects, limited. In the first place, all these measures consist solely of the members' reports of their own perceptions. Although this kind of data is sufficient to determine the influence of most of the member-council related variables, it is more limited when it comes to determining how particular variations in the organizational setting bear on the development of politicization. When it comes to considering, for example, the effects of the power configuration of the councils, survey data is more limited than other available methods, such as participant observation. Moreover, the large number of councils present in the sample presents both distinct advantages and disadvantages for the present analysis. On the one hand, the large number of councils represented enhances the capabilities to generalize about any relationships established. On the other hand, the variety of councils represented and the attendant variety in organizational settings well may obfuscate more idiosyncratic organizational determinants of politicization.

Considering first _personal efficacy_, or a sense of mastery over one's destiny, one finds that this politicization dimension is significantly related (at the 0.05 level or better) to three council variables: power configuration within the council, the respondent's perception of his own influence within the council, and the respondent's activeness within the council. In terms of the first variable, 64 percent of respondents reporting that "everyone has equal influence on the council" also rate "high" on the self-efficacy scale, contrasted with 36 percent of those reporting unequal distributions of influence within the council. Similarly, 74 percent of those respondents who feel that they have "a great deal or a moderate" amount of influence on what gets decided on the council rate high on self-efficacy, compared with 21 percent of those who feel that they have little or no influence. In terms of the member's activeness within the council, 57 percent of those who are highly active within the council are also highly self-efficacious, compared with 28 percent of those who rate either medium or low on the activity index. Those who are more self-efficacious are also more likely to perceive that the council has had significant effects on the community, although this relationship is not statistically significant.

Although it is not within the bounds of this book to entangle the causal path of the association between self-efficacy and the council variables mentioned (that is, which comes first), a possible interpretation of these findings is that an "open" organizational environment coupled with high involvement on the member's part could be conducive to an increased sense of ability to manipulate one's environment. This interpretation parallels findings in studies on industrial democracy in which clear connections between involvement in organizational decision making and increased self-efficacy have been established.[41]

Considering next the correlates of _political efficacy_, one finds that this dimension of politicization appears to be associated with a number of council-related variables, although none of the relationships is statistically significant. First, political efficacy is related to type of council. Sixty-one percent of members from "other" councils rate high on the political efficacy scale, compared with 36 percent of school council members. That is probably because members from "other" councils tend to have more previous experience in community affairs is also suggested by the fact that previous involvement is associated with political efficacy (although the relationship is not statistically significant). As self-efficacy, political efficacy appears to be related to the member's perception of his own influence within the council (57 percent of those who feel that they have a great or moderate amount of influence within the council also rate highly on political efficacy, as compared with 40 percent of those who have little or no influence). Those who are highly efficacious are also more likely to perceive that the council affects the community; and, finally, they are more likely to perceive problems in the council's relations with the agency.

Evaluations of government, which as noted earlier were mostly negative, are related significantly to lack of success of the councils and to perceptions of problems in the operation of the councils. This finding is of interest for it suggests that council members may tend to make generalizations about overall government performance on the basis of their exposure to public agencies in the course of carrying out council goals. Evaluation of government is related (at the 0.03 significance level) to reports of lack of success of projects undertaken by the council. Also, those who are negative about government are more likely to report problems in the relationship between the council and the agency (significant at the 0.05 level).

Other relationships discovered, although not statistically significant, tend to reinforce the association between negative views of council operation and performance and negative views of government. Those who think that the government is not run well or is run "in between" also tend to evaluate the performance of the council in more negative terms. Moreover, those dissatisfied with government are more likely to perceive that the council has failed to affect the community. Finally, members from "other" councils are more likely to express negative views about government, paralleling their generally more negative views of the councils.

Awareness of government's impact on one's life is also significantly related to perceptions of unsuccessful projects (at the 0.05 level). As with negative evaluations of government, awareness of the effects of the government appears to increase when council members face internal or external obstacles to the accomplishment of particular goals. High awareness of government is also more predominant among those who perceive problems in council-agency relations, although this relationship is not statistically significant. Finally, members from "other" councils tend to be more aware of the impact of government on their lives, although this relationship also is not significant.

The similarities between the correlates of awareness of government and of government evaluation are worth brief commentary. These findings suggest that, as conflict levels within the council rise and as council members face internal or external obstacles in the resolution of particular issues or in the accomplishment of particular goals, they become more aware of the power and importance of government and become more dissatisfied with overall government responsiveness and performance. "Negativism" toward government, in this respect, could be reflective of frustration and thwarted attempts to influence the operation of the particular public agency the council is attached to or other, outside agencies. This interpretation can be supported by the fact that only the awareness and evaluation dimensions of politicization are related to evaluations of council performance or to problems in goal attainment. As shall be seen, none of the other politicization dimensions is related to assessments of council effectiveness.

Finally, considering the three remaining dimensions of politicization, participation, perception of increased involvement, and skill learning, one finds that these dimensions appear to be more independent of particular variations in the organizational setting than other dimensions of politicization. No statistically significant relationships between participation and any organizational variables were found. Perceptions of increased involvement were found to be only highly correlated (at the 0.003 level) with activeness within the council; 76 percent of those who rate high on the council activity index perceive that they have become more involved in community affairs, as contrasted with 26 percent of those who are rather inactive within the council. Learning skills, as has been discussed, is largely unrelated to organizational conditions. However, 68 percent of those rating "high" on the learned skills scale also rate high on the activity within the council index. In comparison, only 8 percent of the "inactive" rate high on skill learning.

These findings suggest that the council experience itself and, to a lesser extent, the member's active involvement within the council could be the prime determinants of acquisition of political skills and of increased levels of political involvement. Although this tends to support Verba and Nie's hypotheses about the importance of organizational settings that expose their members to political stimuli in the form of the organization's involvement in community affairs coupled with the member's activeness within the organization, the most important correlate of increased participation and skill acquisition in the case of the advisory councils appears to be the opportunities for exposure to public affairs afforded by the council setting.

In summary, these findings (abstracted in Table 5.22) suggest that some dimensions of politicization are affected by variations in the organizational setting, but others are not. Personal efficacy is associated with "active" membership within an "open" organizational environment. High awareness of government and negative evaluations

TABLE 5.22

Organizational Correlates of Dimensions of Politicization

| Self-efficacy | Political efficacy |
|---|---|
| Power configurations within the council (significant) | Perception of own influence within the council |
| Perception of own influence within the council (significant) | Council has affected the community |
| Council has affected the community | Problems in agency-council relations |
| Evaluation of government | Type of council |
| Unsuccessful projects (significant) | Awareness of government's impact |
| Problems in council-agency relations (significant) | Unsuccessful projects (significant) |
| Negative evaluation of councils | Problems in council-agency relations |
| Type of council | Type of council |
| Acquisition of skills | Perception of increased involvement |
| Activeness within the council | Activeness within the council (significant) |

Source: Compiled by the author.

of government are associated with problems in goal attainment within the organization. Skill learning and increased involvement in community affairs, on the other hand, appear to be primarily a by-product of the exposure to public affairs afforded by the council setting. The relationship between dimensions of politicization and variations in the organizational setting suggested here should be tested further in alternative contexts and through the use of more direct and systematic observational methodologies, particularly participant observation.

Who is Most Affected by the Organizational Experiment

In a final effort to explore the dynamics of the organizational involvement model, this section will focus on the type of individual who is most likely to be politicized as a result of the organizational experience. This question is of great interest for it may offer further insights as to the potential effectiveness of deliberate government policies to raise the level of political participation of low-income individuals.

To see who is most affected, it seems logical to focus on those respondents who report that their attitudes, opinions, or behavior have changed as a result of the council experience. The reader should recall that in earlier parts of this chapter it was noted that on every retrospective pretest measure available, between one-fourth and one-fifth of the responses reported changes in attitudes and orientations toward government, in levels of political involvement, and in self-images as political actors as a result of the council experience. It was further shown that the direction of these changes was, by and large, consistently in the direction of increased politicization.

Efforts to identify a "most changed" group were first made by identifying all those individuals reporting a change on any "before and after" politicization measure. This task proved to be insufficiently discriminating because on two of these measures (perceptions of skill learning and perceptions of increased involvement) the majority of council respondents had reported changes. These two measures thus were eliminated from the analysis to obtain sufficient variation between a "most changed" group and the rest of the sample. Focusing solely on "before" and "after" measures related to (1) awareness of local and national governments, (2) evaluation of local and national government, (3) local and national political efficacy, and (4) political involvement (in the form of joining organizations subsequent to council membership as well as becoming more active in organizations the respondent belonged one finds that 68 percent of the sample reports changes on one or more of these dimensions. This relatively large proportion suggests that the council experience affects _most_ of the respondents on _some_ aspect of politicization, thus adding further credence to the major question posed in this study.

Selection of a "most changed" group was based finally on the following criteria: individuals were classified as "most changed" if they reported two or more instances of changes on any of the eight retrospective pretest measures (this excludes reports of skill learning and reports of increased involvement). According to these criteria, 43 percent of the sample (N = 34) could be classified as "most changed."[42] Discussion of the characteristics of those respondents who appear to be most affected by the council experience is divided into three parts: the first part discusses their personal attributes and characteristics, the second part explores their role as council members, and the third part focuses on their political attitudes and behavior.

Personal Attributes and Characteristics

The respondents who appear to be most affected by the council experience tend to be members of the lower socioeconomic strata. In terms of family income, 77 percent of the "change" group earns less than $10,000 a year compared with 58 percent of the remaining sample. Moreover, 42 percent report incomes under $5,000, compared with 30 percent of the other respondents. This finding is of interest, for it suggests that the much-disputed "maximum feasible participation" policy indeed may be reaching those individuals it aimed to affect: those who are more poor and less educated.

In terms of demographic characteristics, those in the "change" category tend to be older[43] and more female.[44] Additionally, "change" and other respondents are equally likely to have been born in the United States and to be American citizens. Among those who are immigrants,[45] however, "change" respondents tend to have been in the United States longer[46] but are more "newcomers" to the East Los Angeles community.[47]

A final characteristic of interest in this section is the individual's previous involvement in community affairs. No differences between groups were evidenced on this measure; both "change" and other respondents are equally likely to have been previously active or inactive. This appears to support suggestions made earlier that the council experience may work to both activate the previously inactive as well as to further politicize those who are already experienced in politics.

Council-Related Variables

In regard to council-related variables, members of both groups are equally likely to be either school advisory council members or belong to "other" types of advisory councils. Regardless of the type of council to which they belong, however, "change" respondents are more likely to have been members longer.[48] "Change" respondents tend to be more active in council affairs,[49] yet they are equally as likely as other respondents to perceive that they have a high or low amount of personal influence on what gets decided by the council.

Respondents who appear to be most negative in their evaluations of the councils and to report problems in the operation of the council. In this respect, a larger proportion of "change" respondents reports lack of success in implementing council projects[50] and tends to point more readily to problems in agency-council relations.[51] Moreover, fewer "change" respondents believe that the council has affected the community,[52] and fewer evaluate council performance favorably on the summary evaluation probe.[53]

Notwithstanding their generally more negative evaluations of the councils, "change" respondents are considerably more likely than other respondents to rate high on the "learned skills" scale and to perceive that they have become more involved in community affairs.[54]

Two findings reviewed in this section are worth a brief commentary. First, the fact that those who are more affected by the council experience are those who have been on the council for a longer period of time calls attention to length of membership as another relevant variable in the development of politicization. In the previous discussion of the correlates of politicization this variable had not emerged as significant. Second, the fact that those who are affected the most are also more negative about council performance reaffirms a basic assumption underlying this study, that is, whether councils have decision-making power and whether they are effective, the council experience itself is conducive to increases on some dimensions of politicization.

Political Attitudes and Behavior

"Change" respondents tend to be more politically efficacious than "other" respondents,[55] more negative in their evaluations of government at both local and national levels,[56] and more likely to have been participants in protest activity.[57] Although this particular combination of characteristics is supposed to make them more prone to favor radical political activity according to William Gamson, the data are conflicting on this question. On the one hand, "change" respondents are more likely to report that the protests that have occurred in the East Los Angeles community in the previous few years are "good for the community."[58] Yet on the other hand, when asked what strategies should be followed to solve problems in the community, they are less likely to favor what might be called the more radical alternatives: engage in street demonstrations,[59] riot if necessary,[60] and form separate political parties for Mexican-Americans only.[61]

The only other differences between the two groups in regard to political attitudes and behavior are that those in the "change" group appear to be more "ethnically" aware than other respondents. They are, for example, more likely to identify themselves as "Chicano" and "Mexican-American,"[62] more likely to perceive that the dominant society is more discriminatory,[63] and more likely to favor Mexican-American political organizations[64] and coalition formation with black Americans.[65] This raises the possibility that another force, that of group consciousness, could be operative on these council members. This possibility is fully explored in Chapter 6.

## POLITICIZATION: A PRODUCT OF "SELF-SELECTION"?

As has been seen, council members differ significantly from individuals of similar socioeconomic status on most dimensions of politicization. Council members tend to be more politically aware, more self-efficacious, more politically efficacious, and more involved in community affairs than the referent comparison group, the 1972 East Los Angeles panel respondents. Moreover, it has been shown also that the council members tend to perceive that their political attitudes and behavior have undergone changes during membership on the council. These changes were found to be consistently in the direction of increased politicization. The data presented tentatively suggest that there exists a close association between council membership and higher levels of politicization.

Whether higher levels of politicization can be attributed to council membership in a causal fashion will be impossible to ascertain in this study given the lack of appropriate pretest measures. Nevertheless, consideration of plausible rival hypotheses could work to enhance the prospects of the existence of such a relationship. Two major rival hypotheses have been posited. First, higher levels of politicization perhaps could be attributable to a rise in ethnic consciousness. It should be recalled that Verba and Nie have suggested that "group awareness" serves as another substitution mechanism, which "bypasses those processes which lead those with higher SES to participate more and those with lower SES to participate less." They have illustrated this phenomenon with the case of black Americans. As also discussed, manifestations of a rise in ethnic consciousness in the population under study, Mexican-Americans, are numerous. Because of the importance of this alternative explanation and because it requires extensive discussion, group consciousness as an alternative explanation for higher levels of politicization is explored in detail in the next chapter.

The second rival hypothesis posited is that council members, although highly similar to panel respondents on socioeconomic and demographic characteristics, originally differed from panel respondents on politicization measures. This is what has been called the "self-selection" factor. It appears appropriate to explore the explanatory value of this alternative hypothesis at this point, given that the construction and presentation of politicization indices in the second part of this chapter now allow for more parsimonious comparisons.

In the council sample there is an explicit item on the basis of which the member's level of political activity prior to council membership can be categorized; no corresponding measures are available for the panel respondents. Thus one is forced to make some assumptions about the level of communal involvement of the panel sample. Considering then that the panel study represents a cross section of the population

TABLE 5.23

Personal Efficacy Among Council and Panel Respondents
Controlling for Council Members' "Self-Selection"
(in percent)

| Self-Efficacy | Council | Panel |
|---|---|---|
| Low | 24 | 39 |
| Medium | 39 | 45 |
| High | 37 | 16 |
|  | (N = 59) | (N = 44) |
|  | $X^2 = 6.20$ | $(p = 0.05)$ |

Source: Compiled by the author.

POLITICIZATION OF MEMBERS

TABLE 5.24

Political Efficacy Among Panel and Council Respondents
Controlling for Council Members' "Self-Selection"
(in percent)

| Political Efficacy | Council | | Panel |
|---|---|---|---|
| Low | 35 | | 66 |
| Medium | 28 | | 19 |
| High | 37 | | 14 |
| | (N = 60) $X^2 = 10.5$ | (p = 0.01) | (N = 42) |

Source: Compiled by the author.

TABLE 5.25

Awareness of Government Among Council and Panel
Respondents Controlling for Council
Members' "Self-Selection"
(in percent)

| Awareness | Council | | Panel |
|---|---|---|---|
| Low | 28 | | 38 |
| Medium | 57 | | 50 |
| High | 16 | | 12 |
| | (N = 58) $X^2 = 1.28$ | (p > 0.05) | (N = 42) |

Source: Compiled by the author

(and, as such, includes some individuals who are totally uninvolved in community affairs as well as some who are somewhat involved), it seems appropriate to compare the panel respondents solely with those council members who were inactive in community affairs prior to council membership and with those who were "somewhat" involved, excluding from the analysis those individuals who were "deeply" involved in community affairs (who, by definition, were already activists). These comparisons are presented in Tables 5.23 to 5.26.[66]

TABLE 5.26

Involvement in Community Organizations Among Council and Panel Respondents Controlling for Council Members' "Self-Selection"
(in percent)

|     | Council | Panel |
| --- | --- | --- |
| Yes | 70 | 19 |
| No  | 30 | 81 |
|     | (N = 60) | (N = 43) |
|     | $X^2 = 24.47$ | |
|     | (p = 0.001) | |

Source: Compiled by the author.

Tables 5.23 to 5.26 reveal that the council members' higher levels of politicization are not a product of their previous involvement. With the exception of awareness of government,[67] the differences between the two samples on all other measures of politicization remain statistically significant after controls for previous involvement have been introduced. This warrants, it would seem, rejecting the alternative hypothesis that higher levels of politicization can be attributed to a "self-selection" factor.

Next will be a discussion of the other major rival hypothesis, group consciousness, in light of the attitudinal and behavioral changes that have occurred in the community under study since 1965.

NOTES

1. For a discussion of this statistical test, see Sidney Siegel, <u>Nonparametric Statistics for the Behavioral Sciences</u> (New York: McGraw Hill, 1956), pp. 104-111. It should be noted here that five

respondents in the panel study were members of advisory councils. To approximate a "treatment" versus "nontreatment" design (treatment defined as council membership), these cases were dropped from the analysis of panel responses. Unless otherwise indicated, these are not included in any tables or statistical computations.

    2. Percentages may not add up to 100 percent because of rounding. Also, percentages presented in all tables have been adjusted for missing values unless otherwise indicated.

    3. Donald T. Campbell and Julian C. Stanley, Experimental and Quasi-Experimental Designs for Research (Chicago: Rand McNally, 1963), p. 35.

    4. Ninety-four percent of those reporting a change fall in the category of the local government having "great effect" or "some effect."

    5. See Gabriel A. Almond and Sidney Verba, The Civic Culture (Boston: Little, Brown and Co., 1965); and Carl P. Hensler, "The Structure of Orientations Toward Government: Involvement, Efficacy, and Evaluation," paper presented at the Annual Meeting of the American Political Science Association, September 7-11, 1971, Chicago.

    6. No comparable measure is available for the panel respondents in this case.

    7. Kendall's tau and Spearman's rho are generally considered to be the appropriate type of correlation measure for the ordinal data that characterizes this study. However, by no means does agreement exist about what kinds of correlation measures should be used. Although some suggest that only nonparametric correlations (Spearman's rho, and Kendall's tau) should be used with ordinal data, others maintain that Pearson's r correlations, generally necessary for input into more complex multivariate analysis such as factor analysis, yield approximately the same type of results. A comparison of results obtained through the use of parametric and nonparametric correlations on these data tends to support the latter view. The results obtained by alternatively using Kendall's tau, Spearman's rho, and Pearson r correlations on the politicization data are highly congruent and warrant, in the author's opinion, using Pearson correlations to do more complex multivariate analysis. This question is further discussed in a subsequent section of this chapter.

    8. The factor analysis procedures utilized are explained in the second part of this chapter.

    9. This is also further discussed in a subsequent section of this chapter.

    10. The scale reads,

1. "Making plans only brings unhappiness because the plans are hard to fulfill.
2. It doesn't make much difference if the people elect one or another candidate, for nothing will change.

3. With things as they are today, an intelligent person ought to think only about the present without worrying about what is going to happen tomorrow.
4. The secret of happiness is not expecting too much out of life and being content with what comes your way." (Q. 104).

11. For a discussion of the meaning of this scale, see Leo Grebler, Joan W. Moore, and Ralph C. Guzman, The Mexican American People (New York: The Free Press, 1970), pp. 436-438.

12. For a critique of "culture of poverty" theories, see Charles A. Valentine, Culture and Poverty: Critique and Counter-proposals (Chicago: University of Chicago Press, 1968); and Eleanor Burke Leacock, The Culture of Poverty: A Critique (New York: Simon and Schuster, 1971).

13. On this point, see particularly Edward C. Banfield, The Unheavenly City Revisited:(Boston: Little, Brown and Co., 1974).

14. This question follows a direct probe on the respondent's hopes and fears for the future and reads, "Here is a picture of a ladder (HAND RESPONDENT A CARD). Suppose that we say that the top of the ladder (POINT) represents the best possible life for you and that the bottom of the ladder (POINT) represents the worst possible life for you. Where on the ladder (MOVE FINGER UP AND DOWN) do you feel that you personally stand at the present time? Where on the ladder would you say you stood about seven years ago? And where on the ladder do you think you will be five years from now?" Adapted from Hadley Cantril, The Pattern of Human Concerns (New Brunswick, N.J.: Rutgers University Press, 1965).

15. Comparative with the panel and absolute in the sense that 9.5 is very close to the top limit.

16. Following probes as to their own hopes and fears for themselves, respondents were asked to state their hopes and fears for the future of the community and to similarly situate the past, present, and future of the community.

17. Also reported as median levels. The corresponding medians for the panel sample are 4.9, 4.5, and 6.0.

18. See Table 4.1, page 92 above.

19. It can certainly be argued that there is perhaps no better measure of an "ability to defer present gratifications for future goals" than a heavy emphasis on education.

20. For an excellent discussion of the functions and operation of "social trust," see Nicholas P. Lovrich, Jr., "Political Culture and Civic Involvement: A Comparative Analysis of Immigrant Ethnic Communities in San Pedro, California," Ph.D. dissertation, University of California at Los Angeles, 1971.

21. Alexis de Tocqueville, Democracy in America, edited and abridged by Richard D. Heffner (New York: New American Library, 1956).

22. "Less" and "more" are used because some of the panel respondents are also members of organizations.

23. Norman H. Nie, G. Bingham Powell, Jr., and Kenneth Prewitt, "Social Structure and Political Participation: Developmental Relationships, Part II," American Political Science Review 63, no. 3 (September 1969): 808-832.

24. Of those rating "high" and "medium" on previous involvement, 49 percent are trustful on "social trust" item 1 compared with 26 percent of those rating "low" on previous involvement. On "social trust" item 2, the corresponding proportions are 53 percent versus 30 percent; on item 3, 56 percent versus 31 percent.

25. Interviewers were instructed to repeat the choices for each item mentioned.

26. Chapter 3, Note 24.

27. In this respect, it could certainly be argued that even the realization that councils do not have any power requires a minimal amount of political knowledge and sophistication.

28. See Chapter 4, p. 89.

29. They are statistically significant for cognition of the Brown Berets, Chicano Liberation Front, MECHA, TELACU, and Neighborhood Legal Aid.

30. In regard to cognitions of War on Poverty programs, it has already been mentioned that 82 percent of council respondents report having heard about the War on Poverty and that most are able to mention specific programs.

31. Question reads, "As a result of your experience on the advisory council would you say that you have become more involved in community affairs, less involved, or did the advisory council experience make no difference?"

32. Among those joining community organizations after being members of the council, the majority seem to join community service type of organizations and educational groups. Also, 28 percent of those joining community organizations join two organizations; 28 percent join three organizations; and 17 percent join four organizations.

33. The use of factor analysis on the type of ordinal data that characterizes this study, however, is subject to controversy. This controversy revolves primarily around the use of parametric statistics (for example, Pearson correlation coefficients) as input into the factor matrix. As previously mentioned, a comparison of correlation coefficients obtained by alternatively using Spearman's rho, Kendall's tau, and Pearson r correlation coefficients yielded highly similar results. [On this point, Garson, who appears highly critical of the use of factor analysis for other than interval level data, suggests that "although Kendall's tau is not directly comparable to Pearson's r in magnitude, it does tend to be significant at the same level for the same data." (p. 182).] Moreover, no manageable nonparametric statistical tests are available for exploring relationships among a large number of variables. As Verba and Nie put it, "To deal with the question of the

empirical structure of participation in a systematic way implies, almost by definition, the use of parametric statistics." (p. 404). Given the high degree of congruence found among correlational techniques and given the lack of appropriate nonparametric alternative techniques, the use of factor analysis as a data reduction method in this study appears warranted and, moreover, superior to the construction of indices solely based on "face validity." For opposing views on the use of factor analysis on ordinal data, see "Some Methodological Notes on Our Use of Parametric Statistics," in Sidney Verba and Norman H. Nie, Participation in America: Political Democracy and Social Equality (New York: Harper and Row, 1972), pp. 403-410; and G. David Garson, Handbook of Political Science Methods (Boston: Holbrook Press, 1971), pp. 201-212. For a general explanation of factor analysis, see Raymond B. Cattell, Factor Analysis: An Introduction and Manual for the Psychologist and Social Scientist (New York: Harper and Brothers, 1952); and Benjamin Fruchter, Introduction to Factor Analysis (Princeton: D. Van Nostrand Co., 1954).

34. Fred N. Kerlinger, Foundations of Behavioral Research (New York: Holt, Rinehart, and Winston, 1965), p. 650.

35. The SPSS factor analysis programs were utilized (see Norman H. Nie, Dale H. Brent, and C. Hadlai Hull, Statistical Package for the Social Sciences (New York: McGraw Hill, 1970), pp. 208-238. All factor solutions were orthogonally rotated using the Varimax method.

36. The only exceptions were evaluation of government and voting (no significant differences between samples had been found on these variables). Additionally, the SRC political efficacy scale was excluded from the factor analysis for reasons mentioned earlier.

37. Note, however, that the loading of the voting item is fairly low.

38. Scales were created by simply adding together those variables that had loaded together on a separate factor. (These were not weighted).

39. Verba and Nie, op. cit., pp. 186-187.

40. An "activity" index was formulated on the following basis: members were classified as "low" if they reported attending 50 percent or less of council meetings, "medium" if they reported attending 50 to 100 percent of council meetings, and "high" if they (1) attended meetings 50 to 100 percent of the time and (2) had held office on the council or had participated in committees.

41. See Chapter 2, p. 31.

42. That this is a "most changed" group is further suggested by the fact that over 50 percent of this subsample report more than two changes. Moreover, a few respondents exhibit perfect "change" scores (8).

43. Seventy-four percent are older than 35, compared with 60 percent of other respondents.

44. Seventy-one percent are female, compared with 59 percent in the remainder of the sample.

45. Thirty-five percent in both groups.
46. Ninety-two percent have been in the United States longer than 10 years, compared with 62 percent of other respondents.
47. Forty-seven percent have been in the community less than 10 years, compared with 36 percent of the other group.
48. Seventy-one percent have been members longer than a year, compared with 59 percent of the other respondents.
49. Sixty-seven percent rate "high" on the activity index, versus 50 percent of the other respondents.
50. Sixty-one percent versus 50 percent report lack of success in particular projects.
51. Forty-eight percent versus 41 percent report problems in agency-council relations.
52. Eighty percent versus 91 percent believe that the council has affected the community.
53. Thirty-eight percent versus 28 percent evaluate council performance negatively.
54. It should be recalled that these two "change" measures had been excluded from the criteria for selection of the "change" group. Eighty-two percent of the "change" group versus 50 percent of the "other" group perceive that they have become more involved in community affairs (this relationship is significant at the 0.0006 level). Also, 91 percent report learning "new things," versus 67 percent of the remainder of the sample ($p = 0.02$). Finally, 82 percent of the "change" group rate "medium" or "high" on the learned skills scale, as compared with 54 percent of the other respondents.
55. Seventy-eight percent rate "medium" or "high" on the political efficacy scale, compared with 66 percent of the other group.
56. Forty-eight percent report that the government is "not run well," compared with 30 percent of other respondents.
57. Thirty-nine percent versus 21 percent have attended protests.
58. Fifty-two percent versus 42 percent believe that protests are good.
59. Twenty-one percent versus 39 percent favor street demonstrations.
60. Eighteen percent versus 33 percent favor rioting if necessary.
61. Thirty-six percent versus 43 percent favor forming separate political parties for Mexican-Americans only.
62. Forty-nine percent versus 23 percent (in English); 47 percent versus 27 percent (in Spanish).
63. Discrimination:

| | |
|---|---|
| "in this community" | 94 percent agree versus 81 percent of other respondents |
| "in business" | 84 percent agree versus 72 percent of other respondents |

"in politics or govern-    94 percent agree versus
   ment"                    90 percent of other res-
                            pondents.

64. "Mexican-Americans should get together politically:" 78 percent versus 69 percent agree.

65. Thirty-nine percent versus 27 percent.

66. Two measures of politicization previously explored (government evaluation and voting behavior) are excluded from this comparison because, as already noted, the populations did not differ significantly on these measures.

67. The reader should note that even though the differences are not statistically significant on the "awareness of government" dimension, members are still more aware of government than panel respondents.

CHAPTER

# 6

## GROUP CONSCIOUSNESS AS AN ALTERNATIVE EXPLANATION

This chapter explores the major alternative hypothesis posited in this study: higher levels of politicization among the council respondents could be reflective of a rise in group consciousness rather than of the organizational experience. As the Verba and Nie data have illustrated in the case of the black Americans, ethnic identification, by raising the communal consciousness of individuals and by tightening collective bonds, "may substitute for the higher social status that impels citizens into political participation."[1] In fact, it could represent another alternative route to political participation and another explanation for the political attitudes and behavior of the council respondents.

ETHNIC CONSCIOUSNESS IN EAST LOS ANGELES:
AN EXPLORATION OF THE PANEL DATA

Although ethnic consciousness clearly has worked as a political mobilization mechanism more than once in American history, for example, in the case of European ethnic 19th-century immigrants[2] and in the more contemporary case of the black Americans,[3] it is not as clear whether it has worked or will work in the case of the Mexican-Americans. As it has been mentioned, numerous manifestations of a rise in group consciousness among this ethnic group have been evidenced throughout the

---

Part of this chapter is reprinted from Biliana C. S. Ambrecht and Harry P. Pachon, "Ethnic Political Mobilization in a Mexican American Community: An Exploratory Study of East Los Angeles 1965-1972," The Western Political Quarterly 27, no. 3 (September 1974): 500-519. (Reprinted by permission of the University of Utah, copyright holder).

Southwest in recent years. But it is difficult to say how deeply the Chicano movement and its attendant ethnic-based ideology has permeated Mexican-American communities. Empirical studies on this question are notably lacking. Studies of black Americans, of religious groups, and of European ethnics abound in the literature,[4] but studies of the Mexican-American's potential for ethnic mobilization either have been primarily impressionistic in nature or exhortative in character. The difficulties in forecasting the potential for ethnic mobilization among Mexican-Americans are highlighted further when one bears in mind the variegated nature of this ethnic group[5] and its distinctive characteristics, which preclude any facile comparisons to either black Americans or to European 19th-century immigrants.[6]

An effort to ascertain empirically the potential for ethnic political mobilization present in the community under study, East Los Angeles, was made in 1972 by Pachon and this author by conducting a follow-up of a sample of the population originally interviewed in 1965 by the Mexican-American study project[7] (the panel study used here as a control group). The small size of the panel sample ($N = 51$)—while reflective of the problems encountered in panel studies, for example, inability to trace respondents because of high mobility patterns among the population; length of time between the studies; death and senility among some of the respondents and noncooperation among others ("What's the use—nothing has changed since I last answered those questions")—is highly constrictive and highlights the exploratory nature of the panel survey. Although sample size precludes making generalizations applicable to the East Los Angeles community in particular or to Mexican-Americans in general, the unique advantages of the panel technique (that is, true "before" and "after" measures) could enhance the consideration of the alternative hypothesis: group consciousness and its possible politicization effects.

Discussion of the changes that have taken place in the attitudes and behavior of the East Los Angeles respondents reinterviewed in 1972 is divided into two parts. The first section explores whether a reemphasis on cultural distinctiveness has occurred or, in other words, whether a rise in ethnic consciousness has taken place. The second section focuses on whether a rise in ethnic consciousness has been manifested in politically relevant ways, that is, do linkages exist between a rise in group awareness and the political orientations and behavior of the respondents.

## Reemphasis on Cultural Distinctiveness

In their final chapter of <u>The Mexican American People</u>, Grebler, Moore, and Guzman conclude that although the data are highly conflictive, the Mexican-Americans appear to be on the road to full assimilation into American society.[8] The 1972 data for this book suggest

TABLE 6.1

Likelihood of Assimilation into American Society
In 50 Years
(in percent)

|  | 1965 | 1972 |
|---|---|---|
| Agree | 75 | 55 |
| Disagree | 16 | 29 |
|  | (N = 46) | (N = 43) (p = 0.005) |

Source: Biliana C. S. Ambrecht and Harry Pachon, "Ethnic Political Mobilization in a Mexican American Community: An Exploratory Study of East Los Angeles 1965-72," The Western Political Quarterly 27 (September 1974), pp. 500-19.

that a possible reversal of some of the assimilationist trends suggested by these authors has taken place since 1965.

Exploring, first, the respondents' perceptions in this study regarding the likelihood of Mexican-American assimilation into American society 50 years hence,[9] one finds that a significantly larger ($p = 0.005$) proportion of respondents believes that full assimilation will not take place.[10] Moreover, when asked to assess the value of cultural assimilation, fewer respondents evaluate it favorably, although the difference is not statistically significant on this question. Relative frequencies for both questions are abstracted in Tables 6.1 and 6.2.[11]

TABLE 6.2

Value of Assimilation into American Society
(in percent)

|  | 1965 | 1972 |
|---|---|---|
| Good | 82 | 67 |
| Not so good | 10 | 16 |
|  | (N = 47) | (N = 43) (p > 0.05) |

Source: Biliana C. S. Ambrecht and Harry Pachon, "Ethnic Political Mobilization in a Mexican American Community: An Exploratory Study of East Los Angeles 1965-72," The Western Political Quarterly 27 (September 1974), pp. 500-19.

TABLE 6.3

What Children Should Keep of the Mexican Heritage
(in percent)

|  | 1965 | 1972 |
|---|---|---|
| Spanish language | 39 | 27 |
| Mexican way of life | 11 | 27 |
| Manners | 25 | 18 |
| Mexican identity, culture, pride | 5 | 21 |
| Music, cookery | 20 | 7 |
|  | (N = 51) | (N = 51) (p = 0.001) |

Note: Reported adding first, second, and third mentions.
Source: Biliana C. S. Ambrecht and Harry Pachon, "Ethnic Political Mobilization in a Mexican American Community: An Exploratory Study of East Los Angeles 1965-72," The Western Political Quarterly 27 (September 1974), pp. 500-19.

The possibility of a change away from assimilationist tendencies is enhanced when one considers the respondents' views on what aspects of the Mexican heritage they would like to see their children follow. In 1965 most of the responses referred to retention of the mother tongue and to such values as good manners and respect to elders. In 1972, one notes a significant (p = 0.001) shift in the direction of an emphasis on Mexican identity, cultural pride, and the Mexican way of life. Typical commentaries to this open-ended probe were as follows: "keep the Mexican culture strong and have pride in it" (woman, 40 years of age); "learn and be proud of the Mexican culture" (male, 55 years old); "pride in the history of their ancestors" (woman, 38 years old). Relative frequencies for both time periods are abstracted in Table 6.3.

A renewed emphasis on cultural distinctiveness also appears embodied in an increased tendency to draw differentiations between the dominant society and the ethnic referent group. This is evidenced in two major ways: in the form of increased positive self-stereotyping and in the form of increased perceptions of discrimination.

Self-stereotyping, although common to most ethnic groups in America,[12] is a difficult concept to assess. On the one hand, it could be conceived of as largely a defense mechanism or, on the other hand, as reflective of true pride in one's own distinctive cultural makeup. Notwithstanding possible divergent interpretations of the meaning of self-stereotyping, it could be posited that self-stereotyping (which is, by definition, a mark of distinctiveness) would tend to decline as a

## TABLE 6.4

### Self-Stereotypes Among East Los Angeles Respondents
(percent agreeing with statement)

|   | 1965 | 1972 | Percent Change |
|---|---|---|---|
| 1. Mexican-Americans tend to have stronger family ties than other Americans | 59 | 71 | (+12)* |
| 2. Generally speaking, people of Mexican background are very emotional | 77 | 80 | (+ 3) |
| 3. Other Americans don't work as hard as Mexican-Americans | 47 | 51 | (+ 4) |
| 4. Generally, other Americans are more materialistic than Mexican-Americans | 59 | 63 | (+ 4) |
| 5. Other Americans tend to be more progressive than Mexican-Americans | 61 | 57 | (- 4) |
| 6. Mexican-Americans often blame other Americans for their position, but it's really their own fault | 57 | 55 | (- 2) |
| 7. Mexican-Americans often shout about their rights but don't have anything to offer | 41 | 29 | (-12) |

*$P < 0.05$.
Source: Biliana C. S. Ambrecht and Harry Pachon, "Ethnic Political Mobilization in a Mexican American Community: An Exploratory Study of East Los Angeles 1965-72," The Western Political Quarterly 27 (September 1974), pp. 500-19.

group becomes more culturally assimilated. Among the East Los Angeles respondents, assertion of cultural distinctiveness in the form of positive self-stereotypes has increased rather than decreased. Although the changes evidenced between 1965 and 1972 are small and by and large statistically insignificant, their consistency seems worthy of mention. Responses to a series of probes tapping both positive and negative self-stereotypes are abstracted in Table 6.4. The reader should note that negative self-stereotyping (that is, the last three items) has declined.

A greater tendency to differentiate between the dominant society and the referent group also appears evident in increased perceptions of discrimination. Respondents in both waves of the panel study were first asked whether they thought that "it was harder for a Mexican-American with dark skin to get along in the United States than one of light skin." As can be seen in Table 6.5, in 1972 there has been a significant shift in the direction of increased perceptions of discrimination ($p = 0.001$).[13] This trend is further evidenced in responses to a probe tapping whether "it was more difficult for Mexican-Americans to get ahead in this community, in business, and in politics than for Anglo-Americans." These responses, also abstracted in Table 6.5, are of interest for they reveal that, while there has been an increase in diffuse perceptions of discrimination (that is, "in this community") and in terms of the specific referent "business," there appears to be a decreased tendency to view the political realm as discriminatory. Although the change in perceptions of discrimination in politics is not statistically significant, it could be indicative of a tendency to view the political structure as somehow more pliable and open to change than the socioeconomic structure. This is, of course, one of the major questions of interest in this chapter, that is, is increased ethnic consciousness manifested in a politically relevant way? Before turning to this question in the second part of this analysis, however, the presence of a rise in ethnic consciousness (or the lack thereof) must be evaluated first.

A final indicator, which appears to reveal a growth in group consciousness, is cognition of ethnic groups and organizations. As may be seen in Table 6.6, on all Mexican-American organizations for which comparative data are available there has been a significant increase in rates of cognition ($p = 0.05$ or better). This trend is further reinforced when one also considers cognition rates of more recently established ethnic organizations, which were mentioned in the 1972 study only. When these are rank-ordered, three of the top four are Mexican-American organizations[14] (77 percent of the respondents have heard about the La Raza Unida party, 75 percent have heard of the Chicano Moratorium,[15] and 71 percent have heard of the United Farm Workers).

It is somewhat difficult to assess the question posed at the outset of this section: has a rise in ethnic consciousness occurred among the panel respondents? On the one hand, a rise in ethnic consciousness appears to be manifested in a variety of ways—in a tendency to view the referent group as more distinctive and to value it as such, in a tendency to view the referent group as more distinctive and to value it as such, in a tendency to perceive the dominant society as more oppressive, and in an increased awareness of ethnic groups and organizations. On the other hand, other attitudes and orientations have not undergone changes. Patterns of ethnic identification, for example, remain as variegated as ever. In this respect, "the battle of the name,"[16] traditionally a contentious matter among Mexican-Americans, which often

TABLE 6.5

Perceptions of Discrimination
(in percent)

Question: in the United States it is harder for a Mexican-American with dark skin to get along than one of light skin?

|  | 1965 | 1972 |
|---|---|---|
| Agree | 26 | 51 |
| Disagree | 63 | 43 |
| Don't know | 10 | 6 |
|  | (N = 50) | (N = 51) |
|  |  | (p = 0.001) |

Question: people of Spanish-speaking background in the Southwest have to work a lot harder to get ahead than Anglo-Americans. How true is that?

|  | In This Community | | In Business | | In Politics or Government | |
|---|---|---|---|---|---|---|
|  | 1965 | 1972 | 1965 | 1972 | 1965 | 1972 |
| Very true | 31 | 35 | 26 | 43 | 45 | 37 |
| Somewhat true | 28 | 33 | 33 | 22 | 26 | 24 |
| Not very true | 29 | 18 | 18 | 18 | 8 | 6 |
| Not at all true | 8 | 10 | 14 | 10 | 2 | 10 |
| Don't know | 2 | 2 | 8 | 8 | 16 | 16 |
|  | (N = 50) | (N = 49) | (N = 50) | (N = 51) | (N = 49) | (N = 47) |
|  |  | (p > 0.05) |  | (p = 0.05) |  | (p > 0.05) |

Source: Biliana C. S. Ambrecht and Harry Pachon, "Ethnic Political Mobilization in a Mexican American Community: An Exploratory Study of East Los Angeles 1965-72," The Western Political Quarterly 27 (September 1974), pp. 500-19.

TABLE 6.6

Cognition Rates of Ethnic Organizations
(in percent)

|  | MAPA[a]* | | CSO[b]* | | LULAC[c]* | | PASSO[d]* | |
|---|---|---|---|---|---|---|---|---|
|  | 1965 | 1972 | 1965 | 1972 | 1965 | 1972 | 1965 | 1972 |
| Heard | 39 | 67 | 14 | 26 | 14 | 18 | 4 | 10 |
| Never Heard | 61 | 29 | 82 | 67 | 86 | 78 | 96 | 86 |

*$P < 0.05$.
[a] Mexican-American Political Association
[b] Community Service Organization
[c] League of United Latin American Citizens
[d] Political Association of Spanish-Speaking Organizations
Source: Biliana C. S. Ambrecht and Harry Pachon, "Ethnic Political Mobilization in a Mexican American Community: An Exploratory Study of East Los Angeles 1965-72," The Western Political Quarterly 27 (September 1974), pp. 500-19.

TABLE 6.7

Self-Identification (English, Spanish)
(in percent)

|  | English | | Spanish | |
|---|---|---|---|---|
|  | 1965 | 1972 | 1965 | 1972 |
| Spanish speaking | 4 | 2 | * | 4 |
| Latin American | 4 | 2 | 2 | 12 |
| Mexican | 55 | 37 | 26 | 41 |
| Mexican-American | 26 | 31 | 20 | 26 |
| American only | 8 | 14 | 6 | 8 |
| Spanish-American | 2 | * | * | * |
| Chicano | * | 2 | 0 | 2 |
| Other | 0 | 4 | 2 | 4 |
| Don't know | 0 | 2 | 0 | 0 |
| No response | 2 | 6 | 45 | 4 |

*not asked
Source: Biliana C. S. Ambrecht and Harry Pachon. "Ethnic Political Mobilization in a Mexican American Community: An Exploratory Study of East Los Angeles 1965-72," The Western Political Quarterly 27 (September 1974), pp. 500-19.

TABLE 6.8

Orientations Toward Work Performance
(percent saying "very important")

|  | 1965 | 1972 |
|---|---|---|
| **Statements congruent with Protestant ethic** | | |
| 1. The work is important and gives a feeling of accomplishment | 63 | 63 |
| 2. High income | 55 | 53 |
| 3. Chances for advancement | 59 | 63 |
| **Statements contradictory with Protestant ethic** | | |
| 1. No danger of being fired | 63 | 59 |
| 2. Working hours are short, lots of free time | 12 | 16 |
| **Presumed Mexican values** | | |
| 1. You get a feeling of belonging | 43 | 37 |
| 2. People take you as you are[a] | 63 | 55 |

[a]The high rating received by this item, as Grebler et al. point out, "may have been interpreted as much as a plea for an end to prejudice as it is a 'typically Mexican value.'" [The Mexican American People (New York: The Free Press, 1970), p. 434].

Source: Biliana C. S. Ambrecht and Harry Pachon. "Ethnic Political Mobilization in a Mexican American Community: An Exploratory Study of East Los Angeles 1965-72," The Western Political Quarterly 27 (September 1974), pp. 500-19.

has been a roadblock to attainment of ethnic unity,[17] remains unwon. Looking at Table 6.7, where patterns of self-identification in both English and Spanish are abstracted, one sees that, although the category of "Mexican-Americans" has made small gains in both English and Spanish identifications, so has the category "American only." It is also of interest to note here that the name most closely associated with the rise of ethnic consciousness among the Mexican-American, "Chicano," is adopted by only one of our respondents.

The difficulties in drawing conclusions about the presence of a rise in ethnic consciousness are further highlighted when one notes that our respondents are also "typical Americans" in some respects. Considering, for example, those values related to work performance, "often considered the most important characteristic separating the

Mexican American from Anglo-American culture,"[18] one finds that the 1972 respondents appear to be as acculturated in this respect as they were seven years before. A brief glance at Table 6.8 will reveal that the majority of respondents hold value orientations typically viewed as congruent with the Protestant work ethic.[19]

Further indications of conformity to presumably "American" cultural values as evidenced in the respondents' heavy emphasis on education (when asked, for example, their opinions on occupational advice[20] and when expressing their future hopes for themselves and their families[21]). Their great concern with education (which pervades other questioning as well) clearly belies cultural stereotypic notions of the Mexican-American as somewhat passive and present-oriented and as somehow not greatly interested in upward mobility.

In essence, however, the fact that our respondents are both typical Americans in some respects but are also in the process of reaffirming their distinctive cultural values may not be at all conflictive when one considers the distinctions that should be drawn between "acculturation" and "assimilation". Milton Gordon, Michael Parenti, Herbert Gans, and Edgar Litt all have pointed out that the use of these terms interchangeably has obfuscated the meaning and role of ethnicity in American society.[22] These authors distinguish between "assimilation" (the absorption of an ethnic group into the larger society through intermarriage and geographic dispersion) and "acculturation" (the process whereby an ethnic group adjusts itself to the dominant society through the acquisition of language skills and cultural mores). Widespread acculturation and cultural assimilation have taken place among ethnic groups in America, but these authors point out that complete "structural assimilation" has not been achieved. Although the findings of this study do not address themselves to this last point, they are suggestive of another dimension that should be included in this categorization: "selective acculturation." The present findings indicate that, although an ethnic group may adopt particular norms of the dominant society, it also may reject complete acculturation into American society and reaffirm instead its own distinctive ethnic values. Although reemphasis on cultural distinctiveness among the East Los Angeles respondents is not as clear-cut as expected (recall, for example, the low number of respondents identifying with the term "Chicano"), the findings do appear to substantiate the observation that one of the most important aspects of the social movement of the 1960s and 1970s has been the resurgence of cultural pride and its attendant demands for the legitimization of cultural pluralism in this society.

## Prospects for Ethnic Political Mobilization

The second part of this chapter explores whether a potential for ethnic political mobilization exists among our east Los Angeles respondents. This is a somewhat difficult question to explore in the context of the panel data, given the fact that few explicitly political

## TABLE 6.9

### Sense of Neighborliness
(in percent)

|  | 1965 | 1972 |  |
|---|---|---|---|
| Frequency of neighbors' visits to respondent's home | | | |
| Often | 26 | 26 | |
| Sometimes | 22 | 35 | |
| Rarely or never | 51 | 39 | |
|  | (N = 50) | (N = 51) | ($p = 0.02$) |
| Frequency of respondent's visits to neighbors' homes | | | |
| Often | 20 | 20 | |
| Sometimes | 18 | 35 | |
| Rarely or never | 61 | 45 | |
|  | (N = 50) | (N = 51) | ($p = 0.001$) |
| Would neighbors help in case of sudden need? | | | |
| Yes | 71 | 90 | |
| No | 20 | 8 | |
| Don't know | 10 | 2 | |
|  | (N = 51) | (N = 51) | ($p = 0.01$) |

Source: Biliana C. S. Ambrecht and Harry Pachon. "Ethnic Political Mobilization in a Mexican American Community: An Exploratory Study of East Los Angeles 1965-72," The Western Political Quarterly 27 (September 1974), pp. 500-19.

questions were asked in the original 1965 study. In an effort to alleviate this problem, the 1965-72 comparison is bolstered additionally by discussion of political items exclusively probed for in the second wave of the panel study.

It seems reasonable to suggest that political mobilization on the basis of ethnic consciousness would require, among other factors, a capability to engage in cooperative activity and an awareness of the relevance of politics to one's life. Comparison of the 1965-72 data reveal that significant changes have occurred in regard to these orientations: in 1972 the respondents appear to exhibit a higher propensity to engage in cooperative activity and an increased tendency to turn to politics and government and to consider the political arena as relevant to their problems.

An increased tendency to engage in cooperative activity appears to be evidenced, first, in an increased sense of neighborliness. Respondents in both waves of the panel study were asked how often they visited their neighbors, how often their neighbors visited them, and whether their neighbors would help should the need arise. As may be seen in Table 6.9, a significant ($p = 0.02$ or better) increase in neighborliness has occurred. This finding is bolstered additionally when one considers the respondents' answers to a more direct probe tapping "sense of community," or a feeling that others in the community share in the respondent's outlook on community problems. In this respect, 63 percent of the respondents rate "high" on the sense of community scale.[23]

Respondents also were asked (both in 1965 and in 1972) whether they thought that Mexican-Americans should get together politically and, moreover, whether Mexican-Americans should get together with blacks politically. In regard to Mexican-American political organization, a larger proportion of respondents views ethnic group political organization favorably; the changes in this case, however, are not statistically significant. (In essence, the majority already favored this strategy in 1965.) In regard to political organization with black Americans, in 1972 the proportion of respondents favoring this strategy more than doubled (16 percent in 1965 and 39 percent in 1972 agree). Although the majority of respondents still does not favor coalition with black Americans this is an impressive finding when one takes into account traditional animosities marring black-Mexican-American relations, particularly highlighted in the Los Angeles context by the intergroup competition over scarce federal poverty funds in the 1960s and 1970s.[24]

Considering next whether respondents exhibit an increased propensity to turn to politics and government and to consider the political arena as relevant to their problems, one finds that significant changes have occurred on a number of orientations that indirectly tap this dimension. When asked, for example, who or where they would turn to if they "needed some advice on where to go in the local government downtown to get something done," in 1972 one notes a significant change in the direction of a preference for contacting government institutions or officials. In 1965 only 15 percent of the respondents referred to some political or governmental organization (the majority preferring to contact schools, relatives, or the mass media). In 1972, close to 45 percent of the sample named some governmental or political official and/or institution. Similarly, when asked their opinions about the type of occupation "an outstanding young man should follow," one notes that in 1972 close to one-fifth of the respondents mentioned some type of occupation in the public service, in politics, or a "job that helps the community." In 1965 these categories were not mentioned at all.

TABLE 6.10

Opinions on Resolution of Problems in
the East Los Angeles Community (1972)
(in percent)

| | |
|---|---|
| Better education | 15 |
| Enhanced police-community relations | 6 |
| More government spending | 12 |
| Establish avenues of communication between community and government | 15 |
| Enforce laws | 12 |
| Up to the parents and to the individual | 10 |
| Better services (housing, parks, and such) | 6 |
| Miscellaneous | 24 |
| | (N = 51) |

Source: Biliana C. S. Ambrecht and Harry Pachon, "Ethnic Political Mobilization in a Mexican American Community: An Exploratory Study of East Los Angeles 1965-72," The Western Political Quarterly 27 (September 1974), pp. 500-19.

A propensity to consider politics as relevant is further evidenced in the respondents' opinions on how problems in the East Los Angeles community could be resolved. As Table 6.10 indicates, the majority of respondents expressed a preference for political solutions rather than for socioeconomic solutions.

Finally, an increased propensity not only to favor political solutions to common problems but also toward ethnically based political action is evidenced in a series of probes designed to tap "what strategies should be followed to solve problems in this community." In this respect, the overwhelming majority of respondents agrees with the following ethnically based political strategies: "elect Mexican-Americans to office" (90 percent agree) and "get people of Mexican background into government jobs" (98 percent agree).

Summarizing the findings up to this point, a comparison of the 1965-72 data as well as consideration of additional 1972 items appears to indicate that two major changes have occurred in this population since 1965: (1) there has been a renewed emphasis on cultural distinctiveness and (2) there exists an increased propensity to turn to politics and government and an increased tendency to perceive the political arena as relevant. In view of the hypothesized lingage between a rise in ethnic consciousness and increased levels of politicization, the next section explores whether the attitudinal changes evidenced in the 1965-72 comparisons have been embodied in actual changes in political behavior.

## GROUP CONSCIOUSNESS AND POLITICIZATION

Considering first the few 1965-72 items that tap directly political participation behavior, one finds that no significant increases in political activity have occurred. Although voting turnout has increased slightly (55 percent in 1965 and 69 percent in 1972), membership in community organizations has decreased (35 percent in 1965 and 25 percent in 1972). Given the somewhat unexpected nature of these findings, the relationship between group consciousness and levels of politicization was explored further by distinguishing between those respondents who were group conscious and those who were not.

This selection was accomplished on the basis of the following criteria: respondents were classified as "group conscious" if they (1) expressed an awareness and approval of ethnic distinctiveness and (2) perceived the dominant society as discriminatory in some sense.[25] On the basis of this selection process, a new variable, "group consciousness," was created. (Fifty-seven percent of the sample was thus classified as "group aware" and 43 percent was not aware.) To ascertain the effects of ethnic awareness on levels of politicization, the "group consciousness" variable was then cross-tabulated with the previously constructed indices of politicization.[26]

The results obtained through the cross-tabulation procedures are striking, for they reveal that the "group conscious" individuals are either equally or occasionally less politicized than those who are not group conscious on most dimensions of politicization. Comparison of "group conscious" versus "not group conscious" responses on all politicization measures are abstracted in Table 6.11.[27]

The tentative conclusion that must be drawn on the basis of these findings is that a rise in group consciousness by itself does not necessarily lead to increased levels of politicization.[28] The qualifier "tentative" is introduced here because of two major reasons. First, the small sample size clearly limits our capabilities for making generalizations. Second, the sample retested in 1972, while highly similar to the general East Los Angeles population on socioeconomic characteristics,[29] is also considerably older (median age of respondents is 48.5). The Chicano movement, on the other hand, has been seen by

TABLE 6.11

Dimensions of Politicization by Group Consciousness
Among 1972 Panel Respondents
(in percent)

|  | Group Consciousness | |  |
| --- | --- | --- | --- |
|  | Not Conscious | Group Conscious | |
| Awareness of government | | | |
| Low | 25 | 46 | |
| Medium | 63 | 42 | |
| High | 13 | 12 | |
|  | (N = 16) | (N = 26) | ($p > 0.05$) |
| Personal efficacy | | | |
| Low | 50 | 31 | |
| Medium | 33 | 54 | |
| High | 17 | 15 | |
|  | (N = 18) | (N = 26) | ($p > 0.05$) |
| Political efficacy | | | |
| Low | 63 | 69 | |
| Medium | 25 | 15 | |
| High | 13 | 15 | |
|  | (N = 16) | (N = 26) | ($p > 0.05$) |
| Membership in community organizations | | | |
| Yes | 18 | 19 | |
| No | 82 | 81 | |
|  | (N = 17) | (N = 26) | ($p > 0.05$) |
| Voted in last presidential election | | | |
| Yes | 88 | 89 | |
| No | 13 | 11 | |
|  | (N = 16) | (N = 18) | ($p > 0.05$) |

Source: Compiled by the author.

many as a youth-oriented movement. This is particularly true in the urban centers, where such activities as educational reforms, La Raza Unida party efforts, and leadership of the Chicano Moratorium was concentrated primarily in the younger age brackets.

Notwithstanding these caveats, however, the power of group consciousness as an alternative route to political participation, as posited by Verba and Nie, must be questioned and perhaps modified. Possibly the operation of this model can best be elucidated by considering the effects of group consciousness on the political attitudes and behavior of the council respondents, a group that is also considerably older than the general East Los Angeles population (median age, 40.5).

## GROUP CONSCIOUSNESS AND ORGANIZATIONAL INVOLVEMENT: INTERACTIVE EFFECTS

Council members were also classified as "group conscious" or "not group conscious" on the basis of the same criteria previously utilized to make this distinction among the panel respondents. On the basis of this selection process, 71 percent of the council members were classified as "group conscious" versus 29 percent who were "not group conscious."

Cross tabulation of the "group conscious" variable by each dimension of politicization reveals diametrically opposite findings from the results obtained in the panel sample: among those who are organizationally involved, "group consciousness" provides an additional boost to political involvement. Council members who are group conscious are considerably more likely to be highly politicized than those who are not group conscious. The reader may judge for himself by looking at Table 6.12.

Although the relationships abstracted in Table 6.12 are, by and large, not statistically significant, it is readily apparent that "group conscious" council members are consistently more likely to rate higher on all politicization measures than "not conscious" council respondents. Considering other political orientations, "group conscious" members are also considerably more likely to prefer collective and political solutions to community problems (75 percent to 49 percent of other respondents, $p = 0.02$), significantly more likely to favor Mexican-American political organization (82 percent to 47 percent, $p = 0.008$), more prone to favor coalition formation with black Americans (35 percent in favor to 25 percent) and significantly more likely to favor protest activity [55 percent say these are "good for the community" versus 14 percent of other respondents ($p = 0.01$)]

Moreover, it is the "group conscious" council members who perceive that they have been most affected by the council experience. As

TABLE 6.12

Dimensions of Politicization by Group Consciousness
Among Council Respondents
(in percent)

|  | Group Consciousness | |
|---|---|---|
|  | Not Conscious | Group Conscious |
| Awareness of government | | |
| Low | 38 | 18 |
| Medium | 29 | 59 |
| High | 33 | 23 |
|  | (N = 21) | (N = 56) |
|  | $X^2 = 6.05$ $(p = 0.04)$ | |
| Personal efficacy | | |
| Low | 32 | 16 |
| Medium | 41 | 38 |
| High | 27 | 48 |
|  | (N = 22) | (N = 56) |
|  | $X^2 = 3.66$ $(p > 0.05)$ | |
| Political efficacy | | |
| Low | 46 | 27 |
| Medium | 32 | 25 |
| High | 32 | 48 |
|  | (N = 22) | (N = 56) |
|  | $X^2 = 4.49$ $(p > 0.05)$ | |
| Membership in community organizations | | |
| Yes | 67 | 77 |
| No | 33 | 23 |
|  | (N = 21) | (N = 57) |
|  | $X^2 = 0.42$ $(p > 0.05)$ | |
| Voted in last presidential election | | |
| Yes | 91 | 95 |
| No | 9 | 5 |
|  | (N = 11) | (N = 38) |
|  | $X^2 = 0.06$ $(p > 0.05)$ | |

Source: Compiled by the author.

TABLE 6.13

Learned Skills on the Council By
Group Consciousness
(in percent)

|  | Group Consciousness | |
|---|---|---|
| Learned Skills Scale | Not Conscious | Group Conscious |
| Low | 57 | 25 |
| Medium | 30 | 37 |
| High | 13 | 39 |
|  | (N = 23) | (N = 57) |
|  | $X^2 = 8.57$ $(p = 0.01)$ | |

Source: Compiled by the author.

TABLE 6.14

Perception of Increased Involvement in Community
Affairs as a Result of the Council Experience
by Group Consciousness

|  | Group Consciousness | |
|---|---|---|
| Perception | Not Conscious | Group Conscious |
| More involved | 39 | 74 |
| Less involved, no difference, or unable to judge | 61 | 26 |
|  | (N = 23) | (N = 57) |
|  | $X^2 = 7.03$ | $(p = 0.008)$ |

Source: Compiled by the author.

GROUP CONSCIOUSNESS 167

may be seen in Tables 6.13 and 6.14, they are significantly more likely to rate high on the "learned skills from the council" scale and to perceive that they have become more involved in community affairs.

The fact that "group conscious" members are more likely to perceive that they have changed as a result of the advisory council experience is further substantiated when one notes that "group conscious" members comprise 77 percent of the "most changed" group identified in the previous chapter.[30]

The data considered in this chapter suggest some important avenues for further study and research. This analysis suggests that group consciousness by itself is not a powerful independent force leading to increased politicization. However, when combined with council membership, it provides a considerable boost to the independent politicization effects derived from organizational involvement. In this respect, it would appear that, although Verba and Nie are aware of the possibly interactive effects between organizational involvement and group consciousness (in Participation in America they state, "organizational affiliation particularly in Black organizations and a sense of group consciousness would probably mutually reinforce each other"[31]), they do not take this factor into account in their discussion of group consciousness as an independent alternative route to political participation (Chapter 10 of their book[32]). In their discussion of group consciousness they control for socioeconomic variables, but they neglect to control for organizational involvement. It is thus impossible to tell from their analysis whether those "aware" blacks who participate more than their socioeconomic status would predict do so solely because they are more "aware" or because they also are involved organizationally.

TABLE 6.15

"Not Group Conscious" Council Members and "Group Conscious" Panel Respondents Rating High On Politicization Measures
(in percent)

|  | "Not Group Conscious" Council Members | "Group Conscious" Panel Respondents |
|---|---|---|
| High awareness of government | 33 | 12 |
| High personal efficacy | 27 | 12 |
| High political efficacy | 23 | 15 |
| Membership in community organizations | 67 | 19 |
| Voting | 91 | 89 |

Source: Compiled by the author.

The analysis in this chapter suggests that unless group awareness is embodied in organized activity, it is not a sufficient condition for increased politicization. This, of course, highlights the importance of the availability of organizational avenues, which may channel and bring to full political fruition rises in group consciousness and communal identification. Moreover, it points to the desirability of proliferating deliberate government efforts to increase such organizational opportunities. As has been shown, organizational involvement represents a powerful alternative route to political participation. On the one hand, independently, it appears to politicize individuals in multiple and variegated ways. On the other hand, when combined with group consciousness, it actualizes latent propensities for increased political activity and collective behavior. In the council sample both forces were found to be operative (that is, organizational involvement and group consciousness). But it must be noted in conclusion that, although these are mutually reinforcing, the separate effects of organizational involvement should not be confounded.

The independent effects of organizational involvement as a politicization mechanism, which remain even after the group consciousness factor is removed, perhaps can be illustrated best by comparing the "group conscious" panel respondents to the "not group conscious" council members, thus casting, in a sense, the alternative models against one another. Table 6.15, which compares the proportion of "not group conscious" council respondents and of "group conscious" panel respondents who are highly politicized, reveals that (although the differences are not statistically significant) council members are still more politicized regardless of the consciousness factor.

What follows is a discussion of the likelihood of sustained politicization and a speculative analysis of the type of leadership likely to emerge from among the advisory council membership.

NOTES

1. Sidney Verba and Norman H. Nie, Participation in America: Political Democracy and Social Equality (New York: Harper and Row, 1972), p. 151.

2. See, for example, Michael Novack, The Rise of the Unmeltable Ethnics (New York: Macmillan, 1971); Lawrence H. Fuchs, American Ethnic Politics (New York: Harper Torchbooks, 1968); Oscar Handlin, The Uprooted (Boston: Little, Brown and Co., 1952); Andrew Greely, Why Can't They Be Like Us? (New York: E. P. Dutton and Co., 1971); Robert Dahl, Who Governs? (New Haven, Conn.: Yale University Press, 1961); Michael Parenti, "Ethnic Politics and the Persistence of Ethnic Identification," American Political Science Review 61, no. 3 (September 1967): 717-726; among others.

3. See, for example, Joel D. Aberback and Jack L. Walker, "The Meanings of Black Power: A Comparison of White and Black Interpretations of a Political Slogan," American Political Science Review 64, no. 2 (June 1970): 367-388; Marvin E. Olsen, "Social and Political Participation of Blacks," American Sociological Review 35, no. 4 (August 1970): 682-696; Chuck Stone, Black Political Power in America, rev. ed. (New York: Delta, 1970); and Lenneal Henderson, "Black Political Life in the United States: A Bibliographical Essay," in Black Political Life in the United States, edited by Lenneal Henderson (San Francisco: Chandler, 1972), pp. 253-269.

4. For studies of religious groups, see, for example, Gerhard Lenski, The Religous Factor (Garden City, N.Y.: Doubleday and Co., 1961); and Howard Schuman, "The Religious Factor in Detroit: Review, Replication, and Reanalysis," American Sociological Review 36, no. 1 (February 1971): 30-48.

5. Length of residence in the United States, geographical location and its attendant differential political milieux, and differential socioeconomic statuses are some of the factors that account for internal group differences.

6. This point is explored in Biliana C. S. Ambrecht and Harry Pachon, "Ethnic Political Mobilization in a Mexican American Community: An Exploratory Study of East Los Angeles 1965-1972," The Western Political Quarterly 27, no. 3 (September 1974): 500-519.

7. Leo Grebler, Joan W. Moore, and Ralph C. Guzman, The Mexican American People: The Nation's Second Largest Minority (New York: The Free Press, 1970).

8. Ibid., ch. 24.

9. Question reads: "Some people feel that 50 years from now Mexican-Americans will be exactly the same as everyone else in the United States, others disagree. Do you (strongly agree, agree, uncommitted, disagree, strongly disagree)?"

10. The statistical test used to measure the significance of changes between 1965-72 is the chi square "goodness of fit" test; 1965 frequencies are used as "expected frequencies," 1972 frequencies as "observed frequencies." For a discussion of the applicability of this test, see G. David Garson, Handbook of Political Science Methods (Boston: Holbrook Press, 1971), p. 138.

11. In all tables, percentages may not add up to 100 percent because of missing data or because of rounding.

12. See, for example, Greely, op. cit., ch. 3.

13. Perceptions of discrimination were particularly evident in regard to the police. A majority of 1972 respondents consistently reported negative views of police treatment of Mexican-Americans.

14. The best known organization is the PTA. Of respondents in 1972, 88 percent reported having heard of it.

15. The Chicano Moratorium is best known for its leadership role in the protests and demonstrations that have taken place in East Los Angeles in the late 1960s and early 1970s.

16. Grebler, et al., op. cit., p. 385.

17. See examples cited in Alfredo Cuellar, "Perspectives on Politics," in *Introduction to Chicano Studies: A Reader*, edited by Livie Isauro Duran and H. Russell Bernard (New York: Macmillan, 1973), pp. 558-575.

18. Grebler, et al., op. cit., p. 423.

19. For a typology distinguishing between Protestant ethic and nonProtestant ethic values, see ibid., pp. 433-435.

20. This question reads, "Suppose you knew a really outstanding young man here in the neighborhood—what one occupation do you think you would advise him to aim toward?"

21. Respondents were asked a series of questions about their own hopes and fears for the future and their hopes and fears for the community; they were asked further to situate their present, past, and future life conditions (as well as the community's present, past, and future conditions) on the Cantril self-anchoring ladder (ranging from 1 to 10), ten being the "best possible life," one being the "worst possible life"). Adapted from Hadley Cantril, *The Pattern of Human Concerns* (New Brunswick, N.J.: Rutgers University Press, 1965).

22. Parenti, op. cit.; Milton Gordon, *Assimilation into American Society* (New York: Oxford University Press, 1964); Herbert Gans, *The Urban Villagers* (New York: The Free Press, 1962); Edgar Litt, *Ethnic Politics in America*, (Illinois: Scott, Foresman and Co., 1970).

23. Moreover, it should be recalled from Chapter 5 that they also exhibited a high level of social trust.

24. Conflict between these two groups has been highlighted in the Los Angeles area by the fact that both Watts (the black ghetto) and East Los Angeles (the Mexican-American barrio) have qualified as poverty target areas, consequently engaging in intense competion over federal government resources.

25. Operationalization of these two dimensions was as follows: under the first category, respondents were classified as "conscious and approving of ethnic distinctiveness" if they answered any of the following questions accordingly: (1) assimilation is bad; (2) children should keep Mexican cultural identity, ethnic pride; (3) approval of explicitly ethnically conscious organizations (La Raza Unida party, Chicano Moratorium, Chicano Liberation Front, and Brown Berets); (4) identified themselves as "Chicano;" (5) perceived that East Los Angeles had changed positively in the last seven years because of a rise in internal unity; (6) when expressing their hopes and fears for the future of the community, they mentioned either "growth in the cultural awareness of the Mexican-American" or "increased political voice for Mexican-Americans;" and (7) when questioned about problems in the East Los Angeles community and about means of resolving these, they gave some explicitly ethnic-conscious answers, for example, "lack of political representation for Mexican-Americans because of gerrymandering." Under problems and under resolution of

problems, they mentioned "better political representation for Chicanos," "political unification" "promote self-awareness," or "cultural pride." In addition to qualifying as "conscious and approving of ethnic distinctiveness," respondents also had to perceive that the dominant society was in some ways discriminatory, that is, they had to answer any of the following probes accordingly: (1) perception of discrimination "in this community," (2) perception of discrimination "in business," (3) perception of discrimination of darker skin Mexican-Americans in the United States, (4) protests occurred in the community as a result of discrimination and represented a plea for denied equal rights, and (5) perception of unequal treatment by government bureaucracies and by the police. Selection of these criteria to determine "group consciousness" can be justified in two ways: (1) it is on these two major dimensions, that is, reemphasis on cultural distinctiveness (an approval of it) and in perceptions of discrimination, that the greatest changes have occurred between 1965-72; (2) these items were highly interrelated when correlated using Kendall's tau correlation coefficients.

26. It should be recalled that the factor analysis of the politicization data in the panel sample had identified the same factors as the factor analysis in the council sample with only one exception; in the panel sample, voting had not loaded together with belonging to community organizations. Therefore, these measures are analyzed separately.

27. The five respondents who were members of advisory councils are not included in this analysis for purposes of further comparisons with the council sample where the effects of council involvement should be isolated. While most of the council members were group conscious and more politicized, the addition of the five cases did not change the tenor of the findings presented in these tables (see Ambrecht and Pachon, op. cit., pp. 517-518).

28. However, although group consciousness is not related to higher levels of politicization, it is associated with other possibly important variables. Among other factors, group conscious respondents are more likely to view protest activity favorably (52 percent versus 33 percent of the remainder of the sample); they are more optimistic about the future of the community; they are more likely to favor Mexican-American political unification and more likely to favor coalition formation with black Americans.

29. See data presented in Table 4.1 and the text on pp. 92-94.

30. The "change" variable was cross-tabulated with the "group conscious" variable.

31. Verba and Nie, op. cit., p. 206.

32. Ibid., ch. 10.

# CHAPTER 7

## THE LIKELIHOOD OF SUSTAINED POLITICIZATION AND TYPE OF LEADERSHIP LIKELY TO EMERGE

As the discussion of the politicization effects of membership in advisory councils in a low-income Mexican-American community has demonstrated, organizational involvement represents a powerful alternative route to political participation. As the data analysis presented in Chapters 4 to 6 has shown, at the individual level organizational involvement in the form of advisory councils does appear to serve as a compensatory mechanism, which gives the lower-status individual a significant boost in a number of dimensions of politicization: awareness of government, personal efficacy, political efficacy, capabilities to affect government, and political participation.

Although additional empirical support has been provided to the operation of the organizational involvement model in an alternative population (as well as, hopefully, useful reformulation of the Verba and Nie model), there is yet to consider the potential effects of organizational involvement at the <u>group</u> or community level. It should be recalled that Verba and Nie found that, while at the individual level organizational involvement closes the gap between the high- and low-status individual, at the group level it works to increase the disparity between upper- and lower-status groups, simply because upper-class individuals are overwhelmingly more active in organizations than lower-class individuals.

Whether organizational involvement actually can work to eliminate the disparity between status groups on levels of political activity is the subject of the first part of this chapter. Earlier,[1] it was suggested that deliberate government policies to increase citizen participation through such mechanisms as the creation of community advisory councils possibly could be a vehicle to redress class inequalities in rates of political participation at the group level, provided that two conditions were met. First was that such government strategies actually do work to politicize individuals and that the type of politicization engendered by involvement in advisory councils is of a lasting nature. Second, was that governmental strategies to increase citizen participation proliferate and are expanded to involve larger numbers of lower-class citizens.

In regard to the first condition, this study hopefully has established (albeit in a suggestive rather than conclusive manner) that government policies to increase citizen participation do indeed work. In particular, the data analysis presented in Chapter 6 has called attention to the necessity of organizational avenues to channel and to bring to full political fruition other underlying propensities for involvement in politics, such as a rise in group consciousness and communal identification. Yet to be considered is whether the types of politicization engendered by membership in advisory councils are likely to be of an enduring character.

## LIKELIHOOD OF SUSTAINED POLITICIZATION: AN ASSESSMENT

It should be recalled that the original formulation of organizational involvement as an alternative route to political participation by Verba and Nie, and Goldrich's and others' empirical research on the operation of this model in Latin American poverty communities cast some doubts as to the enduring nature of this alternative route to political involvement.[2] According to the original Verba and Nie model, the political participation engendered by organizational involvement is not mediated by those "enabling orientations," which usually are associated with stable and lasting propensities for political involvement. Goldrich, moreover, suggested that the intitial politicization of the poblador was not consistently sustained after initial demands and needs had been met. In light of the possibly sporadic nature of the organizational involvement model, one of the most important aspects of this study was to explore whether organizational involvement actually leads to the development of those attitudinal propensities and capabilities to affect government usually associated with the SES model. In this respect, this study has found that advisory council membership appears to lead to increases in dimensions of politicization other than political participation behavior. The prospects for sustained politicization among the council respondents thus appear brighter than originally anticipated.

The likelihood of sustained politicization among council respondents also appears high when the following additional indicators are considered: (1) council members exhibit a high level of "collective" rather than "individualistic" orientations toward the resolution of common problems, (2) the majority are ethnically aware and hence have a reason for continued political activity, and (3) the majority intend to remain politically active. Each of these indicators is briefly illustrated.

Earlier it was suggested that one way of assessing whether individual politicization is likely to endure is to see whether those who are politicized exhibit a collective rather than individualistic orientation toward the resolution of common problems.[3] That is, it was posited that those exhibiting individualistic orientations would be more likely to pursue self-advancement in nonpolitical ways—such as through better income, jobs, housing, or moving out of the poverty community. On the other hand, those exhibiting collective orientations probably would tend to see self-advancement as intimately related to group advancement and would tend to pursue political strategies to obtain socioeconomic benefits for the group as a whole. Council members appear to perceive a basis for collective political action in their responses to a series of probes designed to identify problems in the East Los Angeles community and to suggest possible avenues for their resolution. Although the type of problems cited were multifaceted and variegated (for example, poverty, lack of law and order, police brutality, youth vandalism, unequal educational opportunities, lack of services, and lack of political representation), the most often cited solutions (43 percent of all responses) were political in nature (for example, more government spending, specific government legislation, establishing avenues of communication between government agencies and the community, and political unification of the community). Moreover, when asked a more specific question as to "which of these groups should have the main responsibility for resolving these problems," an even larger proportion of respondents (65 percent) posits a preference for government and grass roots groups action rather than individual initiative or private enterprise activity.

A propensity toward collective activity is further evidenced in the respondents' opinions as to what strategies should be employed to affect government. Over half the sample mentions some type of collective activity such as "organize," "unite the community," "join community organizations," and "demonstrate," rather than individualistically oriented responses such as "vote," "write letters," or "send petitions." In addition, council members appear to perceive that others in the community interpret common problems in the same light as they do; 67 percent of the respondents rate high on the "sense of community" scale. The high level of collective orientations exhibited by the council respondents, which is evident in other questioning as well, does not appear at all symptomatic of a group on the road to individualistic embourgeoissement. In this sense, Richard Cloward and Frances Piven's contention that "if government bureaucracies affect the poor at all, it will be by raising them one by one into the middle class," does not appear to be particularly applicable to these council respondents.[4]

Prospects for sustained politicization are further enhanced when one recalls the interactive relationship between council membership and group consciousness. As seen in Chapter 6, although group consciousness by itself does not lead necessarily to increased political participation, when combined with organizational involvement it boosts and accentuates already existing tendencies toward politicization. In this sense, it would seem that group consciousness would serve to crystallize and provide a distinctive focus, a raison d'etre for existing collective orientations. When one adds the awareness of a cause, of a reason for collective behavior, to an already high level of exposure of politics and to governmental affairs, the prospects for sustained politicization appear high indeed. Moreover, when one finally considers that the majority of respondents intend to remain active in public affairs (73 percent), it does not appear likely that depoliticization will occur, at least not in the near future.

A final question this study is concerned with is a highly speculative one. If, as the author has suggested, politicization is likely to be of a lasting nature, what type of leaders are likely to emerge from this process? There are no pretensions here about being able to foretell how the individuals studied in this project are likely to behave in the future. Such pretensions clearly would contradict the underlying tone and thrust of this study. As this study itself hopefully has suggested, individuals who one would predict would be low participants on the basis of their low SES status alone are actually highly politicized. That adults do change in their attitudes and orientations, highly deterministic socialization theories notwithstanding, also has been a major emphasis of this study. In contrast with previous discussions, where the author sought to obtain empirically grounded conclusions as to the effects of a new participative process, the remarks in this section ought to be viewed as highly speculative in character.

## TYPE OF LEADERSHIP LIKELY TO EMERGE

In an effort to speculate about the type of leadership likely to emerge from among the rank and file of the East Los Angeles advisory councils, it seems appropriate to focus on those respondents who are potentially most likely to remain politicized: those who are group conscious. As previous analyses have shown, these respondents are more highly politicized than the rest of the sample on most dimensions of politicization. By definition, they are also highly collectively oriented. Moreover, they are predominantly found among those who seem to be most affected by the council experience. They closely reflect, in addition, the socioeconomic and demographic characteristics of the whole council sample.[5] Affected as they are by the twin forces of organizational exposure and group consciousness, these appear to be the leaders of tomorrow.

As was discussed earlier, two principal concerns dominate this speculative analysis of the potential nature of this leadership group. What type of political strategies are they likely to employ to solve community problems both in terms of a vertical referent (strategies directed toward government) and in terms of a horizontal referent (strategies directed toward the ethnic group)? In regard to the first, government, two possible alternative strategies were suggested, radical versus reformist. For the second referent, the ethnic group, two alternative strategies also were posited, ethnic separatism versus coalition formation with other groups. Anticipating our conclusions, the complexity evident in these orientations impedes drawing such facile distinctions.

## Attitudes Toward Government

In an effort to forecast what type of strategies "conscious" council members would be most likely to favor in regard to the vertical referent (government), the respondents' opinions were probed on (1) political strategies that should be pursued to "solve problems in this community," (2) evaluation of protest activity, (3) opinions of community organizations that generally are considered to be radical, and (4) perceptions of anti-Mexican-American discrimination. Responses to these probes are abstracted in Tables 7.1 to 7.4.

Tables 7.1 to 7.4 reveal, first, that the respondents are highly action-oriented, as may be noted by the almost insignificant proportion agreeing with "doing nothing." This reinforces the underlying assumption that this is a potential leadership group. Second, the overwhelming majority perceive that there exists a great deal of anti-Mexican-American discrimination in this society. These perceptions seem to be a further indication of a predisposition for political action; these respondents appear to have strong reasons for engagement in political activity. Third, although the overwhelming majority of respondents appear to favor what generally would be considered "reformist" or "within the system" type strategies (that is, "elect Mexican-Americans to office," "get government jobs for Mexican-Americans," or "work within the established two-party system"), a large number of the respondents also favor what generally would be considered radical political activity. (Note, for example, the high proportion of those evaluating protest activity favorably and those approving of presumably radical organizations.) In fact, what seems clear from these data is that "radical" versus "reformist" orientations are not a zero-sum game. Favorable evaluation of radical activity does not preclude predispositions toward "within the system" type strategies. In fact, "radical" and "reformist" orientations are not at all mutually exclusive. Kendall's tau correlations between all the "radical" activity indicators ("riot if necessary," "form a separate political party," "join in street demonstrations," and favorable evaluation of protests and of radical organizations) reveals that these indicators are correlated significantly with

TABLE 7.1

Strategies that Should be Employed to Solve
Problems in the East Los Angeles Community
(among "conscious" council members)
(in percent)

|  | Agree | Depends | Disagree |
|---|---|---|---|
| Inactive orientation | | | |
| 1. Do nothing because things will work themselves out | 7 | — | 93 |
| Presumably "reformist" inclined orientations | | | |
| 1. Elect people of Mexican background to office | 84 | 4 | 13 |
| 2. Get people of Mexican background into government jobs | 96 | 2 | 2 |
| 3. Work within the Democratic and Republican parties | 73 | 13 | 15 |
| Presumably more radically inclined orientations | | | |
| 1. Form a separate political party for people of Mexican background only | 44 | 7 | 48 |
| 2. Join in public street demonstrations | 34 | 23 | 43 |
| 3. Riot if necessary | 29 | 2 | 70 |

Source: Compiled by the author.

most of the presumably "within the system" strategies ("elect Mexican-Americans to office," "get jobs for Mexican-Americans"). Moreover, both preferences for "radical" and "reformist" political strategies are highly correlated with high perceptions of discrimination.

The one exception to the mutual compatibility between "radical" and "reformist" orientations is "working within the Democratic and Republican parties." In fact, preference for this strategy is either not correlated or inversely correlated with most indicators of "radical" orientations. What this suggests is that those who sanction more radically oriented political activity will not be likely to pursue political goals through the established party system. There are, of course, many reasons for this, some of which already have been discussed.[6] In regard to the Republican party (although it has made some electoral gains in Mexican-American communities), it never has held great appeal for this particular ethnic group. Traditional attachments to the

TABLE 7.2

Awareness of, Attendance at, and Opinions
of Protest Activity
(among "conscious" council members)
(in percent)

| Awareness of Protests | |
|---|---|
| Heard of | Did not hear |
| 95 | 5 |

| Attendance at Protests | |
|---|---|
| Attended | Did not attend |
| 33 | 67 |

| Evaluation of Protests | | | |
|---|---|---|---|
| Good for the Community | Partly Good Partly Bad* | Makes no Difference | Bad |
| 55 | 13 | 8 | 25 |

*As in the panel sample, the major reason cited in justification of this response was that protests were fine unless they resulted in violence.

Source: Compiled by the author.

TABLE 7.3

Evaluation of Presumably Radically Oriented Organizations
(among "conscious" council respondents)
(in percent)

|  | La Raza Unida Party | Chicano Moratorium | Brown Berets | Chicano Liberation Front |
|---|---|---|---|---|
| Good for the community | 64 | 64 | 36 | 60 |
| Makes no difference | 14 | 16 | 11 | 3 |
| Bad for the community | 6 | 8 | 31 | 19 |
| Don't know | 14 | 12 | 20 | 19 |

Source: Compiled by the author.

TABLE 7.4

Perceptions of Discrimination
(among "conscious" council respondents)
(percent agreeing)

| | |
|---|---|
| In this community | 94 |
| In business | 91 |
| In politics and government | 91 |

Source: Compiled by the author

Democratic party among more group-aware Mexican-Americans, moreover, appear to be waning. Particularly in the case of East Los Angeles, where the Democratic party has been notably unresponsive in regard to demands for political representation and for elimination of gerrymandering practices, party defection appears likely.

In essence, what this speculative look at the "conscious" council members' strategy preferences seems to indicate is that these potential leaders will tend to pursue socioeconomic gains for the ethnic group as a whole in a "within the system" fashion without spurning, however, more "radical" strategies should these become necessary. Their relatively high endorsement of protest activity and of presumably radically oriented ethnic organizations does not suggest that this is an easily cooptable group.

### Orientations Toward the Referent Group

Considering next whether ethnically based political activity is likely to be of a "separatist" or of a "cooperative" nature, several dimensions were explored, (1) whether Mexican-Americans should get together politically, (2) whether Mexican-Americans should get together with black Americans, (3) whether Mexican-Americans should get together alone (excluding other groups), and (4) whether Mexican-Americans should form a separate political party. Relative frequencies for each category are abstracted in Table 7.5

As is readily apparent from Table 7.5, most respondents, of course, favor Mexican-American political organization. This is almost definitional in the sense that the orientations of group conscious individuals are being explored. What is of interest here is whether these respondents are likely to favor coalition building with other groups or to spurn such associations. This is a difficult question to assess both

TABLE 7.5

Orientations Toward Ethnic Group Organization
(among "conscious council respondents)
(percent agreeing with statement)

| | |
|---|---|
| 1. Mexican-Americans should get together politically | 82 |
| 2. Mexican-Americans should get together with black Americans politically | 35 |
| 3. Mexican-Americans should form political groups only with other Mexican-Americans | 35 |
| 4. Mexican-Americans should form a separate political party | 44 |

Source: Compiled by the author.

in the context of these data and in the context of the ethnic-based ideology of the Chicano movement. On the one hand, the Chicano movement has emphasized cultural uniqueness and Mexican-American political unification. But it also has manifested tendencies in the direction of "Third World" peoples' consciousness and political unification. The movement itself appears to be torn between separatist and cooperative orientations.

These data also appear to reflect this dilemma. Although 35 percent of the group favors Mexican-American political organization exclusive of other groups, a similar percentage favors political unification with black Americans. The latter is by no means a negligible proportion when one recalls traditional animosities marring relationships between these two groups. The data are not at all clear on this question, but indications of a trend toward increased class consciousness possibly could be in evidence. In this respect, it should first be recalled that such a trend was evident in the 1965-72 panel study comparison: the proportion of those agreeing with political unification with Blacks has doubled since 1972.[7] In the council sample, there are also some indications of this trend. "Getting together with blacks" among the "conscious" group is, somewhat surprisingly, significantly correlated with "forming a separate political party." This finding is of interest, for it may indicate that what on face value appears to be an ethnically exclusionist strategy (that is, "form a separate political party for Mexican-Americans only") could be more indicative of a disappointment with the lack of responsiveness of the two major parties toward the Mexican-American than a sign of racial separatism. This interpretation possibly is reinforced when one notes that preference for coalition formation with black Americans is correlated significantly with most of the "radical" orientations, (participation in protest activity, endorsement of demonstrations, rioting if necessary, with approval of presumably radically oriented ethnic organizations) and, moreover, with every perception of high discrimination. It is thus possible that it is precisely among those who are most ethnically conscious and who endorse radical political activity most readily, that consciousness of class is increasing. Should this interpretation prove to be correct, it would appear that ethnic consciousness, coupled with class-based coalition formation with other ethnic groups, would enhance considerably the prospects for effective political organization.

## CONCLUSIONS

On the basis of this highly speculative look at the future, it would seem that organizational involvement in the form of advisory council membership is conducive to more enduring propensities to participate in politics than had been anticipated. Council members do not appear to be characteristic of a population primarily interested in individual upward mobility. On the contrary, the high level of collective orientations evidenced in the council sample as a whole seems indicative of a tendency to view individual advancement as intertwined with the advancement of the group as a whole, hence auguring bright prospects for sustained politicization.

The type of leadership group likely to emerge from this process is a difficult question to assess. Judging from their stated strategy preferences, it would appear that, although it will be a predominantly reformist rather than revolutionary-oriented group, the potential leaders tentatively identified do not seem to exhibit the characteristics of a readily cooptable group. When one adds their negative perceptions of the responsiveness of the dominant society to their feelings of communal identification and their political experience gained on the councils, this potential group is not likely to be of the "vendido,"[8] easily manipulated type.

Finally, in reference to the question posed at the outset of this chapter—that is, can organizational involvement work to eliminate the class bias in political participation rates in American society—the answer suggested by this study is a qualified "yes". Although at the individual level organizational involvement appears to breed an enduring propensity for political involvement and may be conducive to the emergence of effective indigenous leadership, the class bias in political participation rates is not likely to be eliminated unless opportunities for organizational involvement are expanded sufficiently. Government clearly has a key role in this respect. As has been argued, alternative agents of political mobilization, such as the established political parties, have not been particularly responsive to the needs of the poor, as the evaluations of the more aware council members themselves indicate. Third-party movements, on the other hand, operating under the constraints of an electoral system biased toward the two-party structure (that is, simple plurality single-member districts, as compared with proportional representation) do not appear likely to be capable of mobilizing sufficient numbers and resources to make effective political gains. Moreover, as bureaucratic politics continue to gain preeminence over legislative and electoral processes, it is at the government agency level that interest articulation and citizen representation will have to take place if a semblance of democracy is to be retained. For these reasons, the class bias inherent in the patterns of political participation in this society appear likely to be redressed only if and when deliberate government efforts to do so proliferate.

NOTES

1. See p. 43.
2. See pp. 30-31.
3. See pp. 44.
4. Quoted in Stanford Kravitz, "The Community Action Program in Perspective," in Urban Poverty: Its Social and Political Dimensions, edited by Warner Bloomberg, Jr., and Henry W. Schmandt (Beverly Hills, Calif.: Sage, 1970), p. 301.
5. For example, family income for "conscious" respondents closely parallels the distribution found in the general population, 35 percent have "low" incomes, 44 percent have "medium" incomes, and 21 percent have "high" incomes. Similarly, 35 percent have "low" education, 27 percent have "medium" education, and 37 percent have "high" education. Moreover, they closely reflect the distribution of the overall sample according to type of council; 61 percent are school advisory council members; 39 percent are representative of "other" councils.
6. See pp. 42.
7. As was noted in Chapter 6, 15 percent of the panel respondents agreed with this strategy in 1965; 36 percent did so in 1972.
8. In colloquial Spanish, "vendido" means "sold-out" (generally to the "Anglo establishment").

# CHAPTER 8

## CONCLUSIONS: THE POLITICIZING LEGACY OF THE WAR ON POVERTY

The first major assumption made at the outset of this empirical inquiry into the political attitudes and behavior of advisory council members in the East Los Angeles community was that (recent reversals in federal policy notwithstanding) the practice of including laymen or nonprofessional community representatives in advisory councils to public agencies would last beyond and independently of the longevity of the War on Poverty programs, which fostered this novel practice. It was suggested, in essence, that the much-maligned notion of "maximum feasible participation" had served to institutionalize and diffuse the concept that the layman ought to have an input into the operation of public agencies. This empirical inquiry of advisory councils in one low-income community suggests that this view was indeed correct. In the relatively small community of East Los Angeles, 70 councils were found to be operative at all levels of government and in most functional service areas and, moreover, were found to include a large number of local residents (close to 2,000, or approximately 1 percent of the total population).

The nature of these councils and of their membership also appears to have diverged from practices established by the extensively studied CAP and Model Cities program. The councils surveyed in this study appear to be much less "elitist" than anticipated on the basis of previous research. Seventy-one percent of the membership of these councils is composed of laymen (community people), as contrasted with the one-third poverty representation characteristic of CAP councils. Recruitment patterns, moreover, are highly informal. The ease of membership definition apparent in these councils works to attract previously uninvolved and politically inexperienced individuals. As discussed in Chapter 4, over three-quarters of the advisory council "community" membership is composed of individuals with little or no previous experience in community affairs. Moreover, council members are broadly representative of the socioeconomic and demographic characteristics of the population as a whole. They are, in fact, more economically deprived than the general population, as measured by median family income and family size. In essence, the advisory council members interviewed in this study do not represent an "elite" group, neither in socioeconomic terms nor in political involvement terms. These are, by no means, "the terribly participatory poor" and the "already motivated poor," as numerous previous studies had suggested.

What these findings, in effect, suggest is that advisory councils provide a fertile ground for social science research on alternative means whereby the political involvement of ordinary citizens (particularly of those found in the lower socioeconomic strata of this society) may be upgraded. In particular, more attention should be focused on school advisory councils, for these provide a logical "breaking in" environment for the previously inactive. There exist tangible and readily perceivable self-interest reasons for participation in school councils: the welfare of one's children. As discussed in Chapter 4, it is the school councils that are more likely to attract inactive and politically inexperienced individuals. Moreover, it is the school advisory council members who are consistently more satisfied with council performance and who evaluate the councils most favorably.

The second major assumption motivating this study was that regardless of whether advisory councils held effective decision-making power, the participative process itself would tend to work as a politicizing and skills-acquiring experience. In this sense, organizational involvement in advisory councils was seen as a possible mechanism whereby the rates of political participation of lower socioeconomic groups could be upgraded. The empirical findings of this study clearly suggest that this is so. As shown in Chapters 5 and 6, council members exhibit higher levels of personal efficacy, political efficacy, political capabilities, and political participation than individuals of similar socioeconomic status in the same community. Members also tend to perceive that their attitudes and behavior have changed as a result of the advisory council experience, and these changes are consistently in the direction of increased politicization.

Moreover, the council experience works as a politicization mechanism regardless of the particular power configuration of the councils and regardless of the members' previous levels of involvement. It is precisely those individuals who are most negative about council performance and council operation who report that their political attitudes and behavior have been most affected by the council experience. Those who are most affected are also those who most lack the status resources necessary for political participation: those who are most poor and least educated. Finally, council membership not only appears to politicize the previously inactive but also provides a considerable "boost" to the political involvement of those who already had been participants: members reported learning skills and becoming more involved in community affairs regardless of previous levels of involvement.

As the examination of the two major rival hypotheses in Chapters 5 and 6 suggested, the relationship between council membership and higher levels of politicization than could be expected on the basis of SES status does not appear to be a spurious correlation. The independent politicization effects derived from organizational involvement remain even after the influence of two other major factors, "group consciousness" and "self-selection," have been removed.

Organizational involvement thus appears to be a more powerful independent substitution mechanism for those status resources that generally impel upper-class citizens to participate—more than the alternative route explored, "group consciousness." As the discussion of the 1965-72 data revealed, unless group awareness is channeled through organizational avenues, it does not appear to be a sufficient condition for increased politicization. When combined with council membership, however, it provides a considerable boost to the independent politicization effects derived from the organizational experience.

In addition, the politicization engendered by advisory council membership appears to be of a lasting nature. As discussed in Chapter 7, council members are highly collectively oriented and intend to remain active in community affairs. It thus would appear that the process of involving previously inexperienced and politically unsophisticated individuals in advisory councils to public agencies well may portend better prospects for the development of effective indigenous leadership in low-income communities. That the individuals interviewed in this study are likely to become community leaders is suggested both by their high levels of politicization and by their high collective orientations. Moreover, the leadership group likely to emerge from this process does not appear to be of an easily manipulated type. In this sense, the findings of this study suggest that the legacy of the War on Poverty has perhaps been dismissed too readily and possibly has been unjustly maligned. If the conclusions tentatively derived here are supported in further research able to utilize more rigorous experimental design methodology, it would appear that the variety of procedural innovations introduced by the social programs of the 1960s will prove to have a lasting and important impact on the ability of low-income communities to organize themselves for effective political action.

The broader policy implications of this study thus point to the importance of expanding deliberate government policies to upgrade the level of participation of low-income individuals through such mechanisms as the creation of community advisory councils. As has been shown, this type of organizational involvement appears to portend enduring propensities for political participation at the individual level and to augur better prospects for the emergence of indigenous leaders in poverty communities. Yet, if the class bias in rates of political participation is to be redressed eventually in American Society, organizational opportunities must be greatly expanded and come to involve larger segments of low-income communities.

As a personal postscript, the final point the author feels should be made in this conclusion is that, although throughout this study the politicization of advisory council members has been looked upon primarily as a means to an end (that is, the effective political organization of low-income communities), the intrinsic benefits derived from this type of participative process should not be overlooked. This study's focus on the group benefits that eventually may accompany the politicization of individuals is warranted in view of the fact that individuals in the lower socioeconomic strata must develop group resources to be able to intervene effectively in the political arena. This utilitarian emphasis, although important, should not obscure the intrinsic benefits that the individual gains from the participative process or neglect the fact that opportunities for increased participation also must be expanded for individuals in other social classes in our highly bureaucratized society. Individual powerlessness in a technologically advanced society is not, after all, exclusively a problem of the lower classes, although it is more accentuated there because it is additionally highlighted by group powerlessness. Enlarging opportunities for individual participation in decision making in such spheres as public agencies and work and educational institutions can yield multifaceted benefits in terms of enlarging the individual's sphere of control over his own environment, as well as increasing explicitly participatory tendencies. Yet, social science research on those means whereby individual powerlessness can be alleviated is scant, plagued as it is by a narrow interpretation of the "political" and by an almost exclusive concern with the group rather than with the individual. Extensive empirical research on participatory experiments taking place all over the world, guided by a research orientation willing to go beyond existing reality and to engage in "creative speculation," will have to take place before any solutions to the problem of individual powerlessness can emerge.

# BIBLIOGRAPHY

Aberbach, Joel D., and Jack L. Walker. "The Meanings of Black Power: A Comparison of White and Black Interpretations of a Political Slogan." American Political Science Review 64 (June 1970): 367-388.

Aleshire, Robert A. "Planning and Citizen Participation: Costs, Benefits, and Approaches." Urban Affairs Quarterly 5 (June 1970): 369-393.

_____. "Power to the People: An Assessment of the Community Action and Model Cities Experience." Public Administration Review 32, Special Issue (September 1972): 428-443.

Almond, Gabriel A., and Sidney Verba. The Civic Culture. Boston: Little, Brown and Co., 1965.

Altshuller, Alan A. Community Control: The Black Demand for Participation in Large American Cities. New York: Pegasus, 1970.

Alvarez, Salvador. "Mexican-American Community Organizations." Voices: Readings from El Grito 4 (June 1971): 68-77.

Ambrecht, Biliana C. S., and Harry Pachon. "Ethnic Political Mobilization in a Mexican American Community: An Exploratory Study of East Los Angeles 1965-1972." The Western Political Quarterly 27 (September 1974): 500-519.

Ambrecht, Biliana C. S. "Beyond Bureaucratic Organization: A Case Study of the Yugoslav Experiment in Economic Self-Management." Mimeograph. Los Angeles, Calif.: University of California, 1971.

Anton, Thomas J. "Power, Pluralism, and Local Politics." Administrative Science Quarterly 7 (March 1963): 425-457.

Austin, David M. "Resident Participation: Political Mobilization or Cooptation?" Public Administration Review 32, Special Issue (September 1972): 409-420.

Bachrach, Peter. The Theory of Democratic Elitism: A Critique. Boston: Little, Brown and Co., 1966.

Bachrach, Peter, and Morton S. Baratz. Power and Poverty: Theory and Practice. London: Oxford University Press, 1970.

Backstrom, Charles H., and Gerald D. Hursh. Survey Research. Evanston, Ill.: Northwestern University Press, 1963.

Banfield, Edward, et al. "Nixon, the Great Society, and the Future of Social Policy—A Symposium." Commentary 55 (May 1973): 31-62.

Barrera, Mario, Carlos Munoz, and Charles Ornelas. "The Barrio as an Internal Colony." In People and Politics in Urban Society, Urban Affairs Annual Reviews, edited by Harlan H. Hahn. Beverly Hills, Calif.: Sage, 1972.

Bay, Christian, "Politics and Pseudo-Politics." American Political Science Review 59 (March 1965): 39-51.

Becker, Howard S., and Blanche Geer. "Participant Observation and Interviewing." Human Organizations 16 (Fall 1957): 28-32.

Becker, Selwyn W. "The Parable of the Pill." Administrative Science Quarterly 15 (March 1970): 94-96.

Blalock, Hubert M., Jr. Social Statistics. New York: McGraw Hill, 1960.

Blauner, Robert. "Colonialism and Ghetto Revolts." Social Problems 16 (Spring 1969): 393-407.

Boone, Richard W. "Reflections on Citizen Participation and Economic Opportunity Act." Public Administration Review 32, Special Issue (September 1972): 444-456.

Bottomore, T. B. Elites and Society. London: Penguin Books, 1967.

Boyer, William. Bureaucracy on Trial. Indianapolis: Bobbs-Merrill, 1964.

Brim, Orville G., and Stanton Wheeler. Socialization After Childhood: Two Essays: New York: Wiley, 1966.

Burke, Edmund M. "Citizen Participation Strategies." Journal of the American Institute of Planners 34: (September 1968): 287-294.

California, Department of Industrial Relations, Division of Fair Employment Practices. "Negroes and Mexican-Americans in South and

East Los Angeles: An Analysis of a Special U.S. Census Survey of November 1965." San Francisco, Calif., July 1966.

Camejo, Antonio. "Lessons of the Los Angeles Chicano Protest." In Introduction to Chicano Studies: A Reader, edited by Livie Isauro Duran and H. Russell Bernard. New York: Macmillan, 1973.

_____. "Texas Chicanos Forge Own Political Power." In Introduction to Chicano Studies: A Reader, edited by Livie Isauro Duran and H. Russell Bernard. New York: Macmillan, 1973.

Campbell, Angus, et al. The American Voter. New York: Wiley, 1960.

Campbell, Angus, Gerald Gurin, and Warren Miller. The Voter Decides. Evanston, Ill.: Row, Peterson, 1954.

Campbell, Donald T. "Reforms as Experiments." American Psychologist 24 (April 1969): 409-429.

Campbell, Donald T., and Julian C. Stanley. Experimental and Quasi-Experimental Designs for Research. Chicago: Rand McNally, 1963.

Cantril, Hadley. The Pattern of Human Concerns. New Brunswick, N.J.: Rutgers University Press, 1965.

Cattell, Raymond B. Factor Analysis: An Introduction and Manual for the Psychologist and Social Scientist. New York: Harper and Brothers, 1951.

Chavez, Cesar. "The Organizer's Tale," Ramparts Magazine 5 (July 1966): 43-50.

Clark, Terry N., ed. Community Structure and Decision Making: Comparative Analyses. San Francisco: Chandler, 1968.

Cole, Richard L. Citizen Participation and the Urban Policy Process. Lexington, Mass.: D. C. Heath and Co., 1974.

Crozier, Michel. The Bureaucratic Phenomenon. Chicago: University of Chicago Press, 1964.

Cuellar, Alfredo. "Perspectives on Politics." In Introduction to Chicano Studies: A Reader, edited by Livie Isauro Duran and H. Russell Bernard. New York: Macmillan, 1973.

Cutwright, Philip. "National Political Development." In Politics and Social Life, edited by Nelson W. Polsby, Robert A. Dentler, and Paul L. Smith. Boston: Houghton Mifflin, 1963.

Dahl, Robert A. After the Revolution?: Authority in a Good Society. New Haven, Conn.: Yale University Press, 1970.

_____. "Hierarchy, Democracy and Bargaining in Politics and Economics." In Political Behavior: A Reader in Theory and Practice, edited by Heinz Eulau et al. Glencoe, Ill.: The Free Press, 1956.

_____. Who Governs?: Democracy and Power in an American City. New Haven, Conn.: Yale University Press, 1961.

de Tocqueville, Alexis. Democracy in America. Edited and abridged by Richard D. Heffner. New York: New American Library, 1956.

Dolbeare, Kenneth M. "Public Policy Analysis and the Coming Struggle for the Soul of the Post-Behavioral Revolution." In Power and Community: Dissenting Essays in Political Science, edited by Phillip Green and Sanford Levinson. New York: Random House, 1969.

Dworkin, Anthony Gary. "A City Founded: A People Lost." In Introduction to Chicano Studies: A Reader, edited by Livie Isauro Duran and H. Russell Bernard. New York: Macmillan, 1963.

Easton, David. "The New Revolution in Political Science." American Political Science Review 65: (December 1969): 1051-1061.

Eckstein, Harry. "A Theory of Stable Democracy." Division and Cohesion in Democracy. Princeton: Princeton University Press, 1966.

Ericksen, Charles A. "Uprising in the Barrios." In Mexican-Americans in the United States: A Reader, edited by John H. Burma. Cambridge, Mass.: Schenkman, 1970.

Erwin, Susan, and Robert T. Bowen. "Translation Problems in International Surveys." Public Opinion Quarterly 16, Special Issue (Winter 1952-53): 595-604.

Eulau, Heinz. Class and Party in the Eisenhower Years. New York: The Free Press of Glencoe, 1962.

Festinger, Leo. "Behavioral Support for Opinion Change." Public Opinion Quarterly 28 (Fall 1964): 404-417.

BIBLIOGRAPHY 191

Florence Heller School of Advanced Studies in Social Welfare, Brandeis University, Report 5. "Community Representation in Community Action Programs." Waltham, Mass.: Brandeis University, 1969.

Freeman, Howard E., and Clarence S. Sherwood. "Research in Large Scale Intervention Programs." The Journal of Social Issues 21 (January 1965): 11-28.

Fruchter, Benjamin. Introduction to Factor Analysis. Princeton, N.J.: D. Van Nostrand Co., 1954.

Fuchs, Lawrence H. American Ethnic Politics. New York: Harper Torchbooks, 1968.

Gamson, William A. Power and Discontent. Homewood, Ill.: Dorsey, 1968.

Gans, Herbert. The Urban Villagers. New York: The Free Press, 1962.

Garson, G. David. Handbook of Political Science Methods. Boston: Holbrook Press, 1971.

Goldrich, Daniel. "Political Organization and the Politicization of the Poblador." Comparative Political Studies 3 (July 1970): 176-202.

_____. "The Political Integration of Lower Class Urban Settlements in Chile and Peru," Studies in Comparative International Development (1967): 1-22.

_____. "Toward the Comparative Study of Politicization in Latin America." In Contemporary Cultures and Societies of Latin America, edited by Dwight B. Heath and Richard N. Adams. New York: Random House, 1965.

Golembiewski, Robert T., and Stokes B. Carrigan. "Planned Change in Organizational Style Based on the Laboratory Approach." Administrative Science Quarterly 15 (March 1970): 79-93.

Gordon, Milton. Assimilation into American Society. New York: Oxford University Press, 1964.

Gottesfeld, Harry, and Gerterlyn Dozier. "Changes in Feelings of Powerlessness in a Community Action Program." Psychological Reports 19 (1966): 978.

Grebler, Leo, Joan W. Moore, and Ralph C. Guzman. *The Mexican American People: The Nation's Second Largest Minority*. New York: The Free Press, 1970.

Greely, Andrew. *Why Can't They Be Like Us?* New York: Dutton and Co., 1971.

Greenstein, Fred. "A Note on the Ambiguity of 'Political Socialization,' Definitions, Criticisms, and Strategies of Inquiry." *Journal of Politics* 32 (November 1970): 969-978.

_____. *Personality and Politics*. Chicago: Markham, 1969.

Greenstone, David, and Paul Peterson. "Reformers, Machines, and the War on Poverty." In *Cities and Suburbs*, edited by Bryan T. Downes. Belmont, Calif.: Wadsworth, 1971.

Hallman, Howard. *Community Control: A Study of Community Corporations and Neighborhood Boards*. Washington, D.C.: Washington Center for Metropolitan Studies, 1969.

_____. "Federally Financed Citizen Participation," *Public Administration Review* 32, Special Issue (September 1972): 421-427.

_____. "The Community Action Program: An Interpretative Analysis." In *Urban Poverty: Social and Political Dimensions*, edited by Warner Bloomberg, Jr., and Henry J. Schmandt. Beverly Hills, Calif.: Sage, 1968.

Handlin, Oscar. *The Uprooted*. Boston: Little, Brown and Co., 1952.

Henderson, Lenneal. "Black Political Life in the U.S.: A Bibliographical Essay." In *Black Political Life in the U.S.*, edited by Lenneal Henderson. San Francisco: Chandler, 1972.

Hensler, Carl P. "The Structure of Orientations Toward Government: Involvement, Efficacy, and Evaluation." Paper presented at the 67th Annual Meeting of the American Political Science Association, September 7-11, 1971, Chicago.

Hunter, Floyd, *Community Power Structure*. Chapel Hill, N.C.: University of North Carolina Press, 1953.

Jackson, John S., III. "A Political Socialization Bibliography and Survey of Projects in Progress." Mimeographed. Prepared for the American Political Science Association Committee on Pre-Collegiate Education, September 1972.

# BIBLIOGRAPHY

Jahoda, M., and E. Barnitz. "The Nature of Evaluation." *International Social Science Bulletin* 7: 353-364.

James, Dorothy Buckton. *Poverty, Politics, and Change*. Englewood Cliffs, N.J.: Prentice Hall, 1972.

Josephson, Eric. "Resistance to Community Surveys." *Social Problems* 18 (Summer 1970): 117-129.

Kariel, Henry S. *The Promise of Politics*. Englewood Cliffs: Prentice Hall, 1966.

Kerlinger, Fred N. *Foundations of Behavioral Research*. New York: Holt, Rinehart and Winston, 1965.

Kish, Leslie. "Selection of the Sample." In *Research Methods in the Behavioral Sciences*, edited by Leo Festinger and Daniel Katz. New York: Holt, Rinehart and Winston, 1965.

Kluckhohn, Florence R. "The Participant Observer Technique in Small Communities." *American Journal of Sociology* 46 (November 1940): 331-343.

Kornhauser, William. *The Politics of Mass Society*. New York: The Free Press, 1959.

Kramer, Ralph M. *Participation of the Poor: Comparative Community Case Studies in the War on Poverty*. Englewood Cliffs, N.J.: Prentice Hall, 1969.

Krause, Elliott A. "Functions of a Bureaucratic Ideology: Citizen Participation." *Social Problems* 16 (Fall 1968): 129-143.

Kuhn, Thomas. *The Structure of Scientific Revolutions*. Chicago: University of Chicago Press, 1962.

Langton, Kenneth P. *Political Socialization*. New York: Oxford University Press, 1969.

Leacock, Eleanor Burke. *The Culture of Poverty: A Critique*. New York: Simon and Schuster, 1971.

Lenski, Gerhard. *The Religious Factor*. Garden City, N.Y.: Doubleday, 1961.

Levens, Helene. "Organizational Affiliation and Powerlessness: A Case Study of the Welfare Poor." *Social Problems* 16 (Summer 1968): 18-32.

Lipset, Seymour Martin. Political Man. New York: Doubleday, 1963.

Litt, Edgar. Ethnic Politics in America. Glenview, Ill.: Scott, Foresman and Co., 1970.

Lomax, Louis. The Negro Revolt. New York: New American Library, 1962.

Love, Joseph P. "La Raza: Mexican-Americans in Rebellion." In Mexican-Americans in the United States: A Reader, edited by John H. Burma. Cambridge, Mass.: Schenkman, 1970.

Lovrich, Nicholas P., Jr. "Political Culture and Civic Involvement: A Comparative Analysis of Immigrant Ethnic Communities in San Pedro, California." Ph.D. dissertation, University of California at Los Angeles, 1971.

Lowi, Theodore. "The Public Philosophy: Interest Group Liberalism." American Political Science Review 61 (March 1967): 5-24.

MacCoby, Herbert. "The Differential Political Activity of Participants in a Voluntary Association." American Sociological Review 23 (October 1958): 524-532.

Mainzer, Lewis C. Political Bureaucracy. Glenview, Ill.: Scott, Foresman and Co., 1973.

Marsh, David. "Political Socialization: The Implicit Assumptions Questioned." British Journal of Political Science 1 (October 1971): 453-465.

Marshall, Dale Rogers. "Public Participation and the Politics of Poverty." In Race, Change, and Urban Society, edited by Peter Orleans and William Russell, Jr. Beverly Hills: Sage, 1971.

Marshall, Dale Rogers. The Politics of Participation in Poverty: A Case Study of the Board of the Economic and Youth Opportunities Agency of Greater Los Angeles. Berkeley: University of California Press, 1971.

May, Judy V. "Two Model Cities: Political Development at the Local Level." Paper presented at the 65th Annual Meeting of the American Political Science Association, September 2-6, 1969, New York City.

# BIBLIOGRAPHY

Meier, Matt S., and Feliciano Rivera. The Chicanos: A History of Mexican-Americans. New York: Hill and Wang, 1972.

Meister, Albert. Socialisme et Autogestion. Paris: Seuil, 1965.

Milbrath, Lester W. Political Participation: How and Why do People Get Involved in Politics? Chicago: Rand McNally, 1965.

Miller, S. M., Pamela Roby, and Alwine S. De Vos Van Steenwijk. "Creaming the Poor." Transaction 7 (June 1970): 38-45.

Mills, C. Wright. The Sociological Imagination. London: Oxford University Press, 1959.

Moguloff, Melvin. "Black Community Development in Five Western Cities." Social Work 15 (January 1970): 12-18.

_____. "Citizen Participation: A Review and Commentary on Federal Policies and Practices." Working Papers. Washington, D.C.: The Urban Institute, 1970.

_____. "Citizen Participation: The Local Perspective." Working Papers. Washington, D.C.: The Urban Institute, 1970.

Moore, Joan W. "Colonialism: The Case of the Mexican American." Social Problems 17 (Spring 1970): 463-472.

_____. "Political and Ethical Problems in a Large Scale Study of a Minority Community." In Ethics, Politics, and Social Research, edited by Gideon Sjoberg. Cambridge, Mass.: Schenkman, 1967.

_____. "Social Constraints on Sociological Knowledge: Academics and Research Concerning Minorities." Social Problems 21 (Summer 1973): 65-77.

Moynihan, Daniel Patrick. Maximum Feasible Misunderstanding. New York: The Free Press, 1969.

McClosky, Herbert. "Political Participation," International Encyclopedia of the Social Sciences. New York: Macmillan, 1968.

McConnell, Grant, Private Power and American Democracy. New York: Knopf, 1966.

McCoy, Charles A., and John Playford. Apolitical Politics: A Critique of Behavioralism. New York: T. Crowell, 1967.

Nie, Norman H., G. Bingham Powell, Jr., and Kenneth Prewitt. "Social Structure and Political Participation: Developmental Relationships, Part I." *American Political Science Review* 63 (June 1969): 361-378.

_____. "Social Structure and Political Participation: Developmental Relationships: Part II." *American Political Science Review* 63 (September 1969): 808-832.

"Nixon's Call to Counter-revolution." *Time*, February 5, 1973, pp. 24-29.

Novack, Michael. *The Rise of the Unmeltable Ethnics*. New York: Macmillan, 1971.

Olsen, Marvin E. "Social and Political Participation of Blacks." *American Sociological Review* 35 (August 1970): 682-696.

Parenti, Michael. "Ethnic Politics and the Persistence of Ethnic Identification." *American Political Science Review* 61 (September 1967): 717-726.

_____. "Power and Pluralism: A View from the Bottom." *Journal of Politics* 32 (August 1970): 501-530.

Pateman, Carole. *Participation and Democratic Theory*. Cambridge: Cambridge University Press, 1970.

Payne, Stanley. *The Art of Asking Questions*. Princeton: Princeton University Press, 1951.

Piven, Frances Fox, and Richard A. Cloward. *Regulating the Poor: The Functions of Public Welfare*. New York: Pantheon Books, 1971.

"Political Participation of Mexican-Americans in California." A Report of the California State Advisory Committee to the U.S. Commission on Civil Rights. Washington, D.C.: U.S. Government Printing Office, 1971.

Pollinger, Kenneth J. and Annette C. Pollinger. *Community Action and the Poor: Influence versus Social Control in a New York City Community*. New York: Praeger Publishers, 1972.

Polsby, Nelson. *Community Power and Political Theory*. New Haven, Conn.: Yale University Press, 1963.

Pranger, R. J. The Eclipse of Citizenship: Power and Participation in Contemporary Politics. New York: Holt, Rinehart and Winston, 1968.

Pratt, Raymond B. "Parties, Neighborhood Associations and the Politicization of the Urban Poor in Latin America: An Exploratory Analysis." Midwest Journal of Political Science 15 (August 1971): 495-524.

Presthus, Robert. Men at the Top. New York: Oxford University Press, 1964.

Rendon, Armando B. Chicano Manifesto: The History and Aspirations of the Second Largest Minority in America. New York: Collier, 1971.

_____. "Chicano Culture in a Gabacho World." In Introduction to Chicano Studies: A Reader, edited by Livie Isauro Duran and H. Russell Bernard. New York: Macmillan, 1973.

Robinson, John P., and Phillip R. Shaver. Measures of Social Psychological Attitudes. Ann Arbor: Survey Research Center Institute for Social Research, 1969.

Rose, Stephen M. The Betrayal of the Poor: The Transformation of Community Action. Cambridge, Mass.: Schenkman, 1972.

Rosenberg, Morris. "Misanthropy and Political Ideology." American Sociological Review 21 (December 1956): 690-694.

Rossi, Peter H. "Practice, Methods, and Theory in Evaluating Social Action Programs." In On Fighting Poverty: Perspectives from Experience, edited by James L. Sundquist. New York: Basic Books, 1969.

Roszack, Theodore. The Making of a Counterculture. Garden City, N.Y.: Anchor Books, 1969.

Rubin, Lillian. "Maximum Feasible Participation: The Origins, Implications, and Present Status." Poverty and Human Resources Abstracts 2 (November-December 1967): 5-18.

Sartori, Giovanni. Democratic Theory. Detroit: Wayne State University Press, 1962.

Schuman, Howard. "The Religious Factor in Detroit: Review, Replication, and Reanalysis." American Sociological Review 36 (February 1971): 30-48.

Schumpeter, Joseph. *Capitalism, Socialism, and Democracy*. New York, 1942.

Schwartz, Morris, and Charlotte G. Schwartz. "Problems in Participant Observation." *American Journal of Sociology* 60 (January 1955): 343-353.

Scoble, Harry. "The Political Scientist's Perspective on Poverty." In *Poverty: New Interdisciplinary Perspectives*, edited by Thomas Weaver and Alvin Magid. San Francisco: Chandler, 1969.

Searing, Donald D., Joel J. Schwartz, and Alden E. Lind. "The Structuring Principle: Political Socialization and Belief Systems." *American Political Science Review* 67 (June 1973): 415-433.

Selznick, Philip. *TVA and the Grass Roots: A Study in the Sociology of Formal Organization*. Berkeley, Calif: University of California Press, 1949.

Siegel, Sidney. *Nonparametric Statistics for the Behavioral Sciences*. New York: McGraw Hill, 1956.

Sigel, Roberta S. "Citizen Advisory Groups: Do they Really Represent the People or are They Rubberstamp Decisions of the 'Experts'?" *Nation's Cities* 6 (May 1968): 15-21.

Sjoberg, Gideon, Richard A. Brymer, and Buford Farris. "Bureaucracy and the Lower Class." In *Blacks and Bureaucracy: Readings in the Problems and Politics of Change*, edited by Virginia B. Ermer and John H. Strange. New York: Crowell, 1972.

Spiegel, Hans B. C. and Stephen D. Mitthenthal. "The Many Faces of Citizen Participation: A Bibliographic Overview." In *Citizen Participation in Urban Development*. Vol. 1, *Concepts and Issues*, edited by Hans B. C. Spiegel. Center for Community Affairs: NTL Institute for Applied Behavioral Science, 1968.

Stone, Chuck. *Black Political Power in America*. Rev. ed. New York: Delta, 1970.

Strange, John H. "Citizen Participation in Community Action and Model Cities Programs." *Public Administration Review* 32 Special Issue (October 1972): 655-669.

_____. "The Impact of Citizen Participation on Public Administration." *Public Administration Review* 32 Special Issue (September 1972): 457-470.

# BIBLIOGRAPHY

Suchman, Edward. *Evaluative Research.* New York: Russell Sage, 1967.

Survey Research Center. *A Manual for Coders.* Ann Arbor: Institute for Social Research, University of Michigan, 1955.

Toffler, Alvin. *Future Shock.* New York: Random House, 1970.

U.S. Bureau of the Census. *U.S. Census of the Population: 1960.* Vol. 1, *Characteristics of the Population.* Part 1, U.S. Summary. Washington, D.C.: U.S. Government Printing Office, 1964.

_____. *U.S. Census of the Population: 1960.* Vol. 1, *Characteristics of the Population.* Part 6, California. Washington, D.C.: U.S. Government Printing Office, 1963.

_____. *U.S. Census of the Population: 1960. Subject Reports:* Persons of Spanish Surname. Final Report PC (2) -1B. Washington, D.C.: U.S. Government Printing Office, 1963.

_____. *Census of the Population: 1970. Census Tracts.* Final Report PHC (1) -117. Los Angeles-Long Beach, Calif. SMSA. Washington, D.C.: U.S. Government Printing Office, 1972.

_____. *Census of the Population: 1970. Detailed Characteristics.* Final Report PC (1) D6. California. Section 1. Washington, D.C.: U.S. Government Printing Office, 1972.

_____. *Census of the Population: 1970. General Social and Economic Characteristics.* Final Report PC (1) -C6. California. Washington, D.C.: U.S. Government Printing Office, 1972.

_____. *Census of the Population: 1970. General Population Characteristics.* Final Report PC (1) -B6. California. Washington, D.C.: U.S. Government Printing Office, 1972.

_____. *Census of the Population: 1970. Detailed Characteristics.* Final Report. PC (1) -D1. U.S. Summary. Washington, D.C.: U.S. Government Printing Office, 1971.

U.S. Department of Housing and Urban Development. *Citizen and Business Participation in Urban Affairs: A Bibliography.* Washington, D.C.: U.S. Government Printing Office, 1970.

Valentine, Charles A. *Culture and Poverty: Critique and Counter-Proposals.* Chicago: The University of Chicago Press, 1968.

Verba, Sidney, and Norman H. Nie. *Participation in America: Political Democracy and Social Equality*. New York: Harper and Row, 1972.

Vidich, Arthur J. "Participant Observation and the Collection and Interpretation of Data." *American Journal of Sociology* 60 (January 1955): 354-360.

Warren, Ronald A. "Model Cities First Round: Politics, Planning and Participation." *Journal of the American Institute of Planners* 35 (July 1969): 245-253.

Weiss, Robert S., and Martin Rein. "The Evaluation of Broad Aim Programs: Experimental Design, Its Difficulties, and an Alternative." *Administrative Science Quarterly* 15 (March 1970): 97-109.

Wholey, Joseph S., John W. Scanlon, et al. *Federal Evaluation Policy: Analyzing the Effects of Public Programs*. Washington, D.C.: The Urban Institute, 1970.

Williams, Oliver P., and Charles Adrian. "The Insulation of Local Politics Under the Non-Partisan Ballot." *American Political Science Review* 53 (December 1959): 1052-1063.

Williams, Walter, and John H. Evans. "The Politics of Evaluation: The Case of Headstart." *Annals of the American Academy of Political and Social Sciences* 385 (September 1969): 118-132.

Williams, Walter. *Social Policy Research and Analysis*. New York: Elsevier, 1971.

Wilson, James Q. "Party Organization: The Search for Power." in *The California Governmental Process*, edited by Eugene C. Lee. Boston: Little, Brown and Co., 1966.

_____. "The Changing Political Position of the Negro." In *Assuring Freedom to the Free*, edited by A. M. Rose. Detroit: Wayne State University Press, 1964.

Wood, Robert C. "A Call for Return to Community." *Public Management* 51 (July 1969): 2-9.

Wright, Charles R. "Evaluation Research." In *International Encyclopedia of the Social Sciences*, edited by David L. Sills. New York: Macmillan, 1968.

Zurcher, Louis A. "The Poverty Board: Some Consequences of 'Maximum Feasible Participation,'." *The Journal of Social Issues* 26 (Summer 1970): 85-107.

# APPENDIX: EAST LOS ANGELES ADVISORY COUNCIL QUESTIONNAIRE

EAST LOS ANGELES ADVISORY COUNCIL QUESTIONNAIRE:
ENGLISH VERSION

Loyola University                                              1973

EAST LOS ANGELES ADVISORY COUNCIL SURVEY

Case #_____
Date_____
Time Start _____ Time Finish _____ Time Elapsed _____
Interviewer_____
Advisory Council_____
Respondent's Name_____ Sex_____
Address_____ Telephone_____

    We appreciate the cooperation and the time that you are giving us. As I explained earlier, we are conducting a study of all the advisory councils (USE PROPER SYNONYMS THROUGHOUT) in the East Los Angeles area. As an advisory council member, we are interested in your experiences on the council and in your opinions on important things such as education, politics, and problems in this community. All your answers will be kept strictly confidential; the responses will be compiled statistically and no names or other personal information will appear in the final study. We really appreciate your cooperation.
    First of all, I have questionnaires in both Spanish and English. Would you prefer that we talk in
                Spanish_____1 or in English_____2
            (IF SPANISH, SWITCH TO SPANISH QUESTIONNAIRE)
    Our questions cover several different kinds of things. It is not a test and there are no right or wrong answers. Please feel free to stop and ask me questions at any time. I would like to start by asking you a few questions about your experiences on the advisory council.

1. First of all, do you remember when was the council created?
2. Is the council still in operation?

---

    Items marked by an asterisk (*) are replicated from the 1972 panel study of the population; items marked by two asterisks (**) were included in both waves of the panel study (1965 and 1972).

# APPENDIX

    1. yes 2. no 8. DK 9. NR
    (IF NO) A. Why was the council disbanded?
3. About how long have you been a member of the council?
    years_____ months _____
4. Thinking back, do you remember how you became a council member, that is, did somebody ask you to join, where you elected, did you volunteer, or what?
    1. asked to join (ASK A)         7. other (SPECIFY) (ASK D)
    2. elected (ASK B)               8. DK
    3. volunteered (ASK C)         9. NR
    (IF ASKED TO JOIN) (A. Do you recall who asked you to join?

_____    _____
Name                                Position in organization
(PROBE FOR PROCEDURES FOLLOWED)
(IF ELECTED) B. How were you elected? (PROBE FOR PROCEDURES FOLLOWED)
(IF VOLUNTEERED) C. How did you find out about the advisory council?
(IF OTHER) D. (PROBE FOR PROCEDURES FOLLOWED IN JOINING)

5. Thinking back, do you remember why you wanted to be a council member, that is, for what reasons did you join the council?
6. Do you represent a particular group or agency on the council?
    1. yes, a particular group (ASK A and C)
    2. yes, a particular agency (ASK B and D)
    5. No
    8. DK
    9. NR
    (IF YES, A PARTICULAR GROUP)
    A. What group is that? _____ (NAME)
    (IF NOT CLEAR FROM NAME) C. What <u>kind</u> of group is that?
    (IF NOT CLEAR FROM NAME) D. What <u>kind</u> of agency is that?
7. About how often would you say you attend the meetings of the council? (READ CHOICES)
    1. about 25% of the time       5. never
    2. about 25-50% of the time   8. DK
    3. about 50-75% of the time   9. NR
    4. about 75-100% of the time
8. Have you ever been involved in any special committees of the council?
    1. yes (ASK A) 5. no 8. DK 9. NR
    (IF YES) A. Which ones?
9. Have you ever held any offices on the council?
    1. yes (ASK A) 2. no 8. DK 9. NR
    (IF YES) A. Which ones?

10. In your opinion, what are the most important functions or purposes of the council?
11. What kinds of things has the council done in the past? (ADDITIONAL PROBE IF NECESSARY: To what types of problems has the council addressed itself in the past, what have been some of its projects, can you name a few?)
12. What kinds of things is the council doing _now_?
13. How about in the future? What kinds of things does the council plan to do _in the future_?
14. Can you cite some accomplishments of the council?
15. Let me pursue this question a little further. How did the council go about trying to _____ (DO THIS)? (PROBE FOR ALL ACCOMPLISHMENTS CITED)
16. Are there any projects undertaken by the council which were not successful?
    1. yes (ASK A) 5. no 8. DK 9. NR
    (IF YES)
    A. Can you think of any reasons why the council was not successful in _____ (SPECIFY)? (PROBE FOR CAUSES OF FAILURE)
17. In your opinion, have the activities of the council had any effect on the community?
    1. yes (ASK A) 5. no (ASK B) 8. DK 9. NR
    (IF YES) A. In what ways?
    (IF NO) B. Why do you say that?
18. How would you describe the relationship between the council and the _____ agency? That is, is it generally good or are there occasional problems?
    1. the relationship is generally good
    3. it depends, there are occasional problems (ASK A)
    5. the relationship is generally bad (ASK A)
    8. DK
    9. NR
    (IF "R" MENTIONS PROBLEMS) A. What kinds of problems?
19. Has the agency (SPECIFY) generally been open to suggestions and proposals made by the council?
    1. yes (ASK A) 5. no (ASK B) 8. DK 9. NR
    (IF YES, PROBE) A. In what ways?
    (IF NO, PROBE FOR MANIFESTATIONS AND REASONS) B. Why do you say that?
20. In general, how do things get done on the council, that is, are there some people who seem to have more influence than others, or does everyone seem to have equal influence?
    1. some people seem to have more influence (ASK A)
    3. it depends (ASK A)
    5. everyone has equal influence
    8. DK
    9. NR

APPENDIX 205

    A. What kinds of people seem to have more influence? (PERMISSIBLE PROBE: AGENCY PEOPLE, COMMUNITY REPRESENTATIVES, PROFESSIONALS?)
21. How much influence do you feel you have on what gets decided on the council? Would you say that you have (READ CHOICES)
    1. a great deal of influence      4. none at all
    2. a moderate amount      8. DK
    3. a little      9. NR
22. In your opinion, how well do you think is the council fulfilling its purposes? (READ CHOICES)
    1. very well (ASK A)      4. not at all well (ASK B)
    2. moderately well (ASK A)      8. DK
    3. not very well (ASK B)      9. NR
    (IF POSITIVE) A. In what ways, can you be a little more specific?
    (IF NEGATIVE) B. Why do you say that, can you be a little more specific?
23. Do you have any ideas about how the council could be more effective?

    Now I would like to ask you a few more questions about your own role on the council.

24. How would you describe the role of being an advisory council member, that is, what are your duties and responsibilities?
25. Before joining the council, did you know what you were supposed to do as an advisory council member?
    1. yes 5. no 8. DK 9. NR
26. In the course of your experience as a council member, would you say that you learned any new things, that is, were there any new things that one had to learn in order to get things done?
    1. yes (ASK A) 5. no 8. DK 9. NR
    A. What kinds of new things would you say you learned?
27. Before you joined the advisory council, were you a member of any community organizations?
    1. yes (ASK A) 5. no 8. DK 9. NR
    A. Which ones?
28. How would you describe the extent of your involvement in community affairs <u>before</u> you joined the council? That is, were you (READ CHOICES)
    1. deeply involved in community affairs
    2. somewhat involved
    3. almost not involved
    4. completely not involved in community affairs
    8. DK
    9. NR
29. As a result of your experience on the advisory council would you say that you have become more involved in community affairs, less involved, or did the advisory council experience make no difference?

1. more involved (ASK A AND C)
2. less involved (ASK Why do you say that?)
3. no difference (ASK Why do you say that?)
4. unable to judge
7. Other
8. DK
9. NR
   A. Since you became an advisory council member, have you joined any community organizations?
      1. yes (ASK B) 5. no 8. DK 9. NR
      (IF YES) B. Which ones?
   C. Since you became an advisory council member, have you become more active in organizations you already belonged to?
      1. yes 5. no 8. DK 9. NR
30. Do you plan to be active in community affairs after you leave the council?
      1. yes 5. no 8. DK 9. NR
31. Some people tell us that they have learned many new things on the advisory council. Others tell us that they haven't learned anything at all. How about you? Looking at this list (HAND RESPONDENT A CARD) please tell me (1) whether you are familiar with any of these things or not, and (2) if you are, whether you learned any of them as a result of your experience on the advisory council?

   1. Robert's Rules of Order
   2. How to run a meeting
   3. How to persuade people to your own point of view
   4. How things get done in this particular agency
   5. How different government agencies work
   6. How different community groups work
   7. Who has the power in this community
   8. How to lobby in favor of legislation
   9. How to write a proposal for funding
   10. How to get community support for a new program
   11. How to contact public officials
   12. How to organize a protest march
   13. How to get something reported in the newspapers, radio, or television
   14. How to get out a newsletter
   15. How to quiet a riot

32. Do you belong to any other advisory councils in this area?
      1. yes (ASK A AND B) 5. no 8. DK 9. NR
      (IF YES) A. Which ones?
      B. Do you remember how long have you been a member of the _____ (SPECIFY) advisory council?
                  Years_____ months_____

APPENDIX

Now we would like to ask you some questions about different kinds of things. Again, there are no right or wrong answers, what we are interested in is in your own personal opinions and ideas.

**33. As we go around talking with people in this community, we find that some people prefer to call themselves:
    1. Spanish Speaking      6. Chicano
    2. Americans             7. By other terms (SPECIFY)
    3. Latin Americans      8. DK
    4. Mexicans             9. NR
    5. Mexican-Americans
How do you prefer to be identified? (IF IDENTITY GIVEN IN ENGLISH, ASK IN SPANISH)

**34. Y en espanol, como prefiere Usted ser identificado?
    1. Personas que hablan espanol  6. Chicanos
    2. Americanos                 7. De otra manera
    3. Latino-Americanos        8. DK
    4. Mexicanos                 9. NR
    5. Mexico-Americanos
(INTERVIEWER CHECK:) Understood Spanish\_\_\_\_\_1 Did not understand Spanish _____5

35. About how long have you been living in this community?
    _____ years     _____ months
36. When were you born?_____(year of birth)
37. Where were you born? _____(place of birth) (IF NOT IN U.S.) How long have you lived in the U.S.? (IF BORN IN U.S.) Have you ever been to Mexico?
    1. yes 5. no 8. DK 9. NR
    (ASK OF ALL RESPONDENTS WHO WERE BORN IN MEXICO OR HAVE VISITED MEXICO) **When was the last time you were in Mexico for a visit?

**38. Are you a citizen of the United States?
    1. yes 5. no 8. DK 9. NR

Now we would like to talk to you a little bit about your relatives.

39. Where were your parents born? Father _____ Mother_____
40. Of what descent is your: Father_____ Mother_____
**41. What language do you use when you talk with your family? (READ CHOICES)
    1. Spanish only          5. Both languages
    2. Mostly Spanish       8. DK
    3. Mostly English       9. NR
    4. English only
**42. People have different ideas about how family members should act toward each other. Will you please tell me whether you agree or disagree with the following:

|  | 1. agree | 3. depends, uncommitted | 5. disagree | 8. DK | 9. NR |
|---|---|---|---|---|---|
| Having children is the most important thing that can be done by a married woman. | — | — | — | — | — |
| A husband ought to have complete control over the family's income. | — | — | — | — | — |
| A father should take care of the children when the mother wants some time to herself | — | — | — | — | — |

Now we would like to ask your opinion about people in general.

*43. Generally speaking, would you say that most people can be trusted or that you can't be too careful in dealing with people?
    1. most people can be trusted   8. DK
    3. it depends, uncommitted   9. NR
    5. can't be too careful

*44. Would you say that most of the time, people try to be helpful, or that they are mostly just looking out for themselves?
    1. try to be helpful   8. DK
    3. it depends, uncommitted   9. NR
    5. look out for themselves

*45. Do you think that most people would try to take advantage of you if they got the chance, or would they try to be fair?
    1. try to be fair   8. DK
    3. it depends, uncommitted   9. NR
    5. take advantage

Now we would like to talk about schooling and education. First, do you remember the name of the last school you attended?

**46. What was the last grade that you completed at this school (CIRCLE) 1 2 3 4 5 6 7 8 9 10 11 12 13 14 15 16 17 18 19 20

**47. In your opinion, what are the main things that children need to be taught in the schools today?

**48. Do you feel the same for both boys and girls?
    1. yes 5. no 8. DK 9. NR

APPENDIX

*49. Are the schools in this community teaching these things?
1. yes  5. no (ASK A)  8. DK  9. NR
(IF NO) A. Why is that?

*50. As we go around the community talking to people, we find that everyone wants certain things out of life. When you think about what really matters in your life, what are your wishes and hopes for the future? In other words, if you imagine your future in the best possible light, what would your life look like then, if you are to be happy? Take your time in answering, such things aren't easy to put into words. (IF REQUIRED) ADDITIONAL PROBE: What would your life have to be like for you to be completely happy? (OBLIGATORY PROBE) Anything else? (WRITE ON BACK IF NEEDED)

*51. Now, taking the other side of the picture, what are your fears and worries about the future? In other words, if you imagine your future in the worst possible light, what would your life look like then? (IF REQUIRED) ADDITONAL PROBE: What would make you unhappy? (OBLIGATORY PROBE) Anything else? (WRITE ON BACK IF NEEDED)

Here is a picture of a ladder. (HAND RESPONDENT CARD) Suppose we say that the top of the ladder (POINT) represents the best possible life for you and the bottom (POINT) represents the worst possible life for you.

*52. Where on the ladder (MOVE FINGER UP AND DOWN ON LADDER) do you feel you personally stand at the present time? Step number _____

*53. Where on the ladder would you say you stood about seven years ago? (MOVE FINGER UP AND DOWN ON LADDER) Step number _____

*54. And where do you think you will be on the ladder five years from now? Step number _____

*55. Now, what are your wishes and hopes for the future of this community? If you picture the future of the community in the best possible light, how would things look, let's say five years from now? (OBLIGATORY PROBE) Anything else? (IF NEEDED, WRITE ON BACK)

*56. And what about your fears and worries for the future of this community? If you picture the future of the community in the worst possible light, how would things look about five years from now? (OBLIGATORY PROBE) Anything else? (IF NEEDED, WRITE ON BACK)

*57. Now, looking at the ladder again (POINT), suppose your greatest hopes for the community are at the top (POINT). Where would you put the community on the ladder (MOVE FINGER UP AND DOWN) at the present time? Step number _____

*58. Where did the community stand seven years ago? Step number _____

*59. Just as your best guess, where do you think the community will be on the ladder five years from now? Step number _____
Now I would like to ask you for some more opinions on the future. For example:

**60. Some people feel that 50 years from now Mexican-Americans will be exactly the same as everyone else in the United States, others disagree. Do you:
    1. strongly agree               5. strongly disagree
    2. agree                          8. DK
    3. uncommitted, depends     9. NR
    4. disagree

**61. Do you think such a thing would be:
    1. very good (ASK A)        5. very bad (ASK A)
    2. good (ASK A)             8. DK
    3. in between (ASK A)     9. NR
    4. bad (ASK A)              A. Why do you say that?

**62. What about your children? Is there anything about the Mexican way of life that you would particularly like to see them follow?

**63. It has been frequently said that people of Spanish speaking background in the Southwest have to work a lot harder to get ahead than Anglo-Americans.

|  | 1. very true | 2. somewhat true | 4. not very true | 5. not true at all | 8. DK | 9. NR |
|---|---|---|---|---|---|---|
| How true is that in this community? | ___ | ___ | ___ | ___ | ___ | ___ |
| How about in business? | ___ | ___ | ___ | ___ | ___ | ___ |
| How about in politics, in government? | ___ | ___ | ___ | ___ | ___ | ___ |

*64. Do you feel that things in general in East Los Angeles have changed in the past seven years: that is, have they become better or worse, or have they remained the same?
    1. things have become better (ASK A)    8. DK
    3. things have remained the same      9. NR
    5. things have become worse (ASK A)
    (IF CHANGED, "BETTER" OR "WORSE") A. in your opinion, what accounts for this change?

65. In the past few years, the federal (national) government has been directing its attention to the problems of the poor through a number of programs usually called the War on Poverty. Some people in this community tell us that they are familiar with these programs, while others say that they never heard of them. How about you? Have you ever heard about any of these programs?
    1. heard (ASK A and Q. 66 and Q. 67)
    5. never heard (GO TO Q. 68)
    8. DK (GO TO Q. 68)
    9. NR (GO TO Q. 68)

APPENDIX 211

        A. Which programs have you heard about?
66. Some people say that the programs of the War on Poverty have been successful in helping to resolve the problems of the poor; other people say that, overall, the War on Poverty has been a failure. What do you think?
        1. overall, War on Poverty has been successful (ASK A)
        3. partly success, partly failure (ASK A)
        5. overall failure (ASK A)
        8. DK
        9. NR
        A. Why do you say that?
67. The current administration has recently been cutting a number of programs associated with the War on Poverty. Do you feel that this is a good thing or is it bad?
        1. very good thing (ASK A)     5. very bad thing (ASK A)
        2. good thing (ASK A)         8. DK
        3. uncommitted, it depends (ASK A) 9. NR
        4. bad thing (ASK A)
        A. Why do you say that?
*68. Over the past years, do you remember hearing or reading anything about protests, marches, or demonstrations in the Mexican-American community?
        1. yes (ASK A, B, and C)     8. DK
        5. no (GO TO Q. 69)         9. NR
        *A. In your opinion, why did these protests, marches, or demonstrations occur?
        *B. Did you attend any of these protests, marches, or demonstrations?
           1. yes  5. no  8. DK  9. NR
        *C. In your opinion, do you think these protests, marches, or demonstrations are (1) good for the community, (2) make no difference for the community, or (3) are bad for the community?
           1. good for the community     8. DK
           3. make no difference for the community
           5. bad for the community      9. NR
**69. Now I would like to talk to you about some of the experiences you and your family have had at work. Are you working now?
        1. yes (ASK A, B, and C)     8. DK
        5. no (GO TO Q. 70)         9. NR
(IF YES) **A. What kind of work do you do? (SPECIFIC AS POSSIBLE) Job _____ **B. Generally speaking, how satisfied are you with your present job?
        1. very                 5. not at all
        2. pretty much      8. DK
        4. not very           9. NR

&ast;&ast;C. How would you rate your chances of promotion on your present job?
    1. very good          5. poor
    2. good               8. DK
    4. not very good    9. NR

70. Is your husband (wife) working now?
    1. yes (ASK A)    5. no    8. DK    9. NR
    (IF YES) A. What kind of work does he (she) do? (SPECIFIC AS POSSIBLE) Job _____

&ast;&ast;71. Suppose you knew a really outstanding young man here in the neighborhood—what one occupation do you think you would advise him to aim toward?

&ast;&ast;72. What would you say is the most important single thing for a young man to consider when he is choosing his life's work?

&ast;&ast;73. Now, I am going to read to you some statements about the things some people like on jobs. Please tell me, for each one, whether you think it is (1) very important, (2) important, (3) don't care, (4) not important, (5) not important at all.
    1. High income
    2. No danger of being fired
    3. Chance for advancement
    4. The work is important and gives a feeling of accomplishment
    5. Working hours are short, lots of free time
    6. You really have a feeling of belonging to an organization
    7. People take you as you are

&ast;&ast;74. Counting rents, interests, wages, salaries and things like that, in which of the following categories did your family's <u>total income</u> fall last year before taxes? (HAND RESPONDENT CARD) Please indicate the number under which your salary falls, we don't need your exact salary.
    1. Under $1000 a year or under $20 a week
    2. $1000 to $1499 a year or $20 to $28.50 a week
    3. $1500 to $1999 a year or $29 to $37.50 a week
    4. $2000 to $2499 a year or $38 to $47.50 a week
    5. $2500 to $2999 a year or $48 to $57.50 a week
    6. $3000 to $3999 a year or $58 to $76.50 a week
    7. $4000 to $4999 a year or $77 to $95.50 a week
    8. $5000 to $5999 a year or $96 to $115.50 a week
    9. $6000 to $6999 a year or $116 to $134.50 a week
    10. $7000 to $9999 a year or $135 to $192.50 a week
    11. $10,000 to $14,999 a year or $193 to $288.50 a week
    12. $15,000 and over a year or $289 and more a week

&ast;&ast;75. How many people are supported by this income?

Now we would like to change the subject and talk about the groups you belong to.

APPENDIX

**76. Do you have a religious preference? That is, are you:
    1. Catholic                                   7. No preference
    2. Protestant (ASK A)                8. DK
    3. Something else (SPECIFY)     9. NR
    (IF PROTESTANT, ASK) A. What denomination is that?

**77. How important is religion to you? Would you say that it is: (READ CHOICES)
    1. Very important                  5. Not at all important
    2. Somewhat important           8. DK
    4. Not very important             9. NR

**78. About how often, if ever, have you attended religious services in the last year? I will read from my list; please tell me which one applies.
    1. Once a week or more         6. A special day only,
    2. Two or three times a month        for example, Easter
    3. Once a month                    5. Never
    4. A few times a year or less     8. DK
                                         9. NR

**(INTERVIEWER)                            1. yes  5. no  8. DK
IS A SHRINE VISIBLE?               ____ ____ ____
VIRGIN OF GUADALUPE?             ____ ____ ____
OTHER RELIGIOUS ART?              ____ ____ ____
PERSONAL RELIGIOUS JEWELRY?    ____ ____ ____
PICTURE OF JFK OR RFK?           ____ ____ ____

**79. Are you a member of any religious organizations that meet more or less regularly?
    1. yes (ASK A and B)  5. no    8. DK    9. NR
    (IF YES) A. What are their names?
    B. About how long have you been a member of the _____?
    (SPECIFY ALL RELIGIOUS ORGANIZATIONS MENTIONED BY RESPONDENT)
    NAME OF ORGANIZATION ____ HOW LONG A MEMBER? ____

**80. Are you a member of any other organizations that meet more or less regularly, such as societies, clubs, fraternal organizations, educational groups, unions?
    1. yes   5. no   8. DK   9. NR
    (IF YES, ASK A, B, C, D, and E and <u>ENTER ON CHART</u> BELOW; IF NO, GO TO QUESTION 81) A. What are their names?
    B. What kind of group is that? (IF NOT CLEAR FROM NAME)
    C. About how long have you been a member of _____?
       (SPECIFY ALL ORGANIZATIONS MENTIONED BY R.)
    D. About how often do you attend the meetings of the ____?
       (SPECIFY ALL ORGANIZATIONS MENTIONED, READ CHOICES)
       1. most of the time      4. not very often
       2. sometimes              5. never
    E. Have you ever been an officer in the ____? (SPECIFY FOR ALL ORGANIZATIONS MENTIONED)

The following statements are simply to ask you about your outlook on life in general. As far as we are concerned, there are not right or wrong answers to these questions. We are merely interested in what you think. Would you agree or disagree with the following statements? (CIRCLE NUMBER OF ANSWER)

**81. I don't think public officials care much about what people like me think.
    1. agree    5. disagree    8. DK    9. NR

**82. Voting is the only way that people like me can have any say about how the government runs things.
    1. agree    5. disagree    8. DK    9. NR

**83. People like me don't have any say about what the government does.
    1. agree    5. disagree    8. DK    9. NR

**84. Sometimes politics and government seem so complicated that a person like me can't really understand what's going on.
    1. agree    5. disagree    8. DK    9. NR

Now I'd like to ask a few questions about the way you feel about local government—the government that runs things here in the community.

*85. About how much effect do you think that the activities of the local government have on your day-to-day life? Do they have a great effect, some effect, or none?
    1. great effect (ASK A)    2. some effect (ASK A)    5. none
    8. DK    9. NR
    A. Did you feel the same way <u>before</u> you were an advisory council member?
        1. yes    5. no    8. DK    9. NR

*86. In general, do you think your local government is run the way it should be, or not run the way it should be?
    1. Run the way it should be (ASK A and B)
    3. In between (ASK A and B)
    5. Not run the way it should be (ASK A and B)
    8. DK
    9. NR
    *A. Why do you feel that way?
    B. Did you feel the same way <u>before</u> you were an advisory council member?
        1. yes    5. no    8. DK    9. NR

*87. Some people tell us that there is nothing they can do to affect what the <u>local government</u> does. Other people say they can influence what gets decided in this community if they want to. How about you? Do you feel that <u>you can affect</u> what the local government does, <u>or not</u>?
    1. Yes, can affect (ASK A and C)      8. DK
    3. Sometimes, depends (ASK A and C)    9. NR
    5. No, can't affect (ASK B and C)

APPENDIX 215

     *A. How can you have this effect?
     *B. Why not?
     C. Did you feel the same way before you were an advisory council member?
        1. yes   5. no   8. DK   9. NR

**88. Now I would like to ask you about organizations in the community. Here is a list of organizations which people tell us are around here. I will read them from my list; please follow me on the list I give you. (HAND RESPONDENT CARD) Please tell me if (1) you never heard of the organization, (2) you heard of the organization somewhere, or (3) you belong to it.

| | | 1. never | 2. heard | 3. belongs | 8. DK | 9. NR |
|---|---|---|---|---|---|---|
| **1. | GI Forum | ___ | ___ | ___ | ___ | ___ |
| *2. | LUCHA | ___ | ___ | ___ | ___ | ___ |
| **3. | PTA | ___ | ___ | ___ | ___ | ___ |
| **4. | Alianza Hispano-Americana | ___ | ___ | ___ | ___ | ___ |
| *5. | La Raza Unida party | ___ | ___ | ___ | ___ | ___ |
| **6. | MAPA | ___ | ___ | ___ | ___ | ___ |
| *7. | Chicano Moratorium | ___ | ___ | ___ | ___ | ___ |
| *8. | TELACU | ___ | ___ | ___ | ___ | ___ |
| **9. | Republican clubs | ___ | ___ | ___ | ___ | ___ |
| **10. | Democratic clubs | ___ | ___ | ___ | ___ | ___ |
| **11. | PASSO | ___ | ___ | ___ | ___ | ___ |
| **12. | LULAC | ___ | ___ | ___ | ___ | ___ |
| *13. | Brown Berets | ___ | ___ | ___ | ___ | ___ |
| *14. | Chicano Liberation Front | ___ | ___ | ___ | ___ | ___ |
| **15. | CSO | ___ | ___ | ___ | ___ | ___ |
| *16. | Neighborhood Legal Aid | ___ | ___ | ___ | ___ | ___ |
| *17. | MECHA | ___ | ___ | ___ | ___ | ___ |
| *18. | United Farm Workers | ___ | ___ | ___ | ___ | ___ |

(IF BELONGS TO ANY, ASK QUESTIONS A, B, AND C AND <u>ENTER IN CHART BELOW</u>, IF NO, GO TO QUESTION 89)
    A. About how long have you been a member of the _____?
       (SPECIFY ALL ORGANIZATIONS MENTIONED BY R.)
   *B. About how often do you attend the meetings of the _____?
       (SPECIFY ALL ORGANIZATIONS R. BELONGS TO; READ CHOICES)
       1. most of the time     5. never
       2. sometimes           8. DK
       4. not very often       9. NR

*C. Have you ever been an officer in the _____? (SPECIFY
FOR ALL ORGANIZATIONS R. BELONGS TO)

| NAME OF ORGANIZATION | MEMBER SINCE (A) | ATTEND MEETINGS (B) | OFFICER (C) |
|---|---|---|---|
| 1. | | | |
| 2. | | | |
| 3. | | | |
| 4. | | | |

**89. This list of Mexican-American organizations is incomplete. Have we forgotten any organizations that you are familiar with?
  1. yes (ASK A) 5. no 8. DK 9. NR
 (IF YES) A. What are their names?

*90. People in this community have different opinions about these organizations. Thinking about the organizations you've mentioned, do you think that these organizations are (1) good for the community, (2) don't make any difference, or (3) are bad for the community?
(ASK RESPONDENT HIS OPINIONS ONLY ABOUT THE ORGANIZATIONS HE HAS HEARD ABOUT, THAT IS, REFER TO CHART ON QUESTION 88)

**91. In talking to people about voting, we find that a lot of people were not able to vote because they were not registered or they were sick or they just did not have the time. How about you? Are you registered to vote?
  1. yes (ASK A AND C) 5. no (ASK B) 8. DK 9. NR
 (IF YES) **A. Where did you get registered to vote?
 (IF NO) **B. Why was that?
 (IF YES, DID REGISTER) **C. Did you vote in the last presidential election?
  1. yes (ASK D) 5. no 8. DK 9. NR
 (IF YES, DID VOTE) *C. Who did you vote for president?
 (READ CHOICES)
  1. McGovern 2. Nixon 7. Somebody else 8. DK 9. NR

92. Generally speaking, do you usually think of yourself as a Republican, a Democrat, an independent, or what?
  1. Republican    7. Other
  2. Democrat    8. DK
  3. Independent   9. NR

93. Talking about politics, do you follow the accounts of political and governmental affairs? Would you say that you follow them regularly, from time to time, or never?
  1. regularly 2. from time to time 5. never 8. DK 9. NR

94. Do you follow (listen to, read about) public affairs in the newspapers (radio, television, magazines) nearly every day, from time to time, or never?

APPENDIX 217

   1. nearly every day      5. never
   2. about once a week     8. DK
   3. from time to time      9. NR

Now I would like to ask you some questions about the way you feel about the national government—the government that runs things in Washington, D.C.

*95. About how much effect do you think that the activities of the national government, the laws passed, and so on, have on your day to day life? Do they have a great effect, some effect, or none?
   1. great effect (ASK A)   2. some effect (ASK A)   5. no effect (ASK A)   8. DK   9. NR
   A. Did you feel the same way <u>before</u> you were an advisory council member?
     1. yes   5. no   8. DK   9. NR

*96. In general, do you think that the <u>national</u> government is run the way it should be, or not run the way it should be?
   1. run the way it should be (ASK A AND B)
   3. in between (ASK A AND B)
   5. not run the way it should be (ASK A AND B)
   8. DK
   9. NR
   *A. Why do you feel that way?
   B. Did you feel the same way <u>before</u> you were an advisory council member?
     1. yes   5. no   8. DK   9. NR

*97. Some people tell us that there is nothing they can do to affect what the <u>national</u> government does. Other people say that they can influence what gets decided in Washington if they want to. How about you? Do you feel that <u>you can affect</u> what the national government does or not?
   1. yes, can affect (ASK A AND C)   3. depends (ASK A AND C)
   5. no, can't affect (ASK B AND C)   8. DK   9. NR
   *A. How can you have this effect?
   *B. Why not?
   C. Did you feel the same way <u>before</u> you were an advisory council member?
     1. yes   5. no   8. DK   9. NR

*98. As we go around the East Los Angeles community, some people tell us that there are many problems in this community. In your opinion, do you think that there are important problems facing the East Los Angeles community? (IF NO, OR DON'T KNOW, ASK: EVEN LITTLE PROBLEMS, MAYBE THINGS YOU DON'T PAY ATTENTION TO BECAUSE YOU TAKE THEM FOR GRANTED?)
   1. yes (ASK A, B, AND C)   5. no   8. DK   9. NR
   (IF YES) *A. In your opinion, what are the most important problems facing the East Los Angeles community?
     Problem 1:     Problem 2:     Problem 3:

*B. In your opinion, how could these problems be resolved? (PROBE: ANYTHING ELSE?)
C. There is much talk about whose responsibility it is to solve problems of the sort we have just talked about. Which group should have the main responsibility for solving these problems? (READ CHOICES AND ASK FOR EACH PROBLEM MENTIONED)

Problem 1:  1. the individual and his family
Problem 2:  2. the local government
Problem 3:  3. the state government
            4. the national government
            5. community grass roots groups
            6. private business

**99. Some people say that all people of Mexican background should get together politically, and other people disagree. Which would you say?
   1. agree (ASK A)   5. disagree (ASK A)   7. other   8. DK   9. NR
   **A. Why do you say that?

**100. Some people say that all people of Mexican background should get together with Negroes politically, but others don't agree. Which would you say?
   1. agree (ASK A)   5. disagree (ASK A)   7. other   8. DK   9. NR
   **A. Why do you say that?

*101. Some people say that <u>only</u> people of Mexican background should get together politically, that is, form political groups <u>only</u> with other Mexican-Americans; other people disagree. Which would you say?
   1. agree (ASK A)   5. disagree (ASK A)   8. DK   9. NR
   *A. Why do you say that?

*102. Here is a list of things that some people think should be done to solve problems in this community. As I read them, would you please tell me with which ones do you strongly agree, agree, are undecided, disagree, or strongly disagree?
   1. do nothing because things will work themselves out
   2. elect people of Mexican background to office
   3. join in public street demonstrations
   4. work within the Democratic or Republican parties
   5. riot if necessary
   6. get people of Mexican background into government jobs
   7. form a separate political party for people of Mexican background only

*103. When thinking about your opinions on community problems, do you think that other people in the community think the same way that you do? Which of the following statements best describes your own feelings? (CIRCLE THE ANSWER AND READ RESPONSES)

APPENDIX 219

      1. I think that I am pretty much alone in my way of thinking about problems in this community.
      2. Although not alone, I feel that only a small minority of people think the same way I do about problems in this community.
      3. I feel that most people think the way I do about problems in this community.
    *A. Why do you say that?

**104. Now there are a few more things I would like to get your opinion about. Once again, there are no right or wrong answers, we would just like to get your opinion. For each of the following statements, please tell me whether you agree, or you disagree.

| | agree | depends | disagree | DK | NR |
|---|---|---|---|---|---|
| Making plans only brings unhappiness because the plans are hard to fulfill. | ___ | ___ | ___ | ___ | ___ |
| It doesn't make much difference if the people elect one or another candidate, for nothing will change. | ___ | ___ | ___ | ___ | ___ |
| With things as they are today, an intelligent person ought to think only about the present without worrying about what is going to happen tomorrow. | ___ | ___ | ___ | ___ | ___ |
| The secret of happiness is not expecting too much out of life and being content with what comes your way. | ___ | ___ | ___ | ___ | ___ |

**105. Finally, to wind up, could you please tell me what you read and see on television. What is your favorite television station—the one you watch most often?
      1. Mexican                5. no favorite
      2. Mexican-U.S. origin    6. no television
      3. network                8. DK
      4. other                  9. NR

**106. What is your favorite radio station—the one you listen to most often?
      1. Mexican                5. no favorite
      2. Mexican-U.S. origin    6. no radio
      3. Network                8. DK
      4. Local or other        9. NR

**107. And what newspaper do you read most often?
      1. Mexican                5. no newspaper
      2. Mexican-U.S. origin    8. DK
      3. major daily newspaper  9. NR
      4. neighborhood

**108. And what magazines do you read or subscribe to?
**109. Thank you very much. Your opinions have been very valuable to us. Should it be necessary, may we come back and talk to you again at some future time?
    1. yes   5. no

**INDEX**

advisory councils: activities of, 87-89; definition of, 65; early use of, 2; effectiveness of, 89-91; effects of involvement in, 11-12, 30, 31, 33-34, 36-42, 43, 99-142, 164-167, 173, 184; [acquisition of political attitudes, 12, 30, 31, 34-38, 100-114, 128; acquisition of political skills, 11-12, 30, 38-40, 87-88, 91, 114-119, 121-122; behavioral changes, 12, 30, 40-42, 122-128; formation of indigenous leaders, 10-12, 42-45, 175-181, 185]; functions of, 86; internal operation of, 89; membership of, 68-72, 84-98 [characteristics of, 70-72, 84, 92-95, 99; overlap in, 69-70; overrepresentation of females in, 70-72; previous involvement of, 40-41, 95-98, 125, 127, 140-142, 183, 184; recruitment patterns for, 85-86, 91, 95-98, 183; representativeness of, 11, 84, 92-95, 183]; power of, 4-5, 6-7, 8, 10, 139, 184; type of, 65, 84-85, 88, 89, 91, 132, 134, 138, 184 [governmental level of, 65] (see also, citizen participation, organizational involvement, politicization, self-selection factor)
Aleshire, Robert, 5
Almond, Gabriel A., 23, 29

Bachrach, Peter, 10
Banfield, Edward C., 11
Baratz, Morton S., 10
Becker, Selwyn W., 33
Brim, Orville G., Jr., 26

Campbell, Donald T., 48

citizen participation: in advisory councils, 2-3, 5, 16 (see also, advisory councils, political participation)
Cloward, Richard A., 174
Community Action Programs (CAP), 2, 3, 6, 8-9, 10, 64, 68, 84, 86, 88, 183 (see also, Economic Opportunity Act, War on Poverty)
community organizations, 41, 90-91, 121, 122-123, 125-127, 154, 164, 174 (see also, Mexican-Americans, community organizations)

Dahl, Robert A., 24
data collection procedures: conduct of field work, 74-75; definition of community, 61-64, 76, 79; definition of universe of advisory councils, 65-66; design of questionnaire, 72-73; drawing of sample, 72; obtaining lists of members of advisory councils, 67-68, 79-80; problems of, 67-68 (see also, self-selection factor)

East Los Angeles: characteristics of, 61-64; problems in, 139, 161, 174.
Economic Opportunity Act (1964), 1, 2, 8 (see also, War on Poverty)
ethnic consciousness (see, group consciousness)
evaluative research, 46-47

factor analysis (see, politicization, indices of)

Gamson, William A., 37, 139

Gans, Herbert, 158
Glazer, Nathan, 6
Goldrich, Daniel, 30, 128, 173
Gordon, Milton, 158
Grebler, Leo, 48, 64, 96, 150, 158
Greenstein, Fred, 25
Greenstone, David, 42
group consciousness: among blacks, 32, 140, 149-150; among Mexican-Americans, 33, 62, 139, 140, 149-161; as alternative route to political participation, 32-33, 139-140, 149, 162-164, 168, 185; related to organizational involvement, 164-168 (see also, Mexican-Americans; political participation, as a function of group consciousness)
Guzman, Ralph C., 48, 64, 150

Johnson, Lyndon B., 1

Kahn, Tom, 11
Kerlinger, Fred N., 129
Krause, Elliott A., 4

leadership. (see, advisory councils, effects of involvement in, formation of indigenous leaders; organizational involvement, group effects of)
Litt, Edgar, 25, 158

Marsh, David, 26
maximum feasible participation, 2-3, 6, 7-8, 64, 138, 183; consequences of, 3, 7, 8, 12, 183; effects on power distribution of, 3-5, 7; effects on quality of service of, 5-6; long-range effects of, 6-7, 8, 9; operationalization of, 2-3; short-range effects of, 3-6, 9. (see also, Economic Opportunity Act, War on Poverty)
Mexican-Americans: cultural distinctiveness of, 150, 152-154, 157-158, 162, 180; community organizations, 39, 122-123 [perceptions of, 45, 90, 120, 154, 178]; political attitudes of, changes in, 42, 61-62, 139, 150-158, 179; political mobilization among, 33, 61-63, 158-162; political strategies of [cooperation with other groups, 45, 160, 164, 176, 179-181; ethnic separatism, 45, 160, 176, 179-181]. (see also, community organizations; group consciousness, among Mexican-Americans)
Mexican-American study project (1965), 48, 64, 73, 150
Milbrath, Lester W., 23
Miller, S. M., 8
Mills, C. Wright, 47
Mittenthal, Stephen, 4, 5
Model Cities program, 2, 3, 8-9, 47, 64, 79, 84, 85, 87, 183 (see also, Economic Opportunity Act, War on Poverty)
Moore, Joan W., 48, 64, 150

Nie, Norman H., 22, 27, 28-30, 31, 32, 112, 128, 132, 135, 149, 164, 167, 172, 173

organizational involvement: as alternative route to political participation, 29-32, 33, 127-128, 168, 172, 173, 184; as independent variable, 33-35; group effects of, 12, 32, 43, 44-45, 172-173, 181; individual effects of, 12, 32, 42-44, 172, 181, 184; related to group consciousness, 164-168. (see also, advisory councils; political participation, as function of organizational involvement; politicization)

Pachon, Harry P., 48, 64, 73, 150, 152, 153, 155-156, 157, 159, 161
Parenti, Michael, 13, 14, 158
participation. (see, political participation)

# INDEX

Pateman, Carole, 23
Peterson, Paul, 42
Piven, Frances Fox, 174
political attitudes and cognitions: awareness of impact of government, 27, 36, 100-102, 129-131, 134-135, 136, 137, 140, 162, 165, 167; evaluation of government, 37, 102-105, 129-130, 131, 134, 135-136, 137, 139; political efficacy, 27, 37-38, 105-108, 129-130, 131, 133-134, 136, 137, 138, 139, 168, 184; self-efficacy, 22-23, 109-111, 129-130, 131, 133, 135, 136, 139, 165, 167, 184; social trust, 27, 38, 111-113. (see also, politicization, dimensions of, indices of)
political capabilities: political knowledge, 40, 119-121, 129; political skills, 39-40, 114-119, 121, 131, 135, 136, 137, 138, 166-167. (see also, politicization, dimensions of, indices of)
political participation, 13-15, 21, 22-25, 27-33, 172-173; as a function of "enabling antecedents," 27, 28, 29, 128; as a function of group consciousness, 32-33; as a function of organizational involvement, 29-32, 127-128, 181; by lower-status groups, 21, 22-24; related to SES or class, 22-24, 27-28, 127-128; studies of, 21-25 (see also, citizen participation)
political participation behavior: electoral activity, 41, 42, 124-125, 131, 164, 168; local community involvement, 40-41, 123-124, 131, 136, 137, 138, 139, 168;perception of increase in, 125-128, 129-131, 135, 136, 137, 139, 166, 184; protest activity, 41, 124, 139. (see also, politicization, dimensions of, indices of)
political parties, 25, 36, 41, 42, 123, 176-177, 179, 181
political socialization, 21, 25-26; during childhood, 21, 25-26; as adult, 21, 25-26, 52, 175. (see also, politicization)

politicization: as dependent variable, 33-35; dimensions of, 34-36, 100-127, 128, 129, 134, 136 [capabilities to affect government, 38-40, 114-122, 128, 129; political participation behavior, 40-42, 122-128, 129, 131; propensity to affect government, 36-38, 100-114, 127-128, 129]; indices of, 128-131; likelihood of sustaining, 42-43, 173-174, 175, 185; member-related correlates of, 136-142; operationalization of, 34-45; organizational correlates of, 131-136 [council-member-related, 132-133, 134, 135, 136; council-related, 132-136]
Powell, G. Bingham, Jr., 22, 28, 29-30
Prewitt, Kenneth, 22, 28, 29-30

quasi-experimental design, 46, 47-49

Rein, Martin, 47
Rendon, Armando, 71
research strategy, 46-50
Rossi, Peter H., 8

self-selection factor, 91, 95-98, 140-142, 184-185
socialization. (see, political socialization)
Spiegel, Hans, 4, 5
Stanley, Julian C., 48
Strange, John, 2

Verba, Sidney, 23, 27, 28, 29, 31, 32, 128, 132, 135, 149, 164, 167, 172, 173

War on Poverty, 1, 2, 3, 4, 5, 6, 36, 37, 40, 42, 56, 57, 73, 104-105, 145, 183, 185; studies of, 3-13, 47, 84, 102, 104, 105, 119, 121-122. (see also, Economic Opportunity Act)
Warren, Ronald A., 5
Weiss, Robert S., 47
Wholey, Joseph S., 47

**ABOUT THE AUTHOR**

BILIANA C. S. AMBRECHT is an assistant professor of political science at the University of California, Santa Barbara, where she teaches courses in urban politics, public policy, and political socialization. Previously, she was on the faculty at Loyola Marymount University.

Professor Ambrecht received her Ph.D. from the University of California at Los Angeles in 1973 and subsequently completed postdoctoral studies in urban and ethnic politics at Harvard University. She has been the recipient of a number of research grants and fellowships from the National Endowment for the Humanities, the Ford Foundation, the Sea Grant Program, and the American Political Science Association. Her major research concerns currently are focused on the prospects of increasing the scope of citizen participation in the work organization and in the local community.

**RELATED TITLES**
Published by
Praeger Special Studies

ETHNICITY AND SUBURBAN LOCAL POLITICS
David J. Schnall

THE IMPACT OF FEDERAL ANTI-POVERTY POLICIES
Charles Brecher

MINORITY ACCESS TO FEDERAL GRANTS-IN-AID:
The Gap Between Policy and Performance
John Hope II

SOCIALIZATION OF CHICANO CHILDREN:
A Comparative Study with Anglos in
California Schools
F. Chris Garcia

POVERTY, POLITICS, AND HEALTH CARE:
An Appalachian Experience
Richard A. Couto